CW01111203

Lancia *Stratos*
thirty years later

Andrea Curami

Lancia
Stratos
thirty years later

Giorgio NADA EDITORE

Giorgio Nada Editore

Editorial director
Luciano Greggio

Editing
Leonardo Acerbi

*Graphic design,
layout and cover*
Isabella Gianazza

English translation
Warren McManus

Photographs
Archivio Bertone
Archivio Fiat
Archivio Giorgio Nada
Archivio Andrea Curami
Archivio Franco Varisco

© 2003 Giorgio Nada Editore, Vimodrone (MI)

Surrupuit currenti cursori solum
He's can steal the soles off the shoes
of a person running at full speed
(Plautus, *Trinummus*, 1023)

Printed in Italy
ALL RIGHTS RESERVED

*Apart from any fair dealing for the purpose of private
study, research, criticism or review, no part of this
publication may be reproduced, stored in a retrieval
system, or transmitted, by any means, electronic,
electrical, chemical, mechanical, optical photocopying,
recording or otherwise, without prior written consent.
All enquiries should be addressed to:*

Giorgio Nada Editore s.r.l.
Via Claudio Treves, 15/17
20090 VIMODRONE (Milano)
Tel: +39 02 27301126
Fax: +39 02 27301454
E-mail: info@giorgionadaeditore.it
http://www.giorgionadaeditore.it

*The catalogue of
Giorgio Nada Editore
publications is
available on request
at the above address.*

Lancia Stratos - thirty years later
ISBN: 88-7911-300-3

Content

Foreword		6
Sandro Munari		
Introduction		8
Andrea Curami		
Chapter 1		10
Background		
Chapter 2		36
"Today Lancia, tomorrow FIAT"		
Chapter 3		56
Family infighting		
Chapter 4		68
Arrival of the Stratos		
Chapter 5		100
Separated at home		
Chapter 6		112
An engine in search of a master		
Chapter 7		122
The Stratos HF and the races		
Stratos facts and figures		164

Foreword

Few cars have left their mark on the history of motor sports like the Lancia Stratos HF.

Retracing its birth and development is almost like reading a wonderful fairy tale from our childhood, populated only with good wizards and sprightly elves.

We had to overcome the crisis that had overtaken Lancia and was threatening its very survival. Cesare Fiorio handed me a blank sheet of paper, like the one he gave to the engineers, test-drivers, the other drivers and navigators of the racing team. We had to respond to just one question: describe a replacement for the glorious Fulvia HF, pinpoint the requisites necessary to make this automobile a winning weapon in rally competition, a sector on which Lancia was focusing and in which intended to continue competing. The company management had decided that such a car, besides being an excellent test bench, could be transformed, through victories, into a powerful publicity vehicle.

Now many people feel that racing has no affect on series cars, but the Fulvia HF was a striking demonstration of the contrary. Its production, which was to cease in 1972, continued for four more years after my win with Mario Mannucci at the Rally of Montecarlo that same year; 161,000 units of that model were produced, 51,000 of them following our victory at Montecarlo.

Participating in the realization of a car right from the initial phases of design specification was to overturn the concept of rally cars then in vogue: they had always been selected from series touring cars, based on their "racier" characteristics. What's more, we could not overlook the fact that the FIA had also opened rally racing to grand touring cars, and there was talk that it would be gradually liberalized toward other highly competitive categories of automobiles.

I clearly recollect the responses I provided on that sheet: I wanted a rear-wheel-drive car, light but tough and versatile, with a rear-mounted engine of at least 300 bhp, a front-meshing gearbox, and a short wheelbase, to provide maximum handling in tight corners. The design had to allow quick changes in setup and final drive ratios, to fit the type of special stage, permitting maximum accessibility to the mechanicals during servicing.

All my desires were fulfilled, and the car deliberated, which in the meantime had taken the monocoque chassis and aerodynamic appendages from Formula 1, had lost all similarities to the dream-car Bertone had presented at the 1970 Turin Auto Show. But the total

weapon for rally racing was born, enabling us to win everywhere and to hold uncontested sway over the world championship in that specialty for three years.
In this regard, I can affirm without hesitation that the Stratos proved to be the ideal, most versatile car for that purpose I had ever driven. It immediately proved unbeatable, whether it was racing at Montecarlo (the rally best suited to 'chameleon cars', since no two special stages had the same road surface), or in Sweden (a snow-covered layout with temperatures of -40°) or the Safari (a race unsuitable on paper, in the opinion of the big 'experts', because the car was considered too sophisticated, due in part to its suspensions which had too little bounce). It failed to win the Safari at its debut in Kenya — that was in 1975 — because of negative factors unrelated to its quality. The result was still clamorous. Lancia was the only marque that had all three cars entered reach the finish-line. That edition of the Safari was one of the toughest, considering that of the 75 cars that started only 14 took the checkered flag. We finished second with this writer, third with Bjorn Waldegaard, and 11th with Prestom Junior, who drove the backup car and was piloting the Stratos for the first time. Unfortunately, due to commercial requirements, the Stratos was set aside, because the FIAT group, which had taken over Lancia some time before, decided to push the FIAT 131 Abarth, derived from a series model that proved a winner in the absence of an "official" Stratos. The logical evolution of technology exaggerated even more the concepts underlying the Stratos, which each of us regarded as his own for having participated in its conception, taking recourse to other devices that later helped open the way to even more sophisticated technical solutions.
But speaking only of the technical side also means downsizing what was a marvelous adventure by a closely-knit group of men in a successful attempt to restore a historical marque to its former splendor.

Introduction

When I was asked to prepare a text on the Lancia Stratos HF, I felt flattered but at the same wondered what new I could add to what had already been recounted over the years in the monographs by Piero Casucci, Nigel Trow and Graham Robson.
The Stratos, as a car, had already been analyzed from the technical standpoint in every aspect and its trophy case amply commented. Less attention had been devoted to the situation in which Lancia found itself when it set out to study the new project and why that HF was added to the car's name.
In this book I shall attempt to fill these voids but without necessarily rewriting the history of the company from its origins. I shall dwell, rather, on the reasons that led to the suffered acquisition by FIAT in 1969 and the meaning of that symbol that characterized all the racing cars produced at Chivasso, with the exclusion of the Lancia 2000 HF, improperly designated in my opinion.
I shall then review the human events, rather than the horsepower and handling of this or that car. I shall therefore necessarily speak not only of personal weaknesses but also of the vital demands that have often uselessly complicated relations between individual companies that in fact belong to the same group.
This must be grasped especially to interpret the relationship — not always easy and cordial — that was established between engineers Sguazzini and Gobbato, both driven by a desire to do well at the tasks assigned to them. Unfortunately, the dichotomy that came to be created found origin in the obvious quest for victory in the competitions in which the cars of both marques participated, where first place in the overall classification was and is normally only one and can rarely be shared.
This fact was then affected by the emotional involvement of this writer not only in reporting the information but also in elevating to the role of real news the men and the hopes that the protagonists of these events privately shared with him.
We realized, for example, the untruth of the news carried by several newspapers at the time that the Stratos had been put into production with an engine derived from that of the 132 (they went so far as to confirm the actual completion and even published the probable list price). It now seems that that engine version was never tested nor built in prototype form. In the surreal, almost Pirandello-like situation of the prototype of the Stratos presented in 1971 at the Turin Auto Show, that of a bodied chassis in search of an engine, it is possible that someone

even considered using such an engine, but it all remained in the realm of pure imagination without even an executive design.
Even though the reporting of the time was of fundamental assistance in tracing the chronological sequence of the individual events recounted, the opinions and comments expressed at the time are not always respected in these pages. I have preferred to base my text, wherever possible, on my firsthand recollections of the protagonists of those episodes, who with extreme patience have tolerated my effrontery and impertinence.
Obviously, this writer is responsible for the opinions, unavoidable errors and insufficiencies.

Andrea Curami

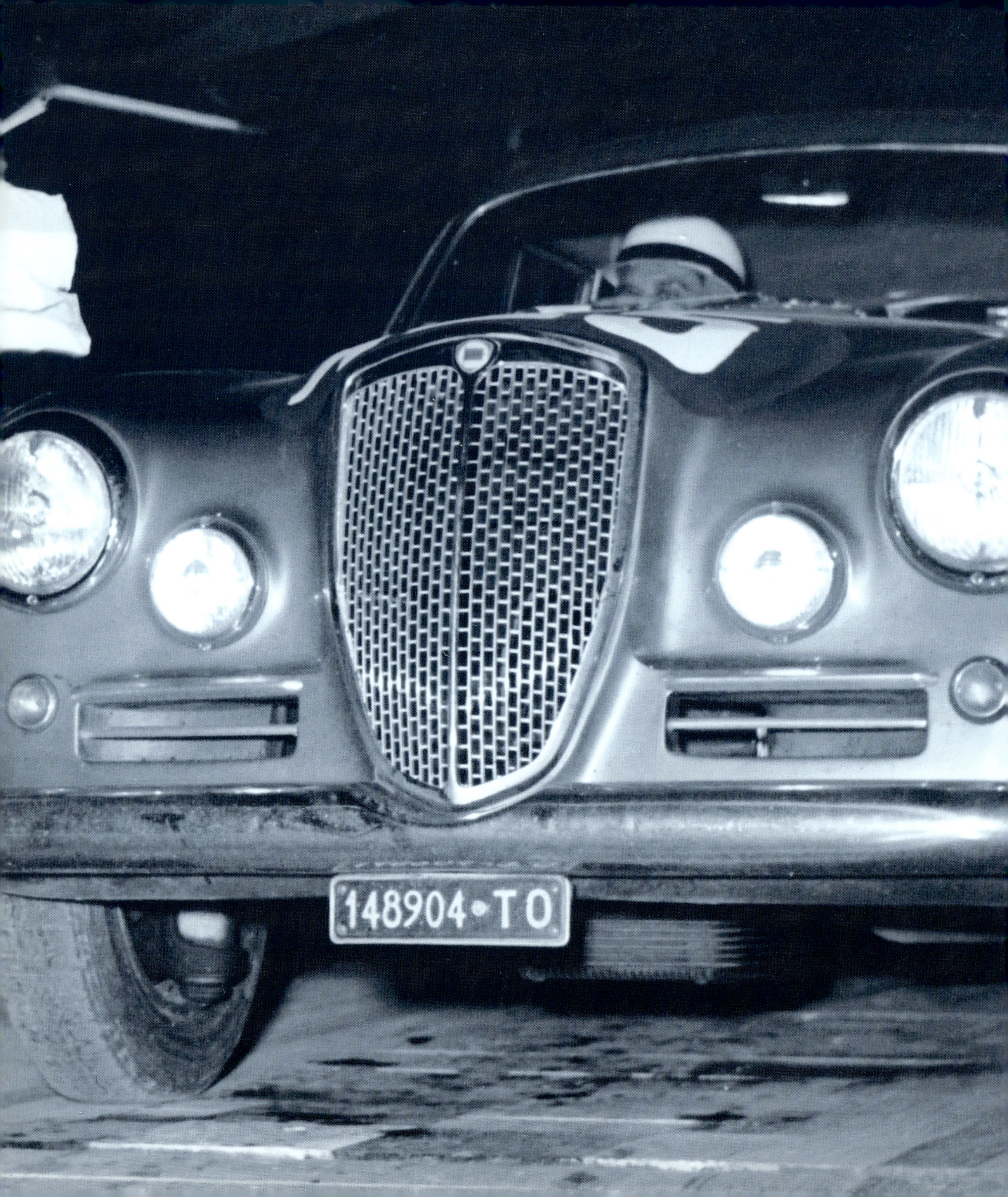
148904 TO

Chapter 1

Background

The birth of a competition car is closely linked to changes in the FIA sporting and technical regulations, and this was also the case with the Lancia Stratos. To better create the history and evaluate in detail the human and professional factors that conditioned its initial design concept and subsequent development, we must backtrack in time to that fateful November 1971, when at the Turin Auto Show coachbuilder Bertone presented the prototype, almost definitive, of a car intended for rally racing, called the Lancia Stratos HF.
In these brief notes, we would remind the reader of the history behind each of the words that make up the official designation of the car.

From Hi.Fi. Club to HF Racing Team

During the 1960 Geneva Auto Show, Lancia promoted the creation of a club that would bring together its most assiduous customers, those who had owned at least ten factory-new Lancias, and that association took the name of Hi.Fi., i.e. high fidelity to the marque. The club soon ventured into racing,

Sandro Fiorio, paired with Piero Avalle, at the start of the 1950 Mille Miglia. With their ALF 750 they placed third in their class, later winning the 750 cc Sport class at the Tuscan Cup. The partnership with the tuner from Turin was abruptly halted by a tragic accident at Pontelagoscuro during the 1952 Mille Miglia, which cost Piero Avalle his life.

Chapter 1 Background

The badge given to Hi.Fi. Sport members. The one shown below belongs to Luigi Cabella.

The Lancia Appia Sport Zagatos of Giorgio Dacrema (no. 8), Herbert Demetz (no. 7), and the Flaminia Sport Zagato of Elio Zagato, a.k.a. "Scansa" (no. 48) grouped on the Monza circuit during the 13th edition of the Intereuropa Cup on 4 September 1960. The race was won by another Flaminia Zagato driven by Giuseppe Rota.

animated by Sandro Fiorio, the Lancia public relations manager at the time, and his son Cesare.

Sandro, formerly an important figure in the leather industry, had been a good sports car driver in the up to 750 cc class and in the early 'fifties had even developed the ALF, an acronym formed of the initials of Turinese tuner Avalle, the Turin-based company Lancia (because of the downsized Ardea engine mounted on it), and Fiorio, of course. His son had earned distinction with an Appia Zagato, and in 1961 had dominated the Italian championship in the hotly contested 1150 cc Grand Touring class, with the enviable achievement of five victories in the five races he entered, despite strong opposition from other young drivers, such as Neapolitan Corrado Ferlaino and Gianni Lado of Veneto, whose racing handle was "Matich".

That same year Giulio Cabianca, driving a Flaminia Sport, had won the Italian title in the up to 2500 cc GT class, after capturing second place overall in the last speed-based Mille Miglia, organized that year with racing regulations similar to those of modern rallies, with speed stages linked to legs with imposed averages.

With the approval of Alfredo Della Seta, Lancia commercial director, but without the direct involvement of the company, the club activity of the racing customers was consolidated in 1962 with overall victory in the Rally dei Fiori, the current

Giulio Cabianca climbing into the first Flaminia Sport managed by Hi.Fi. Sport (right). With this car (TO 340516) the driver from Verona participated in the 30th Rally of Montecarlo in 1961, paired with Ghino Longo, halted by a spinout. Driving this car, with bodywork reconstructed after Aldebaran's accident at the 1962 Targa Florio, Leo Cella captured the Italian 2500 GT Championship in 1963.

The Team's first Flaminia Sport was soon joined by this lighter, more aerodynamic car (TO 372685), which Elio Zagato had previously raced in 1960 (right, below). This car captured the Italian 2500 GT Championship with Cabianca in 1961 and with Piero Frescobaldi in 1962.

Souvenir photo of a historical win at the Nürburgring in 1962 (bottom left). Standing between the two Flaminia coupes (the left one, with the different grille, prepared by Facetti) are, left to right, Dante Marengo and "papà" Pietro Facetti. Mario Angiolini is leaning on the fender of Bosato's car. Kneeling, left to right, are Piero Frescobaldi, Marcello De Luca di Lizzano, and a young Cesare Fiorio.

Rally of Sanremo, won by a Lancia Flavia sedan driven by Piero Frescobaldi and Dorando Malinconi and the class victory at the Rally of the Acropolis, valid for the European Rally Championship, by Luigi Cabella, winner of the Italian title in 1961 for the 1150 cc Touring class with a FIAT 1100 TV tuned by Samuele Baggioli, and who on that occasion had raced at the wheel of a series III Appia tuned by Almo Bosato of Turin.

Besides the Hi.Fi. Sport emblem on the grille, this car bore a blue baby elephant inscribed in a white round at the base of the

Chapter 1　　　Background

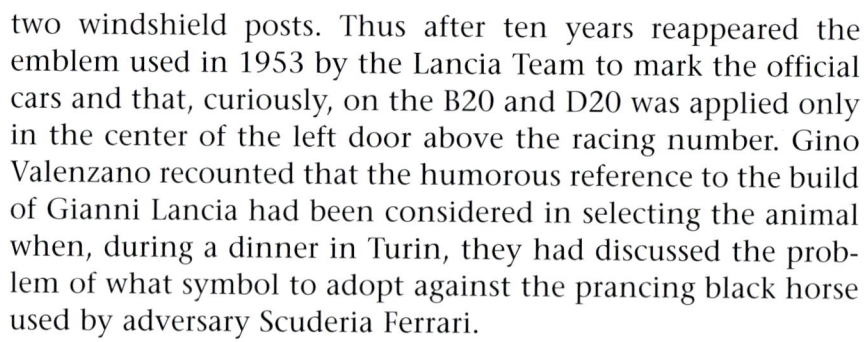

two windshield posts. Thus after ten years reappeared the emblem used in 1953 by the Lancia Team to mark the official cars and that, curiously, on the B20 and D20 was applied only in the center of the left door above the racing number. Gino Valenzano recounted that the humorous reference to the build of Gianni Lancia had been considered in selecting the animal when, during a dinner in Turin, they had discussed the problem of what symbol to adopt against the prancing black horse used by adversary Scuderia Ferrari.

In preparation for the European Touring Car Challenge, which was to begin in 1963, the gentleman drivers of the Hi.Fi. Club performed more than honorably with the Flaminia Pininfarina coupe prepared by Pietro Facetti, winning second place overall behind a Jaguar 3.8 MkII at the 12 Hours of the Nür-

Top: the dark-blue baby elephant on white background placed in 1962 and 1963 at the base of the windshield on all the cars entered before the Hi.Fi. Sport and then used by the HF Racing Team.

12 Hours of Nürburgring, 1962: Piero Frescobaldi, shown in the pit area, next to his Lancia Flaminia prepared by Facetti. Destiny was cruel to him: at the 24 Hours of Spa in 1964 he lost his life in an accident while driving a Flavia Sport.

The Flaminia Bosato of Luigi Cabella and Marcello De Luca ahead of a Mercedes-Benz on the tortuous layout of the Nürburgring. De Luca was also unlucky, dying in an accident at the 4th Junior Cup at Monza in September 1962.

Lancia Stratos

A rare photo of the tubular Flaminia Sport entered by the Jolly Club in the 1962 Targa Florio with the team Frescobaldi-"Kynder". Entered as a prototype, it retired during lap seven with driveline problems.

An indiscreet photo taken inside the Zagato coachworks in early 1962 (below): detail of the tubular frame prepared for the Lancia Flaminia prototype that debuted at the Targa Florio.

The Lancia Flaminia Sport Zagato (plate TO 372685) photographed at the start of the Targa Florio on 5 May 1963 (below right). Driven by Luigi Cabella and Luciano Massoni it finished 22nd in the overall classification.

burgring in 1962, with Luigi Cabella and Marcello De Luca di Lizzano. Piero Frescobaldi and Cesare Fiorio, protagonists until the final minutes at the Nürburgring with an identical car prepared by Almo Bosato, revenged their loss in the 6 Hours of Brands Hatch, finishing fifth overall and first in their class. They were again driving the Flaminia coupe tuned in Cormano (MI) by Piero Facetti. Luigi Cabella recently recalled that this car was more powerful that the one prepared by Bosato which, however, in his opinion, held the road better. Although the cars had been prepared for competition outside the company, and worked through the organization of the Jolly Club of Mario Angiolini for the two victorious expeditions abroad, the ties with Lancia remained close. This is demonstrated by the fact that the cars used were the property of Lancia and that the Hi.Fi. drivers raced the Flaminia Sport with tubular frame, the prototype which apparently raced only once, at the 1962 Targa Florio. It was to be Lancia's secret weapon for the World GT Manufacturers' Championship in 1963, but it was pure fantasy to think it could beat the Ferrari GTOs, despite the skill of drivers like Piero Frescobaldi and Cesare Fiorio.

After two years of experience, the Hi.Fi. Club gave official status to this group of drivers by forming the HF Racing Team. The team's creation was announced on 12 January 1963 during the annual awards ceremony for racing customers. Giovanni Bracco was the unanimous choice for Team president, while Dante Marengo became its organizational manager and Cesare Fiorio its racing manager. The Team had a highly ambitious goal: to participate with Lancia cars in the international road races valid for the GT Manufacturers' Championship and those reserved to touring cars. As their emblem, the side panels of the Team cars would bore a white "HF" on a field of black surmounted by four galloping red elephants. That animal, in light blue, had been the symbol of the Lancia Team from 1953 to 1955, and adorned the certificates Della Seta had been presenting since the award ceremonies of 1962 to drivers who had earned particular distinction.

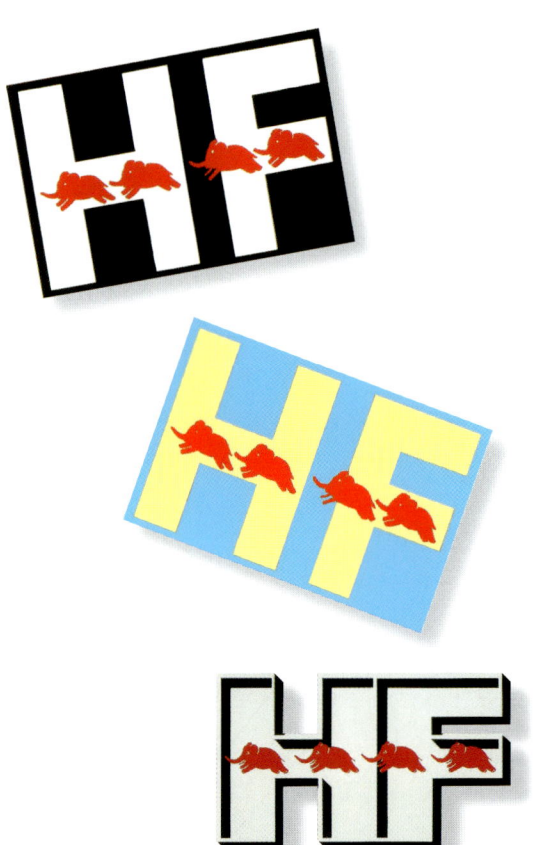

For the first edition of the Touring Challenge of 1963, the HF had acquired other new cars, all of them owned by Lancia&C: at least five Lancia Flavia 1500 coupes prepared da Almo Bosato, two of which were entrusted to Leo Cella and Franco Patria, as well as the two Flaminia coupes used the previous year, one of them reserved to Luigi Cabella.

An examination of the international licences issued by the CSAI in 1963 curiously reveals that the new Turin-based club never applied for a competitor licence, which were obtained, along with racing licences, by drivers Luciano Massoni, Luigi Cabella, Leo Cella and Gianfranco Patria with serial numbers 1003 to 1006. Thus the HF racing team never had any legal liability in the competitions, just the drivers, who were therefore regarded as racing on their own. This significant commitment, financial and otherwise, was rewarded at season-end with class

Facing page, left: evolution of the HF Squadra Corse emblem over the years: the paperweight presented to Luigi Cabella at the end of the 1963 season with the emblem carried on the cars from 1963 to 1965. From 1966 the phrase "Squadra Corse" disappeared from the emblem. In 1968-69 the emblem received an initial face-lift, with yellow lettering on a light-blue background. At the end of 1969 came the final revision, also used on the Lancia Stratos.

Almo Bosato with the five Lancia Fulvia Coupes he prepared for the 1963 racing season (facing page, bottom right). They were used both in rallies and on the track, dominating the 1600 Touring class in both the European Challenge (with Leo Cella) and the Italian Championship (with Franco Patria).

21 April 1963, Touring GP at Monza: on the first Lesmo curve Luigi Cabella in a Lancia Flavia precedes Carlo Zuccoli driving the Alfa Romeo Giulia TI tuned by Facetti. Although comparable in weight and horsepower (around 115 bhp), the Alfa was soundly defeated by the Lancias. Cabella came in second behind Patria, overtaking Cella on the last lap when the latter's car suffered a mechanical breakdown.

Gianfranco Patria, 1963 Italian champion in the 1600 Touring class, in action at the 3rd Cesana-Sestrière in July of that year. The young driver from Turin was also struck by the misfortune that seemed to plague former HF drivers. Moving to the official Abarth team the following year, he died at only 21 years of age during the 1000 Km of Paris in 1964. A similar fate befell Leo Cella: the Italian champion in the 700 Touring class in 1961 and 2500 class in 1963, after transferring to Alfa Romeo in 1967, lost his life testing a 33 Sport on the Balocco track in 1968.

victories by Leo Cella (ninth overall) and Luigi Cabella (eighth overall). In addition to this international success, they also captured a class victory in the World Grand Touring Manufacturers' Championship with the Flaminia Sport, which repeated the win of the previous year ex aequo with Triumph.

Worthy of note were the two triumphs obtained among the cars of the competition Touring category (Group 2), since the Flavia outpaced the Alfa Romeo Giulia TI and the Vauxhall VX 4/90, while the Flaminia bettered the Ford Zodiac and FIAT 2300 S, the latter entered by Abarth. These were still normal production cars, however, tuned within the prescriptions of

Chapter 1 — Background

Appendix J to the FIA sporting regulations and not "homologation specials", as the British began to humorously describe aberrations like the Mini Cooper S 1071, which appeared in March 1963, conceived expressly to create a modern engine for the Junior Formula and to compete in the increasingly popular Touring category.

The final outcome of that season was hapless, particularly for the FIAT Abarth, whose victories in competition were proportional to the financing received each year from FIAT. It was soundly defeated by the sibilant Saab 96s in the up to 850 cc class, while the DKW Junior, also a two-stroke, bested it in the next higher class.

The pickings were also slim for Alfa Romeo, whose Giulia TI was a loser in the up to 1600 Touring class, both internationally in the Challenge and in the Italian championship, won by Franco Patria with the HF's other Flavia coupe. Of modest consolation was the Italian title captured by the Alfa Romeo 2600 Sprint of Franco Concari. That victory was gleaned fortuitously in the last race with the outside help of the Jolly Club to the detriment of Luigi Cabella, for which Cesare Fiorio had perhaps underestimated the parallel commitment in the two championships, European and Italian, and the consequent calendar conflicts.

While Lancia was ably exploiting its victories in the specialized press, Abarth and Alfa Romeo could do no more than roll up their sleeves. Abarth thus began to add bulk to the homologation fiches of its 850 TC and 1000 sedan with many pages of photos, most of them unintelligible, illustrating new technical features. For its part, Alfa Romeo followed the example of BMC and Ford, which had homologated the Cortina Lotus, by presenting the Giulia TI Super in 1963. The car's production was halted in 1964 after only 501 cars had been assembled, so it miraculously obtained racing homologation in the Touring category well before it had built the 1,000 units required.

It remained to be seen whether those empirical and costly attempts had served to return the two Italian firms to success in the international field. The results of the second edition of the Challenge seemed to negate that. In fact, the Abarth 1000 sedans found an unbeatable adversary in the Mini Cooper S 970. Built perhaps in a total of 1,000 examples between June

Top: in the early '60s the exploits of the HF Racing Team and its drivers were exploited as an advertising vehicle to promote Lancia products in the leading car magazines. In issue 40 of 3 October 1963, «Auto Italiana» carried this ad celebrating the victory of Gianfranco Patria in a Flavia coupe at the Florence-Consuma and the Premio Campagnano that year.

Gianfranco Patria, on the left, next to Giorgio Pianta, Leo Cella and Luigi Cabella, leaning against a Lancia Flavia coupe 1500 Pininfarina, certainly contributed most in this sense, capturing important wins in rallies, hillclimbs and track events. Lancia played an active role in those years promoting the participation of young drivers in competition.

Lancia Stratos

6 October 1963, 8th Leopoldo Carri Cup. Driving the Alfa Romeo 2600 Sprint tuned by Facetti is Mantua's Franco Concari, entering the Junior chicane ahead of Luigi Cabella in his Lancia Flaminia with engine also prepared by Facetti. To protect its chances for the Concari title, the Jolly Club entered two other Alfa 2600 S of Facetti driven by talented Paolo Colombo, among the few "heavy feet" with the cantankerous Ferrari 250 GTO, and ever-fast Elio Zagato, who finished ahead of the driver from Mantua.

1964 to April 1965, it was mysteriously homologated in time to compete in the 1964 European series, capturing not only its class, against the Abarths, but also the overall classification with driver Warwick Banks. The Giulia TI Supers, which Alfa Romeo, like Lancia, had been assigned to the Jolly Club team of Milan — which had them prepared in Turin by Almo Bosato and by Virgilio Conrero — found a superior adversary in the Ford Cortina Lotus. At year-end, despite a few partial successes, they were defeated not only in the international series but also — the crowning blow — in the national championship, which was gradually becoming less provincial.

The HF Racing Team was more fortunate in its moves. After abandoning the Flavia 1500 coupe (on the road layout at Monza, it had proved over five seconds per lap slower than the

Chapter 1 — Background

better TI Supers and Cortina Lotuses), they put up the new Flavia Sport 1.8. This was another miracle of precocious homologation, with only 507 units produced from 1963 to 1966, that managed to capture seventh place overall in the European series and victory in the up to two liter class coupe over the BMW 1800 TISA, thanks to Marco Crosina. The Flaminia 2.8 coupe's season was not as fortunate. Though benefiting from a few generous gifts on the homologation form, such as the three carburetors of the Flaminia Sport, light-alloy doors and covers, as well as oversize wheels, it found itself competing in the same class as the Mercedes-Benz 300 SEs.

In the Italian Championship, the HF Racing Team did not participate directly in the two-liter class, leaving customers to contend final victory with the Flavia 1.8 coupes, lightened and with the two-carb engine of the Sport. The attitude was different in the higher class, with a repeat of the duel with the more powerful but less manageable Alfa Romeo 2600 Sprint, expertly driven by Gian Carlo Galimberti. This was not an official car, but was specially supported by the Alfa dealers of Lombardy, which Pietro Facetti had equipped with an extremely powerful engine. Against him, the HF Racing Team marshalled

Luigi Cabella left Lancia at the end of 1963 and went to South America. Before leaving Italy, he raced one last time with the official FIAT 2300 S of Abarth which had attempted some records and, as he recalled, was taken to Monza for him by friend Franco Patria.
He won the 2500 cc class but was preceded at the opening Criterium in Monza on 19 March 1964 by the more powerful Alfa Romeo 2600 S of Andrea De Adamich, Franco Concari and Ezio Selva.

Marco Crosina shortly after the start of the Trento-Bondone on 11 July 1965. His Flavia Sport was preceded at the finish-line by an identical car driven by Claudio Maglioli, who set a new record for the Touring category and at season-end won the Italian class title, repeating the feat the following year. Crosina won the Mountain Trophy for the Touring class in 1966, driving a Flavia Sport.

the equally valid Luciano Massoni with a Flaminia 2.5 coupe, which had enjoyed the same homologations as its sister car with larger displacement.

The first "evil deed" came three-quarters through the regular season at the Nissena Cup, third-from-last event of the championship. Massoni found that only one other competitor was entered, so he could not have a valid score. But suddenly four other Turinese drivers appeared on the scene, driving four Flaminias: they were exceptionally slow on this occasion, permitting the designated driver to capture the maximum points and the lead in the classification.

The Carri Cup, held on the Junior track at Monza under a driving rain, was favorable to the Alfa Romeo driver who preceded his rival. Thus he came to the last race of the season (to be held this time on the road layout at Monza) again with a slight point advantage but not sufficient to ensure him the Italian title if he placed behind Galimberti.

On Saturday during the official trials of the 3rd Cup of Autumn-100 Miles of Monza, it seemed clear that Massoni, barring unforeseen breakdowns to his adversary, would not be able to beat him, nor would teammate Giorgio Pianta (driver

Turin's Luciano Massoni, Italian champion of the 500 Touring class in 1961 with a FIAT prepared by Almo Bosato, reached first overall in the Touring category at the Mugello circuit in 1964 with the Lancia Flaminia coupe of Facetti. The wheel-wells had been modified to accommodate the new homologated wheels, which gave the car a more aggressive look than the Flaminia driven by Cabella the two previous years.

who had raced the European series for the Turinese team with the Flaminia 2.8) be able to do so. Thus the "plot" perpetrated against Cabella and the HF Racing Team in 1963 was repeated, with roles reversed, and it was comic to watch the starting grid procedure on Sunday afternoon, with drivers lining up and then, palgued by second thoughts, returning to the pits.

In the end, with considerable delay, the start was given for the up to 3000 cc class with a single starter, good Gian Carlo Galimberti, who honored automobile racing by winning the overall victory and establishing a new track record for Touring category cars, but without gaining a single point on the field valid for the Italian Championship.

The event had an unfortunate epilogue, when the National Appeal Tribunal of the Italian Automobile Club appealed against the final classification. The judges, introducing clear interpretations of the difference between "starting" and "started", "officially" assigned to the Alfa Romeo driver the score that he would have earned if all the competitors in the official trials had actually taken the start of the race.

Birth of the Lancia HF Racing Team

In no time the races had undergone an unexpected transformation. To make a good showing, it was no longer enough to secure the services of an outside preparer, however expert, like Bosato or Facetti, who precisely because of their recognized art were overwhelmed with requests from customer, including some adversaries like Galimberti in 1964. The teams had to continue development on the engines and setups of the existing models, continuously proposing new features to homologate in the first FIA session, and to work alongside the engineering offices so that future models would include those characteristics that would make them easy to transform into competition cars. Our carmakers had finally learned the lessons of the Mini Cooper S, the Cortina Lotus and the FIAT-Abarth, but also the Renault Dauphine 1093, though with some delay.

Alfa Romeo thus created a free-standing racing department in the form of a joint-stock company controlled by Alfa:

Lancia Stratos

The Alfa Romeo Giulia TZ of Jean Rolland and Gabriel Augias, winner of the scratch classification for GTs at the 25th Coupe des Alpes in 1964. Though not designed specifically for rallies but for speed, the TZ (tubular Zagato) expressed itself best in road endurance racing, where its robustness and reliability could prevail over the lightness of the Lotus Elans, engineered to race on smooth tracks.

Autodelta S.p.A. with head offices in Settimo Milanese. It was a transformation of the firm Delta Auto, later Autodelta, created in Udine in 1963 by engineers Carlo Chiti and Ludovico Chizzola to assemble 100 Alfa Romeo Giulia TZs.

Lancia followed the same path in early 1965, probably burned by the disastrous Argentine expedition at the end of 1964 to participate in the Argentine Grand Prix, a 4,800 km marathon, almost an attempt to revive the marque's success at the Carrera Panamericana over ten years earlier. All the cars entered by the HF Racing Team were forced to retire due to the suicidal conduct of the drivers, who seemed to have forgotten how long the race was, and to the inexperienced, disorganized assistance provided.

The HF Racing Team thus ceased to exist as a formally independent structure and was transferred to the plant on Via

| Chapter 1 | Background |

Caraglio, former site of the glorious racing department dismantled ten years before, on 26 luglio 1955. Cesare Fiorio retained his position as racing manager, linked to Lancia by a consulting relationship, while for engine preparation, the collaboration with Bosato and Facetti continued. Lancia&C also applied for a competitor license, which was granted by the CSAI with number eight, thus officially reentering motor racing competition.

Dusting off its glorious racing team emblem of the early Fifties (the green four-leaf clover), Alfa Romeo had presented the Giulia GTA at the Amsterdam Auto Show in mid-February. Externally, for commercial reasons, it duplicated the lines of the series-production Giulia Sprint GT by Bertone, but it had an all-aluminum body, often including an aluminum floor pan, as well as an engine with a twin-ignition cylinder head. Lancia, on the other hand, was totally unprepared for the racing season. Its product range, in fact, offered nothing that could be entered in a speed race with any hope of success, especially after it abandoned the experimental short-wheelbase Flavia Sport: the car had the unpleasant habit of lifting its inside rear wheel on corners and an engine bored out to two liters had debuted unhappily among the prototypes at the Targa Florio. The Flaminia 2.8 coupe was heavy and underpowered compared to the competition. Despite its victory at the Rally dei

Claudio Maglioli at the Stallavena-Boscochiesanuova on 4 April 1965. His Lancia Fulvia 2C, though its power was comparable to the Mini Cooper S 1071's, was too heavy. Piero Conte, with the British car prepared by Almo Bosato, bettered him by 20 seconds on the fast hillclimb of over 15 kms. He only finished fourth in the 851-1150 Touring class, however, behind Paolo Lado and three other FIAT Abarth 1000 sedans. Climbing in 8'04"4 at an average of over 113 kph with a private car prepared by Trivellato, Lado was 17" faster than the Cooper S and 29" faster than the comfortable sedan entered by the HF Racing Team. The Abarth 1000 Berlina was not yet equipped with the radial head and the two two-barrel carburetors.

The Lancia Fulvia 2C of Enzo Martini, entered by the Jolly Club and prepared by Samuele Baggioli at the 2nd Rally Lazzaroni in 1965 (Rome, 25 April 1965); the same driver won the Italian rally title at season-end. The Lancia 2C sedan with dual-carb engine extended the limited racing possibilities of the Lancia Fulvia before it entered the coupe field with its debut at the Tour de Corse (7 November 1965).

Fiori with Leo Cella and Sergio Gamenara, the new Fulvia 2C was heavy and had little power and an unfortunate displacement for the 1300 cc limit for the international class in which it was entered.

At the 4 Hours of the Jolly Club of Monza, first event on the European Challenge calendar, Giorgio Pianta finished ninth overall in the grouping from 1001 to 2000 cc, separated by only four laps from the Cooper S 1300 Broadspeed of John Terry and by less than a lap from the Cooper S 1100 Bosato of Piero Conte and Roberto Benelli. That day many watched the pantomime of Mario Poltronieri with his Flaminia 2.8 coupe, who interpreted his usual role as manager in an ideal race "behind-engines" of the smaller Fulvia, awaiting it in each lap and literally sucking it up on the long straights of Monza.

The Flavia Sport had also reached the end of its brief racing career. Only Almo Bosato had succeeded in the titanic undertaking of squeezing a few more horses from the delicate horizontally-opposed pushrod engine, and only tightrope walkers of the caliber of Marco Crosina, Claudio Maglioli and Carlo Facetti, still cornering on three wheels, could pilot it to a few results in national competition, where the official BMW 2000s were not entered.

Both cars, belonging to the second group of the European Touring Challenge, were outclassed, however, by "rockets" like the Cortina Lotus and challenged by the more modest Alfa Romeo Giulia TI Supers. Even more embarrassing were the clashes with the superior Giulia GTA, miraculously homologated on 1 August 1965, and the super-light Mini Cooper S 1300, which in the hands of a few British specialists could generate annoying headaches on the sinuous tracks.

The final classification for manufacturers in the 2nd division of the European series confirmed the values on the track: it was won by Ford, in front of Alfa Romeo (recovering after homologation of the GTA,) BMW, BMC with the Mini, and Lancia. The racing manager of the fledgling Lancia HF team probably suffered an attack when the Lancia Fulvia Coupe was unveiled at the 1965 Geneva Auto Show. It was definitely elegant and rakish, thanks to the skilled pen of Piero Castagnero, well finished like all the Lancias, but it spotted the Mini Cooper S 1300 almost 300 kg on the scales. The engine, a narrow

Chapter 1 — Background

Facing page: two views of the elegant Lancia Fulvia Coupe prototype (top), designed by Piero Castagnero. Compared to the definitive model presented at the 1965 Geneva Show, this car differs in the roofline, the shape of the rear lighting groups and the front turn indicators.

Facing page, bottom: Luigi Cabella, back from Brazil in 1966, resumed racing for the Jolly Club, which assigned Roberto Angiolini this Fulvia Coupe prepared by Gino De Sanctis, then riding the crest of the wave for his fast Lancia Appia GTs. The photo shows the Angiolini-Cabella team during the 4 Hours of the Jolly Club held at Monza on 20 March 1966. They finished 17th in the 1001-1600 cc group and seventh in the 1300 cc sub-class, almost 10 laps behind the Cooper S of Julian Vernaeve and four from the Cooper S 1100 of Piero Conte and Spartaco Dini. The trim of the car here taking the Parabolic corner at Monza leaves much to be desired.

V4, was also apparently not conceived for competition. It had been derived from the super-square 2C sedan by increasing the bore from 72 to 76 mm for a total displacement of 1216 cc, well below the class limit of 1300 cc. And the cylinder head, configured with intake on the right and exhaust on the left, a characteristic of the Appia, also inherited its defect of having different length intake and exhaust ports on the two banks. A step forward had been taken with two overhead camshafts, chain-driven, but the valves were actuated by rockers, and the arrangement of the cylinders did not seem designed for running the engine a high rpms. The gearbox, with only four gears, was also rather "non-racy", not to mention the long wheelbase that promised the same three-wheel cornering behavior as the Flavia.

It was no surprise, therefore, when on the complete Monza layout (road section plus high-speed), during the official trials for the 4 Hours of the Jolly Club of 1966, the opening event of the European Touring Challenge, the fastest of the Fulvia Coupes, driven by Carlo and Giuliano Facetti, accumulated a gap of exactly eight seconds from the official Mini Cooper S driven by Belgian Julien Vernaeve. At the end of the race, the two brothers, sons of famed Pietro, finished almost two laps behind the British car, even though the track was more favorable to the Lancia than to the less aerodynamic Mini.

With the possibility of international success in speed precluded, all that remained was the Italian Championship, where the private Minis were perhaps not as fast as the British ones. After the surprise showing by Sandro Munari at the Imola race, however, where he clocked the best time in qualifying (according to the commentator of «Autosprint» because he was "reprieved by the timekeepers" for that incredible time), the Italian championship in the up to 1300 Touring class also proved too difficult for the semi-official car of Roberto Angiolini, always forced into secondary positions. With yet another round of sparring, in fact, the Jolly Club's relation with Alfa had gradually cooled due to the natural overlapping in races between the roles of the Mario Angiolini and Autodelta teams. Angiolini had meanwhile begun competing in the fledgling Italian Rally Championship, just launched in 1961, notching his first victory with Arnaldo Cavallari in a Giulia TI Super in

Lancia Stratos

Chapter 1 — Background

Rally dei Fiori, third event in the 1966 European Rally Championship: the victory went to the Fulvia HF of the team Leo Cella-Luciano Lombardini, after the exclusion on complaint of the Ford Cortina Logus of Elford-Davenport for nonconformity of the gearbox ratios with the actual number of teeth and a discrepancy between the metric and British weights of the con-rods ("both mathematically in error" stated the report of the racing commission). The Italian team won the combined Montecarlo-Rally dei Fiori classification in a tie with Andersson-Dahlgren, also in a Lancia Fulvia HF.

Leo Cella was among the first drivers to race the new Lancia Fulvia Coupe, in the 10th Tour de Corse in 1965, even before the car was homologated, teamed with Sergio Gamenara, finishing in eighth place overall. For the Fulvia this was an interesting test bench, since it was able to contend with cars that had become habitual adversaries over the years, such as the Alpine-Renault A110 and the agile, fast Mini Cooper S's.

1964 and then with Enzo Martoni in a Fulvia 2C the following year, paralleling the efforts of the HF team in national events. The only successes were obtained by the Sicilian «Radec», (acronym with the immodest meaning of Rizzo Antonino Dominatore e Conquistatore) with his first place of class at the Belmonte Cup in Siracusa, where he had preceded the obsolete Giulietta TI and a FIAT 1300, and at the Jolly Hotels Trophy, where he finished first and only in his class after driving the entire race behind the old Alfa Romeo Giulietta TI of Vallardi and Ferrari, as long as they remained in the race.

The high point coefficient assigned to this event, however, enabled «Radec» to leap to the top classifications in the Italian championship with two victories, so Lancia HF decided to enter him paired with Sandro Munari at the Mugello Circuit, a grueling event still raced on the classic road layout and also assigned a high point coefficient. The strong driver from Veneto gave a good performance, overtaking the Minis and boosting «Radec» even higher in the championship ranking.

As we mentioned earlier, the greatest obstacle to racing success was the excessive weight of the production car, so the Lancia racing team set to work on the coupe's monocoque, but without going as far as Autodelta with the GTA, which built an extreme version with an all-aluminum floor pan. Everything superfluous was eliminated, the lids and doors were replaced with light-alloy versions, achieving a 150 kg reduction with respect to the series car, while thanks to new carburettors and intake and exhaust manifolds the power rose to about 90 bhp. The car, later commercially designated the Fulvia HF to indicate its competitive vocation, debuted in 1965 among the prototypes admitted to the 10th Tour de Corse with Leo Cella and Sergio Gamenara: they placed eighth overall. The more attentive did not fail to notice the second and fourth places overall of two Renault Alpine A 110s, crowning the success the French firm had gleaned with the victory of the Renault R8 Gordini of Corsicans Orsini and Canonici. Both these cars joined the Mini Cooper S in making life difficult for the fledgling Fulvia HF in the rallies in subsequent years.

The racing Fulvia was homologated first in Grand Touring on 1 February 1966 in time for the Rally of Sanremo, where Leo Cella was paired with the late Luciano Lombardini. That;

Lancia Stratos

homologation, with an incredible and unlikely effort, was extended to the Touring category on 1 August 1966, since someone accepted as true the declaration that 1,000 identical units had been built while, according to company data, construction was halted after only 435 cars had been produced.
Not coincidentally Reinhard Klein, in the his book Rally Cars, described the racing homologation procedure and the art of seeing what is not there.
This fact enabled Leo Cella to participate in the 500 km of Snetterton and win the up to 1300 cc class, preceding a Mini Cooper S. This victory over the stronger adversaries was clamorous, but no one remembered that there was virtually no competition: from the start of the year in Britain, the Touring championship had been governed by the Special Touring technical regulations, and certainly no British team had the spare cash to specially prepare a car for a single race — not valid for the national championship — in accordance with the restrictive regulations of Prepared Touring.

A Fulvia HF shown during the severe initial tests on snow, one of the surfaces on which the Lancia coupe displayed its best virtues. The car in the photograph is one of those with a 1216 cc engine used by the Lancia press office to promote testing in the car magazines.

The gap with respect to the Cooper S's raced by the Italian drivers had almost completely narrowed, and «Radec», now with the Fulvia HF, was able to capture the Italian title in the up to 1300 cc Touring class. Leo Cella captured the Italian title in the Italian rally championship by winning the San Martino di Castrozza event.

From the Fulvia HF to the Fulvia HF Rallye 1.6

The basic defects of the car remained, however. Competing for the international championships required a car with a lower weight-to-power ratio and an engine with more torque at low rpms.
At the 11th Tour de Corse in 1966, Leo Cella, again paired with Luciano Lombardini, was entered with a new Fulvia HF prototype. Let us review, in this regard, a few technical notes that Franco Lini wrote for the weekly «Auto italiana»:
"…it is a Fulvia Coupe mounting a special engine with greater displacement than stock, 1322 cc to be precise. Fueled by two Weber horizontal dual-barrel carburetors, this engine should deliver 15 more horsepower than the normal Fulvia HF (90 CV), i.e. a 15% increase in power. Attention has been focused on the power avail-

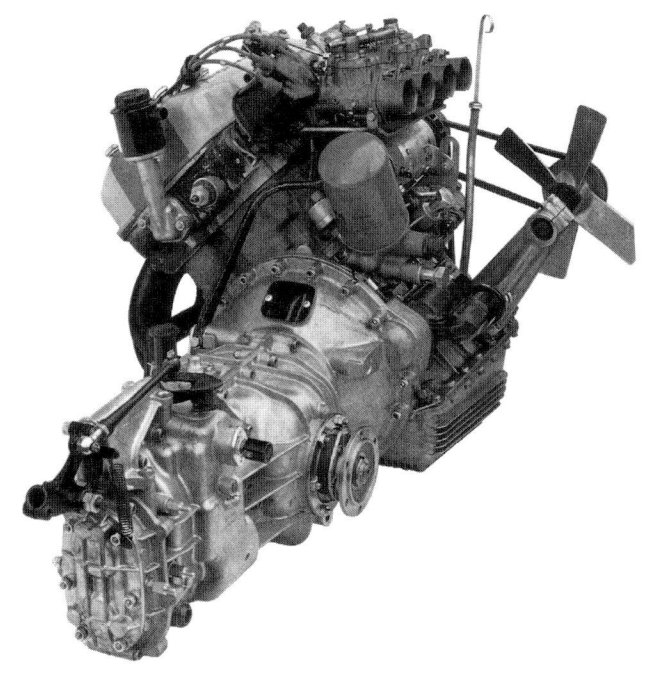

able at low rpms, with special cam profiles that produce loads of torque. Overall, the car is much lighter, with total weight reduced to around 750 kg, greatly increasing its acceleration potential, an essential feature in races like the Tour de Corse. [...] The performance offered by Cella and his special HF was exciting, and in fact the Italian pair was leading the race when the car went off the road and was forced to stop. We don't know whether this car will have a follow-up, but one thing is certain: at least in the prototype category it can still offer great satisfaction".

Then the Fulvia HF Rallye 1.3 (or HFR) was presented at the Geneva Auto Show of 1967, incorporating many of the engine modifications adopted on the Corsica prototype, even though displacement was reduced to 1296 cc to drop it down into the up to 1300 cc class. The increased stroke (from 67 mm to 69.7 mm), as well as a new cylinder head and camshafts, helped increase maximum torque in the version marketed to the public to 12.8 kgm at 5100 rpm, versus 10.5 kgm at 5000 rpm in the Fulvia HF. Unfortunately, the drivers' requests for an even lighter car, like the prototype in Corsica, with more gearbox speeds, given the high maximum torque speed, had not yet been satisfied.

The HF Rallye 1.3, as the new version was called, almost declaring its use, was homologated in GT on 1 March 1967. But Cesare Fiorio had realized from the start of the year that if they wished to compete internationally, having the best cars was not enough: as had already been demonstrated, they also

The 4-cylinder engine of the Fulvia Coupe Rally 1300 (1289.26 cc) had two chain-driven overhead camshafts and two Solex C35 PHH9 twin-barrel carburetters. It generated 87 bhp at 6000 rpm.

"*Excellent the performance of the small Lancia Fulvia 1300, 14th overall with Cella-Munari*" wrote the report of «Auto Italiana» at the 12 Hour International of Florida in 1967, better known as the 12 Hours of Sebring. Pity that "*also noteworthy was the result of the BMC team, which with MG Sprites driven by reliability specialists Hopkirk, Makinen and Alltonen, obtained 11th, 12th and 13th places*".

Claudio Maglioli in a Fulvia HF at the 1967 Tourist Trophy: he was forced to retire. His diligence in the championship events earned him a well-deserved continental title in the 1300 class, but this did not absolve the car, which had reached the end of a brief career in speed competition.

needed drivers with greater experience than the young talents in the fledgling Italian rally school. Cella and Munari already possessed international status, but the arrival of drivers of the caliber of Ove Andersson, Pauli Toivonen, Vic Elford and Sobieslaw Zasada to the team enabled the Fulvia HF to take a leap forward in the overall classifications.

The important thing was winning, and only first place in the general classification could justify the increasing financial involvement associated with participation in the European or world championships. The only one approachable for a racing department like Lancia's, and for the types of car available, was the European Rally Championship for drivers, which beginning in 1968 was to be joined by an international rally championship for manufacturers. From 1968 the European Touring Challenge was to be opened up to cars in Group 5, or Special Touring, resulting in a massive return of the British cars (which had been racing with those technical regulations since 1966) and the sure participation of the unbeatable Mini Cooper S's with fuel injection and the super-fast Ford Anglia Supers in the up to 1300 cc class. It was best to take advantage of the additional year of British sabbatical in 1967 and seek to win the up to 1300 cc class in division II, from 1001 to 1600 cc, and then abandon speed racing, except for participation in a few prestigious events with great publicity impact, like the Targa Florio.

It was a wise choice to pursue a European class title, with Claudio Maglioli and the Fulvia HF, which though of minimal visibility was the last one Lancia was to capture in speed racing for many years. On 1 April 1967 Alfa Romeo homologated the

Lancia Stratos

A snapshot taken during the 1300 cc class of the exciting 13th Leopoldo Carri cup on 13 October 1968. On the finish-line straightaway we see Giuliano Facetti (Lancia Fulvia HFR Facetti no. 86), Maurizio Zanetti (Lancia Fulvia HFR Bosato no. 85) and Enrico Pinto (Alfa Romeo Giulia GT Junior Autodelta no. 81). It was won by "Nanni" Galli (Alfa Romeo Giulia GT Junior Autodelta), at least 10" ahead of Giuliano Facetti. Enrico Pinto set the best lap time of 2'03"5, bettering the pole position time (2'04"7) clocked by Eugenio Foschetti in a Lancia Fulvia HFR Facetti, who finished third.

| Chapter 1 | Background |

Sandro Munari smiling after his victory in the 1967 Italian Rally Championship.

In the 1967 season the Fulvia Coupes were protagonists in the European Touring championship. At the 500 Kilometres of Snetterton, on 17 September 1967, the Mini of Roger Heavens leads the Fulvia of Leo Cella (in the photo), but the Italian driver prevailed in the end.

GT Junior in Touring, but fortunately for Squadra Corse Lancia it was too late to alter the destiny of the Italian 1300 cc class Touring championship, won by the HF of Giuliano Facetti. For many of us it was a real displeasure to see the three official cars of Autodelta, driven by Nanni Galli, Spartaco Dini and Teodoro Zeccoli, humble all the other competitors at Monza, during the Carri Cup, and lap in only 27 laps the best of the Fulvia HFs, driven by Piero Conte, preceded to the finish-line not only by the private GT Junior of «Ans» (Ansano Cecchini.) but also by the Mini Cooper S of Silvano Pittini.

In the rally championships, the admittance of cars from the Grand Touring category broadened the field of competing manufacturers, with the threatening presence of the Porsches and the Renault Alpines. On the other hand, the smaller production volume required for homologation permitted development of models with less investment on the part of the carmakers. Furthermore, the difficulties of the circuits made the quest for horsepower less decisive for occupying the top position in the overall classification, and at the same time the press placed less importance on the class and category in which the cars were competing.

Perhaps this is why, at the 1967 Tour de Corse, Lancia entered a team of Fulvia Rally 1.3 HFs, light like the one used the previous year but with engine bored out to 80 mm for total displacement of 1401 cc. It was a team victory, with the overall

Facing page: the Fulvia HF of Pauli Toivonen and Marrti Tiukkanen at the 1967 Tour de Corse. The car was entered as a Prototype, since it mounted an engine bored out to 1401 cc. They placed second in the overall classification behind the twin car driven by Sandro Munari and Luciano Lombardini.

The Fulvia with 1584 cc of displacement was derived from the 1401 cc. It debuted as a Prototype at the 1968 Tour de Corse (right). The new car, also called the "fanalone" because of its large front lighting groups, finally mounted the five-speed gearbox as standard.

win by Sandro Munari and Luciano Lombardini, in front of the twin car of Toivonen and Tiukkanen, while Leo Cella and Sergio Barbasio, piloting another Fulvia prototype, finished sixth overall.

Thus began the third and last phase of evolution of the Fulvia Coupe, which ended with racing homologation of the Fulvia Rallye 1.6 HF on 1 October 1969 in Special Grand Touring. The new car had grown in displacement up to the limit of the 1600 cc class and was finally equipped with a five-speed gearbox and the possibility of mounting a self-locking differential.

To reach the final version, then deliberated, HF also raced the HFR with an absurd seven-speed gearbox, obtained by installing a two-gear reduction downstream from the series four-speed gearbox. This certainly did not facilitate driving, since the drivers had to actuate two levers each time they shifted gears.

Then victory finally came in the European Drivers' Championship with Harry Kälsström in 1969 and in the International Manufacturers' Championship in 1972.

MILLE MIGLIA
COPPA FRANCO MAZZOTTI
MILLE MIGLIA
COPPA FRANCO MAZZOTTI
CEAT
602
162250-TO
540

Chapter 2

"Today Lancia, tomorrow FIAT"

This is how Giuseppe Berta entitled a chapter of his book *Fifty Years of Industrial Relations at Lancia (1919-1969)*. As the author recalls, it was:

"... the effective slogan coined by the initial groups of political intervention in the factories when protests broke out anew in the old company on Via Monginevro in early 1962. This byword intended to emphasize, at the same time, the deep roots of the demands addressed to Lancia and their general scope, which was to fuel the resumption of a massive new cycle of worker protests, such that they also totally engulfed the fortified citadel of the Turin industrial system, FIAT, where no strikes had been proclaimed in almost ten years".

Improperly transposing it in time, that bellicose proclamation marked a sequence of events from 1937 to 1969, during which the ownership of Lancia changed hands from the heirs of Vincenzo Lancia to the management of FIAT at Corso Marconi.

The decline of a family-owned company

When the founder of Lancia suddenly passed away on 15 February 1937, the helm the company passed to Ms. Adele Lancia Miglietti, wife of Vincenzo and formerly his secretary at the company. Formally, no major changes in the management resulted, as she continued to work with her husband's closest collaborators, i.e. Oscar Ravà, who directed the commercial side but was soon forced to leave his position due to racial laws; Ernesto Zorzoli, chief financial officer; and Manlio Gracco de Lay, the technical manager. This left the purely entrepreneurial and planning function uncovered, however, as it had been filled by Vincenzo Lancia.

The hiring in February 1938 of Vittorio Jano, who had left Alfa Romeo due to the inability of the cars he designed to compete with the powerful, technologically advanced Mercedes-Benzes and Auto Unions, seemed to offer a measure of security about the quality of the new products that were to replace the Aprilia and the Ro truck. He still possessed the latent capacity of

A famous photograph of Vincenzo Lancia. He was born in Fobello (Val Sesia) on 24 August 1881. At only 17, though from an affluent family, he decided to leave school and become a helper in the bicycle shop Giovanni Ceirano had opened in the home of his father, Giuseppe Lancia. Along with friend and contemporary Felice Nazzaro, a mechanic at Welleyes, he went to work at FIAT, becoming its official tester and driver until 1908. After the success of the first car designed by him, he abandoned racing to form his own automobile factory. He died in Turin on 15 February 1937.

Chapter 2   "Today Lancia, tomorrow FIAT"

Vittorio Jano shown at the pits on the Monza circuit. He was born on 22 April 1891 in San Giorgio Canavese, son of the technical director of one of the two arsenals in Turin. At the age of 18, after completing his studies at Turin's Istituto Professionale Operaio, he found work at Rapid as a draftsman. In 1911 he was hired by FIAT and in 1921 became head of the engineering design office. He worked on the 805, a 2-liter racecar, and developed a friendship with Luigi Bazzi, whom he later followed to Alfa Romeo in Milan, where Jano designed the famous P2 (1924) and P3 (1932) Grand Prix cars. Hired by Lancia in 1938 at the death of its founder, he designed the revolutionary D50 Formula 1 car in 1953-54, following its fortunes to Maranello when Ferrari absorbed the Lancia Racing Team. Vittorio Jano died by his own hand in 1966 at the age of 75, following the death of his son.

charismatic manager capable of conducting relations with the political power, an essential function at a time when Lancia, the first company to comply with the laws on industrial decentralization, had to cope with a new requirement: open the new plant in Bolzano, where it had to position the industrial vehicles to be produced there.

In search of a valid technical manager for the company, Adele Lancia extended unproductive feelers to the managing director of Alfa Romeo, but Ugo Gobbato declined them, as he was busy turning around the Milan-based company, an assignment given him by the Prime Minister in person. She then tried unsuccessfully with Gaudenzio Bono, former assistant general manager of FIAT from 1931 and then director of SPA in 1939. In April 1941 an attempt was made to resolve the lack of management by replacing the sole administrator with a board of directors, still under the presidency of Adele Lancia, but joined by Pompeo Vaccarossi, representing his family (which had always been a minority shareholder), Vittore Palchetti, manager of the Bolzano plant, Manlio Gracco and Ernesto Zorzoli. The new board immediately sustained the idea of introducing economies of scale and industrial synergies, seeking to reach an accord with Alfa Romeo to produce compressed air brakes and shock absorbers through SABIF, a company purposely formed with ownership split 60% Lancia and 40% Alfa Romeo. Gobbato was to be the chairman and Peano managing director (proposals to create a company to produce aeronautical engines and extend the collaboration to auto marketing and assistance, as well as the manufacture of a midsize truck derived from the 3Ro, were never confirmed).

The difficult situation was created by a government veto that eliminated the production of automobiles, and a military veto that reduced and then suspended the production of heavy tanks in favor of light and medium tanks. This threw Lancia into a state of profound crisis, aggravated by its heavy financial exposure, due in part to the subsidies requested for the construction of the now useless Bolzano plant.

The end of the war brought a new management team and a deepening of the debt structure. Between 1943 and 1945 the board of directors lost first Palchetti, then Zorzoli and then

(cont. to page 42)

Lancia Stratos

Giovanni Bracco taking the checkered-flag in the 1951 Mille Miglia at the wheel of a Lancia Aurelia B20. He finished second overall behind Luigi Villoresi in a Ferrari with more than twice the displacement.

The dazzling performance of the Aurelia was completed by the placement of two other identical cars among the top ten finishers: *Ippocampo*-Mori fifth and Valenzano-Maggio sixth.

Chapter 2 "Today Lancia, tomorrow FIAT"

Lancia Stratos

Facing page: a photo of Piazza Vittoria in Brescia during technical scrutineering prior to the 1953 Mille Miglia, second event in the world manufacturers' championship instituted that year by the FIA. The Lancia Team participated en masse, with the D20 berlinettas and the Aurelia B20 GTs, all with blue-and-ivory livery. Note that the elephant emblem appears on the open left door of Valenzano-Margutti's B20 GT (no. 559) but is absent on the right door. The same good-luck symbol is also absent on the right door of Bonetto-Peruzzi's D20 (no. 606).

The elephant appeared on the left door of Bonetto-Peruzzi's D20 (no. 606), third overall in the Mille Miglia and shown here passing through Reggio Emilia (top left), and on Piero Taruffi's D20 (no. 635, above right) and Valenzano's B20 GT, shown again at the start of the Tour of Sicily that year (no. 347).

At the 1953 Dolomiti Cup, held on 12 May and won by Paolo Marzotto with a Ferrari 250 MM, Taruffi came in second, 1'33" behind, driving the Lancia D23 Sport roadster (below left), sporting a gaudy light-blue livery with red flames on the trailing edges of the fenders.

Below right: the Lancia D23s, having dropped the two-tone livery they had in the Grand Prix of the Autodrome in Monza on 6 June 1953, were entered two months later at Merano for the 1st Supercortemaggiore GP with the traditional red color. The Lancia contingent included Eugenio Castellotti, forced to retire at lap seven.

41

Chapter 2   "Today Lancia, tomorrow FIAT"

Gianni Lancia had a deep passion for racing and felt it represented the ideal platform for launching new series models. He was the principal author of the company's return to competition, first promoting participation in the GT category with the Aurelia B20s, then in Sport with the D20, D23 and D24 and lastly, in the maximum formula with the D50 single-seater, challenging Ferrari and Mercedes-Benz.

Facing page: the Lancia D24, logical evolution of the D23, was used in the 1954 racing season (top left). In the world manufacturers' championship it proved to be the chief antagonist of Ferrari, winning the Mille Miglia with Alberto Ascari (in the photo), among other events.

The D50 single-seater with which Lancia was to race in Formula 1 took to the track for initial testing with Alberto Ascari on the runway at Turin's Caselle Airport.

(cont. from page 38)

Gracco. Zorzoli was replaced by Aldo Panigadi, nominated by Vaccarossi, while the position of general manager was assumed by Arturo Lancia, *"...a technical type with experience in major American corporations"*. But in the intentions of Adele Lancia, his role was destined to disappear when her son Gianni, only 21 at the time, was ready to take the reins of the firm. The sudden death of Arturo in 1948 hastened the management change, but in the meantime Lancia was falling more deeply into a state of crisis. Hopes of a turnaround through the production of industrial vehicles were dashed by the ARAR operation, which threw 9,000 war surplus trucks onto the market, 16 times the truck production volume of Lancia in 1948, for a value of around ITL 15 billion, totally satisfying demand.

At that time Lancia asked the competent ministries to have IRI take over the Bolzano plant or, as an alternative, to dismiss over 2,000 redundant workers, another burden of the Turin-based company.

Fortunately American support arrived in the form of a loan of over three million dollars between 1948 and 1951, but unfortunately only a small part was used to upgrade the Turin facilities. In fact, in 1951 over 36% of the machine tools on hand had been purchased in the 'Thirties, 20% in the '20s and 5% even before, resulting in an inevitable drop in productivity.

Thanks to the De Gasperi-Grüber agreements for renovation of the South Tyrol, the Bolzano plant suddenly became important for the government in Rome, and this enabled Lancia to acquire first right of refusal on military and civil contracts.

In 1953, in addition to the presentation of the Lancia Appia I series, which proved a total failure due to the modest technical characteristics and uncertain handling of the cars, Lancia became heavily involved in racing competition with purposely designed cars that had nothing in common with normal production models.

This was a personal success for Gianni Lancia against all those who had criticized him, as the D24s won the 12 Hours of Sebring and the Mille Miglia in 1954, vying with Ferrari for the world Sport title right up to the last event. The D50 Formula 1, an authentic prodigy of Vittorio Jano, was the only car that could compete with the Mercedes-Benz W196, probably supe-

Lancia Stratos

The first major victory of the D50 single-seater was captured by Alberto Ascari on 27 March 1955 on the Valentino Circuit in Turin. Teammate Eugenio Castellotti (above) finished fourth. Lancia's Formula 1 adventure was halted by the death of Ascari at Monza on 26 May. In July of that same year all the Lancia material was transferred to Scuderia Ferrari, which won the World Championship with that car the following year.

rior to it despite the limited budget available. Ceded to Ferrari and banalized there, it still permitted Juan Manuel Fangio to capture another world drivers' title in 1956.

The management of Gianni Lancia aroused considerable criticism even within the family, ever inclined to invest all the company earnings in real property outside the company. On close examination the financial situation of Mercedes-Benz, which could be considered a rival to Lancia because of its product category and market segment and which also returned to racing in 1952, was also anything but bright, partly because the German defeat in war was still fresh.

Unfortunately, short historical memory causes many to forget that after the second place overall captured by the Lancia Aurelia at the Mille Miglia and the brilliant performance at Le Mans in 1951, FIAT had presented the 8V at the Geneva Auto Show of 1952, entering a numerous team of them in the Mille Miglia. Likewise, Alfa Romeo had sent its competition 1900 Sprints to Brescia, assigning one to Juan Manuel Fangio himself. Both companies were irreparably defeated by the Aurelia B20s. Alfa repeated the defeats in 1953 by creating the so-

Chapter 2   "Today Lancia, tomorrow FIAT"

called "Flying Saucer", in an ill-fated attempt to capture the first World Manufacturers' Championship organized by the FIA, against Lancia and Ferrari.
Then came the new skyscraper office building, with the gigantic "Lancia" on top, dominating all of Turin: another moral blow to the other Turin-based automaker. As Aldo Panigadi recounts:
"…Gianni realized that production required a face-lift… the company equipment had become too antiquated. He had family problems…Find me someone to buy the whole operation, he told me, I'm tired, look for someone in Milan. I'm leaving for Brazil".

The Pesenti management

Panigadi had little difficulty finding in his co-tenant Carlo Pesenti, alias "Carletto Grab-all", from Bergamo, owner of Italcementi and Italmobiliare, the buyer who for less than ITL 10 billion purchased the interest of Gianni Lancia, his two uncles, and the Vaccarossis, in June 1956. Gianni's two sisters, Anna Maria and Eleonora, in conflict with their brother, kept their shares until 1958.
During the negotiations for sale, the Lancia technical management had changed, and in April 1955 the professor, Antonio Fessia, arrived on the scene. Dante Giacosa, who had worked under him at FIAT, recalls him in his book «My 40 Years of Engineering at FIAT» with these rather unflattering words:
"Fessia had a strong, singular personality. His discourse was brilliant, lively, varied, always intelligent and cultured. And he often abused these qualities. He did not conceal his great regret that he had not studied the classics, and often quoted Latin phrases to demonstrate that he also knew that language. He had a great passion for music and, from what one could gather from his words, was a good amateur pianist. His greatest gift was an infallible memory, electronic, always quick, immediate. This made it easy for him to speak effortlessly in other languages, and he was proud of this. Ambitious, he loved to speak of himself, and I listened. He was an excellent manager: he was easy to work for, demonstrated respect and total confidence in me. He the mathematician and I the designer were in full agreement. He impulsive and open-minded, I calm and reflective made a highly efficient team.

In 1955, via Caraglio in Turin became, along with the Fiat headquarters on corso Marconi, another place-symbol of the Italian automotive industry. A modern new office building was erected there for Lancia, which in the meantime had come under the financial and industrial control of Carlo Pesenti, who acquired the equity interest of the Lancia family, reaching total ownership in 1958.

He was a friend to the employees who went along with him. With his peers he was extremely combative and always behaved in a way that made him enemies. Ambitious, he would find a topic that let him demonstrate his superiority, even if it was extraneous to our field of work: he was never charitable with his rivals, which he never lacked. He had outbreaks of impatience, infuriating whims and sometimes strange reactions that seemed crazy, and he couldn't repress them".

In any case, he was known for his passion for front-wheel-drive cars and, like Vincenzo Lancia,, who came from the same environment, for his deep-seated aversion to motor racing, a fact that had created a gelid atmosphere around him prior to his resignation from FIAT. Among other things, Fessia had removed Carlo Salamano from his position as head of testing for prototypes, because he did not tolerate the test-driver's habit of going over his head and reporting directly to Senator Agnelli and to Prof. Valletta.

Giacosa:

"In informing me of his decision, Fessia told me that with the evolution of the automobile toward a more utilitarian use, it was not admissible that the person responsible for the final judgment was a former race-driver who assigned importance only to the resistance of the mechanical parts, performance, roadholding, steering quality and brakes".

After leaving FIAT, in 1945 he joined Cemsa Caproni, where he designed the F11, the first front-drive car of his life, an architecture Fessia was to repeat in 1960 with the Lancia Flavia.

With his egocentric, arrogant character, at the limits of tolerability (all his cars at Lancia had names beginning with the letter F, from Flaminia to Fulvia, passing through Flavia), it took no great prophet to foresee that he was to make life difficult for many at Lancia. This came to pass when Pesenti in May 1958 called Eraldo Fidanza to Turin as chairman and managing director. Fidanza was a "taskmaster" who had succeeded in the hopeless undertaking of turning Terni around.

There were multiple reasons for conflict, and not just with Fessia. From his arrival at Lancia, Fidanza made no friends among the trade unions: in 1958, to treat the chronic overstaffing, 1,500 workers were dismissed in just five months. Many in Turin were surely disappointed with the concentration of

Carlo Pesenti, right in the photo together with Alfredo Della Seta, Lancia sales manager, had built his fortune in real estate and, after taking control of Lancia, launched an ambitious expansion program, with the introduction of new models like the Flavia and the Fulvia. A similar turnover occurred in the management of the technical department, where Vittorio Jano, transferred to Maranello along with the Lancia D50s, was replaced by Antonio Fessia, engineer from Turin Politecnico. A fervid advocate of front-wheel-drive, a solution he applied to the Cemsa-Caproni F11, he introduced this concept to Lancia cars as well.

Chapter 2   "Today Lancia, tomorrow FIAT"

roles, especially professor Fessia. Fidanza further alienated the opinion of a certain local middle class when, in a special shareholders' meeting in March 1959, the share capital was halved by nullifying 500,000 shares of company equity, including 429,795 of the Lancia heirs, and then reinstated to its initial value of ITL 6 billion through the subscription of 500,000 new shares by Union de Banque Suisse and Pesenti's Credito Lombardo. Curiously, a new shareholder appeared, the result of Pesenti's relations in the real estate sector: the Istituto per le Opere di Religione, later sadly known by the acronym IOR.

But the greatest cause of conflict with the engineer was created by the Appia III series, a Fessia-improved version of the model designed by Jano and, precisely for this reason, never accepted by Fessia, who would have replaced it with a front-drive car of similar dimensions designed by him. Fidanza, however, seeing the success the car had finally achieved, with 19,500 units sold in 1959 and 16,000 the following year (a record in the history of Lancia), wanted to put into production a re-styling of it, already prepared by Pininfarina.

Equally unacceptable to the technical manager was the presence of quality controllers and production programmers, who

The Cemsa-Caproni F11, which appeared in 1946, was the first opportunity for Fessia to produce a car with front-wheel drive. This car can be regarded as precursor of the concepts that Fessia expressed almost 15 years later in the Lancia Flavia. The Cemsa possessed a horizontally-opposed 4-cylinder engine (1254 cc, 45 bhp) mounted overhanging the front axle, and a 4-speed gearbox with shift lever on the steering column. The chassis was floorplate-based, and the suspension were independent-wheel front and rear. The unitized body had four doors and four seats.

The Lancia Flavia berlina 1500 made a few sporadic appearances in racing, penalized with respect to the competition by its dimensions, modest aerodynamics and horizontally-opposed engine (78 bhp at 5200 rpm), which left little opportunity for tuning. The photo shows driver Luigi Cabella at the Vergato-Cerelio hillclimb on 31 March 1963.
Among the Lancias designed before Fessia took the reins of the technical office was the Appia III series, which appeared in 1959 and remained in production until 1963. Luigi Cabella participated with this car in the Rally of the Acropolis in 1962 (photo right).

through design revisions and changes in materials, had reduced by 41% the average hours required to produce a Lancia: from 1,055 in 1959 to 621.6 in 1960, despite an increase of only 5% in the hours worked in production.

Forgetting the example offered by Henry Ford in the 'twenties, Fessia thus began to attack Fidanza accusing him *"...of betraying the company spirit in his fury to rationalize"*.

In a Board meeting of 30 April 1960, Eraldo Fidanza responded harshly to the self-serving criticism of Fessia and Mario Bencini, closely linked to the professor: *"Undoubtedly much remains to be done, and it would be illusory to believe that no serious problems exist for the future of the company. It is especially a work of organization, familiarity with and control of costs, standardization, simplicity of design, that must be confronted and resolved"* and during the next Board meeting of 31 May he submitted his resignation.

The post of chairman went to Massimo Spada, a figure of Vatican finance, with the motivation of *"...satisfying the desires of a strong group of shareholders not yet represented on the Board"*, while the role of general manager was assigned to Guido Calbiani, who came from the steel industry.

Relations between Calbiani and Fessia must not have been

Chapter 2 "Today Lancia, tomorrow FIAT"

Massimo Spada addresses the guests at the traditional awards ceremony for outstanding Lancia gentlemen drivers in 1962. At his right are Italian champion Piero Frescobaldi and Lancia general manager Guido Calbiani. Seated to his left are driver Silvano Stefani, Lancia sales manager Alfredo Della Seta, Stefano Marsaglia of the CSAI and, last, journalist Giovanni Canestrini.

Following the period of Pesenti, who left the Lancia management in 1969, Pierugo Gobbato (shown in the photo at Monza with Giovanni Agnelli), son of engineer Ugo Gobbato of Alfa Romeo, was engaged by FIAT to make an appraisal of Lancia's plant and equipment, with an eye to launching a bid to acquire the Turin-based firm, then on the verge of bankruptcy. On 24 October 1969 an official press release from FIAT announced the acquisition of total ownership in Lancia.

idyllic, if the former, in commemorating him after his death in August 1968 due to an incurable disease, wrote:
"Thinking of him in the often difficult moments of our long coexistence in the company, I had come to consider him a man who had more "inside him" than his mantle could contain: hence his exuberance, the power of his will, the authority of his discourse, which occasionally went beyond apodictic discourse".

The death of Fessia came at the moment of greatest difficulty for Lancia. Sorely damaged by the Italian auto crisis of 1964, and with the failure of the attempted salvage by Alfa Romeo ordered by the government, the real estate empire of Pesenti was also exposed, in 1968, to the attack of operator Michele Sindona, sadly known to the newspapers in Italy and also linked to IOR, which later found in Archbishop Marcinkus one of its most widely publicized leaders.

Pesenti was thus forced to liquidate the burden of Lancia at the earliest. Thus FIAT, in January 1969, engaged Pierugo Gobbato, son of Ugo Gobbato, to begin appraising the plant and situation of Lancia. Gobbato had been the architect of the FIAT-Ferrari deal and had managed Ferrari in 1965-66, thus joining the ranks of those disliked by Enzo Ferrari, according to the gossips of Modena, because of his recognized talent and professional background.

The Lancia 1600 Competizione by Ghia

In addition to the alarming news on the Lancia situation, the pages of the car magazines began allotting increasing space in 1969 to two other topics: the official return of FIAT to competition and the preparation of a Lancia car for the 24 Hours of Le Mans.
The first news item was immediately clarified by a press release published during the Montecarlo Rally: the return was limited to rallies and was based essentially on a series of special prizes to be awarded to drivers finishing first and second in their class (ITL 100,000 and 75,000, respectively) and in their group (ITL 200,000 and 150,000) and to the first three in the overall classification (ITL 500,000, 300,000 and 200,000), providing, of course, they were driving FIATs. In addition, *"... a group of qualified rally drivers (13 in all) who race with FIAT cars will be granted free assistance for the entire season, the reimbursement of personal expenses during the events, as well as the aforesaid prizes in case of success",* as reported by the weekly «Autosprint».
Although FIAT strove to explain that this did not constitute fhe creation of an official team, in effect this operation represented a sharp change of course compared to the 1967-68 season, when in a few races the press and propaganda office has asked the auto technical assistance office to deploy a team to assist drivers of FIAT cars. Now the fact was formalized with the automatic presence, beginning with the rally of Sanremo, of a number of teams from DATA (the assistance department) at the Italian and European championship races.
It was at Sanremo that Urbano Rattazzi, nephew of Gianni Agnelli, and Luca Cordero di Montezemolo debuted in the rallies with an excellent seventh place overall, winning the up to 1600 cc class in Group 2, obviously not attracted to the specialty by the mirage of FIAT's ITL 100,000 special prize. Although the fact was publicized with discretion, the FIAT rally cars, at their first "assisted" outing, captured the first four places in Group 1 (Series Touring) and the first two in Group 3 (Grand Touring).
Regarding the other news item, the Lancia racing teams had participated in the 24 Hours of Daytona with a Lancia Fulvia Sport, entered in the Sport Prototype category, since it mounted the engine-gearbox group of the Fulvia Rallye 1.6 HF. At the end of the race, Claudio Maglioli and Raffaele Pinto found

Chapter 2   "Today Lancia, tomorrow FIAT"

themselves in 11th place overall and first in the Sport Prototype category, since the Matras, the Alfa Romeo 33s, the Porsche 908s and a solitary Ferrari Dino 206 were forced to retire. The Fulvia, preceded over the finish line by five cars in the Touring category, was sixth among the cars competing in the World Manufacturers' Championship, thus capturing an unexpected point in the FIA classification, erroneously compiled initially by a few Italian journalists.

Although the company issued no official announcement, a rumor began circulating persistently that, after Daytona and Sebring, Lancia would also participate in the Targa Florio and the 24 Hours of Le Mans. For the Sarthe circuit, according to «Auto Italiana», Lancia was preparing a special Fulvia Rallye 1.6 HF that would be bodied by Ghia and would be unveiled at the Geneva Auto Show.

Ghia owner Alejandro De Tomaso, interviewed by «Autosprint», did not deny the news:

"I cannot hide the fact that our relations with Lancia are excellent'. De Tomaso revealed nothing further, and we are therefore forced to write for our readers that this Lancia coupe will have 'sporting' characteristics, will be built for racing, and its possible presence at the Targa and Le Mans cannot be ruled out. De Tomaso clearly is not in a position to confirm or deny, but the news is true. We do not know, however, whether the car will be displayed at the Geneva Auto Show by Ghia or by Lancia. This remains to be seen. We think we also heard that, if a Lancia-Ghia agreement is reached, a certain number of these cars (25-30 units) may be produced".

Journalist Mario Morselli also alluded to the possibility it might be homologated in the Sport category. In Geneva the car, designed by Tom Tjaarda, was exhibited on the Ghia stand, and its only "sporting" characteristics were a curious rear wing, extendible by command from the cockpit with an electrical telescoping actuator, activated by a button on the dashboard, while the angle of attack could be altered via a level located above the clutch pedal. *"The interior is barebones, essential, typical of race cars, with a reinforcing roll bar against the roof,"* stressed the obtuse, anonymous author of the caption accompanying the photo in «Autosprint». Pity that the so-called roll bar, probably aluminum from the look of it, was drilled like a flute along

(cont. to page 53)

Lancia Stratos

The Fulvia Sport Competizione of Claudio Maglioli-Emanuele Pinto shown at the start of the 12 Hours of Sebring in 1969. It is preceded by a Porsche 911 S and followed by a Lola T70 and two MG Cs.

Chapter 2   "Today Lancia, tomorrow FIAT"

The Carrozzeria Ghia stand at the 1969 Geneva Auto Show displayed this unusual coupe built on the chassis of the Fulvia Rallye 1600 HF. Designer Tom Tjaarda conceived of a car that "had to be at the same time a racecar and an advertisement" to exhibit at the shows as well as a prototype of a possible series production model. The racing vocation of the car, along with its highly aerodynamic lines (compared to the standard of the day, of course) was confirmed by the mounting of a rear wing with telescopic actuator.

The racing concept of the Fulvia Rallye 1600 HF was also enhanced by large glazed areas of Plexiglas rather than glass, by the stripped-down interior, and by the lightening holes in the internal structure of the doors and on the central pillar, perhaps of aluminum, which did not serve as roll-bars (the small photo shows how precariously it was anchored to the body) but only as decoration.

(cont. from page 50)

its height, visible through the glazed side panels.

The rival publication «Auto Italiana» meanwhile published a list of the 55 cars sent to *Le Mans*, which included, with racing numbers 49 and 50, two Lancia Sport Prototypes (displacement 1584 cc, equal to that of the Fulvia Rallye 1.6 HF), entered by the Lancia racing team. The reporter concluded his commentary as follows, with a certain tone of satisfaction for the scoop by his magazine:

"Lastly, the list of entries includes confirmation of the advance news of a Lancia Fulvia prototype designed by Ghia".

The two Lancia F&Ms participated in the Targa Florio, driven by Fiorio and Maglioli, i.e. two HF coupes with the engine and gearbox of the 1.6 HF, the interior blocked off behind the driv-

Chapter 2   "Today Lancia, tomorrow FIAT"

At the 1000 Km of the Nürburgring on 1 June 1969, the HF Team also entered two topless Fulvias, none other than the two 1.3 HFs brutally cut off at the beltline and called F&M Specials (Fiorio-Maglioli), mounting the 1.6 HF engine. The cars raced that edition of the German classic with Rauno Aaltonen and Sandro Munari (car no. 50); an identical car was assigned to Claudio Maglioli-Raffaele Pinto (car no. 51).

er and the body shorted in the rear by 21 cm, with a benefit in weight of around 100 kg over the original version. Despite the encouraging ninth place overall obtained by Sandro Munari and Rauno Aaltonen, it seemed clear that not much more could be expected under normal racing conditions.

The Fulvia Competizione 1600 was mentioned a couple of time more: it was finally tested at the aero-autodrome of Modena and then, after major modifications by Gian Paolo Dallara, it was retested by Luigi Bertocco, before appearing at the Turin Auto Show, announced by the same Mario Morselli in «Autosprint» in his reports from Modena.

No photo of the car in testing was ever seen. At Geneva it was presented as a static prototype, and there is no evidence it was exhibited at the Turin Auto Show. Thus the suspicion emerged that the move had been designed to lend greater force to some rumors that Ford, the new home of both De Tomaso and Ghia, was interested in purchasing Lancia.

This deal-making atmosphere might also explain the announcement of the rally operation by FIAT, thus vulgarly declaring that the Lancia racing team, with its organization, represented useless value added, despite the assessment of Gobbato who, even in recent times, did not hesitate to declare during a press conference devoted to the Lancia Stratos:

"In October 1969 I entered Lancia along with FIAT. I had participated in the appraisal of the plant and equipment of the three facilities at Turin, Chivasso and Bolzano, plus a small auxiliary shop in Omegna. The situation was dramatic: a collapse of sales, cars well designed but superceded, no project for the future, in either the automotive field or in industrial vehicles. In other words, the coffers were empty. The only positive points were the great capacity and great attachment of the company's employees, office staff and workers, their great desire to work, even if the opportunity was offered to them by the historical competitor located in the same city. Little good blood flowed between the two companies, but the entry of FIAT into Lancia was viewed as the company's salvation.

The situation left me little time to dream, so I did not immediately consider the idea of salvaging what was still functioning well, though with great effort, i.e. the racing department. With reduced means, but with great skill and desire, this department was sending the sport version of the Fulvia Coupe, feared competitor in the vari-

The F&M Specials had debuted at the Targa Florio (4 May 1969). In the photo, the car of Rauno Aaltonen and Sandro Munari in the Cerda pits at the 1969 Targa Florio. At the finish they placed ninth in the overall classification, only 4'23" behind the Porsche 908/2 of Mitter-Schutz that won that edition of the Sicilian race.

ous rallies of the period, around Europe with considerable success". Amid all these hypotheses, we should note an item published in «Autosprint» in the column 'La zanzara' [The Mosquito] of «Marcellino», i.e. editor Marcello Sabbatini:

"Our anticipation was right on the money: FIAT has concluded the acquisition of Lancia. The official news is expected at the Turin Auto Show. The disruptive action by Ford was blocked because, when the cards were on the table, it was discovered that the control effect of the group headed by Pesenti (anti-FIAT) was not as significant as thought. Decisive, rather, was the ... countdown of Lancia shares in the hands of Opere Pie (the Vatican)".

HF

F & M
SPECIAL

Chapter 3

Family infighting

As announced by Marcello Sabbatini at the 1969 Turin Auto Show, a brief press release announced the amalgamation of Lancia by FIAT.
During his press conference, Gianni Agnelli was the target of several questions about the future of Lancia, including:
"Q. I'd like to know the financial terms of the Lancia deal, unless they are particularly confidential. More precisely, how much did FIAT pay for Lancia?
A. Lancia was taken over by FIAT for the symbolic price of ITL 1 per share. Since there were a million shares, the price paid was one million liras.
Q. What were the accumulated losses of Lancia and how will they be covered?
A. The debt position of Lancia was just over ITL 100 billion. The creditori are covered by our commitments.
[…]
Q. Considering the success achieved by Lancia in the racing field, and precisely in a sector quite close to series cars and thus of high publicity value, do you feel that this racing activity must be continued and, if so, in what form?
A. This activity will certainly be pursued at Lancia through the same staff currently assigned to it, with the same drivers and with the same type of budget. Along with the racing activity of Lancia, we shall provide that unofficial assistance to FIAT production cars in rally competition, just as we have this year".
Thus the survival of the team managed by Cesare Fiorio is guaranteed by the chairman in person. It was the racing customers who complained of the competitive result of the FIATs. They were disappointed with the new 124 coupe and roadster presented in Turin. All of them were expecting a 1600 cc version so they could compete at the displacement limit of the class. Instead, they received a 1608 cc, which for those stupid 8 cubic centimeters more relegated them to the role of smallest in the up to two liter class. Was this the first sign of a new "non-aggression pact", never ufficialized, with Lancia, which raced with the 1.6 HF in the up to 1600 class, or simply a final gesture by those inside FIAT opposed to racing, headed by Oscar Montabone?
With the 1970 Montecarlo Rally two facts clearly emerged.

Two of the fiercest rivals of the Lancia Fulvia 1600 HFs in the rallies of the early '70s: the Porsche 911 S (below top) shown at the 1969 Montecarlo Rally with Waldegaard-Holmer, and the Renault Alpine A110 of Thérier Callewaert (bottom), shown at the 1970 Montecarlo Rally, raced that year almost entirely over paved and dirt roads, due to the almost total absence of snow.

Chapter 3 | Family infighting

The engine of the FIAT 125, presented in May 1967, was a 1608-cc in-line 4-cylinder with dual overhead camshafts driven by cogbelts and hemispheric combustion chambers. With a compression ratio of 8.8:1 and a two-barrel carburetor, it developed top power of 90 bhp at 5600 rpm. The 125 S (100 bhp at 6200 rpm) was launched at the 1968 Turin Auto Show.

With 5,000 units produced by 20 November 1968, the Fiat 125 S obtained homologation in Group 1 on 1 January 1969 and was entered in competition that season. Prepared by Ceccato Rally Racing of Schio (Vicenza), the 125 S officially represented FIAT in rallies, often competing with the 124 Spyders, a real family feud that characterized the late 60's and early '70s.

Firstly, with good weather and asphalt, the Fulvia 1.6 HF could not consider beating the Porsches, the Alpines and the Ford Escorts. The German car, in the 2.2 liter version, boasted a weight-power ratio of 4 kg/bhp, versus the 4.4 of the French berlinetta with the 1600 cc engine and the 4.8 kg/bhp of the Ford Escort TC. Lancia was blocked at 6.0 kg/bhp, penalized by an engine of moderate power (140 bhp against the over 170 of the Ford Escort and the Alfa Romeo GTA with the same displacement) and by signficant weight (840 kg). Excluded from any chance of success in the overall classification were the FIATs, at 8.1 kg/bhp with the 124 roadster of Group 4 and over 9.0 Kg/bhp with the 125 S of Group 1.

If the HF team was to continue competing for overall in the international championship, it seemed necessary to homologate a much lighter version of the Fulvia, like the 1969 Ghia prototype, or design a car ex novo without front drive and with a more powerful engine.

The environment at FIAT had also changed. The Technical Assistance Service had been created, at the orders of Gianfranco Sguazzini which, like the DATA team of 1969, was to follow the racing customers in the rallies valid for the Italian championship and in a few highly visible foreign events, such as Montecarlo. The prizes earmarked for the competitions in which Assistance Service was present were the same as those of

At the 37th edition of the Montecarlo Rally (19-22 January 1968) the FIAT 124 Spyder of Paliero-Bossa also participated with no. 38: it finished 49th. The race was won by a Porsche 911 T driven by Elford-Stone.

previous years: those assigned to competitors making a good showing in the overall classification remained unchanged, the third finished in the group was also rewarded with ITL 50,000, while ITL 75,000 were reserved just for the class winner. The prizes were not cumulable but were still richer than those offered by Lancia for the 1970 season: ITL 500,000 to the winner of the championship or CSAI trophy, except that pure regularity, for which only ITL 300.000 was offered. For each race the prizes were ITL 50,000 to the first of class and 150,000 to the first overall, except for regularity, where the first overall received only 50.000. This largesse was not available to the drivers of official Lancia cars, which did not count for classification purposes. Other sums were destined to the drivers who participated in at least six races, escluding those of pure regularity, placing in the top 15 in the general classification.

Although Sguazzini emphasized: *"Please, don't talk of a FIAT team..."*, alluding to the fact that there was not official commitment of the company, one detail was clear to one and all: the eight cars "assisted" at the rally of Montecarlo all had Turin license plates and progressive numbering, unlike what has occurred the previous year, when Rattazzi and Montezemolo drove a car with Grosseto plates, while Ceccato and Eisendle raced with the abbreviation of Vicenza, the province of Schio, site of the Ceccato FIAT dealership, advertised on the car's side panels. In 1970, then, the four FIAT 125 S's and the 124 Spiders were identical not only in livery but also because they bore the same accessories, the same advertising messages applied in the same place on the body and the same number-plates as well. This was the visible sign of an admirable work of coordination and standardization, worthy, it should be said, of a true official team.

At the end of 1969 the weekly «Auto Italiana» disappeared from newsstands after 51 years of publication; the only print source available was therefore its competitor «Autosprint», sometimes less technical but much more present on the racing circuits in Italy; it was perhaps too sensitive to corridor gossip, with verifying its authenticity, as we have seen and will have more occasion to see.

Rallies tinged with mystery?

It all began with the 1st Rally of Italy Sanremo-Sestrière, when the three official Lancia Fulvias of Lampinen-Davenport, Ballestrieri-Audetto and Barbasio-Mannucci were forced to drop out immediately after the start due to fuel system woes (Ballestrieri did not even start, as they were unable to get it running). According to the Lancia press release:

"A check of the fuel filters, fuel pumps and carburetors revealed the present of foreign bodies (pieces of perforated cloth) that probably represented the covering of some harmfujl substance. Laboratory analyses are being performed to identify the chemical characteristics of the substances.

These coverings were obviously introduced into the fuel tanks by unknown saboteurs before the start of the race".

Lancia thus filed a statement against unknown parties to the courts of Sanremo, but the was was still lost to the Alpine 1600 of Jean Luc Therier; the FIAT 125 S of Smania-Zanchetti, sixth overall, captured the first point in the International Manufacturers' Championship for the Turin-based company. In presenting the rally of Elba, the next event in the Italian championship, «Autosprint» entitled the article "Troubles for those who break down at Elba", recalling:

"...the difficulty of the layout, almost entirely on unpaved roads (at

Facing page: at the end of 1968, when the 125 Special was launched, FIAT published a two-page ad in the principal car magazines exalting the racing achievements of the 125. The photo shows the car of Smania-Zanchetti that participated in the 3rd International Rally of Elba in 1970, where it finished 7th overall.
At the 12th edition of the Automobile Rally of Sestrière (FIAT Trophy), the FIAT 125s derived from the production sedan proved highly efficient (the photo shows no. 90 driven by Sonda-Manfrotto) in a race plagued by a constant downpour that transformed the race layout into a muddy bog. Sandro Munari won the event at the wheel of a Lancia Fulvia HF, after a long duel with Ove Andersonn in a Ford Escort.

least in the decisive sections)" and that ... the continual controls will prevent competitors from accumulating time for major repairs".
Thus it happened that at the end of the race the panel of racing commissioners empowered the technical commissioners to check the first seven finishers in search of any chassis reinforcements, not permitted by Appendix J to the international racing regulations. The two Lancia Fulvias of Barbasio -Mannucci and Rattazzi-Bernacchini were found to be non-compliant due to the presence of reinforcements to the front chassis crossmember and thus excluded from the race. In addition to the poor impression made by the Lancia Racing Team, due to the violation and the exclusion of Rattazzi, nephew of Gianni Agnelli, who thanks to the change in ownership was able to move from "assisted" driver for FIAT to official driver for Lancia, the manner in which the parts to be officially inspected were selected suggested some other competitors had "ratted" to the officials.
This writer has frequented the race courses for many years, also as a technical commissioner of the CSAI, and when such targeted checks take place I know that they are almost always motivated by "radio pit", i.e. by drivers or adversaries who, without officially filling a formal complaint, which could be embarrassing if it proves unfounded, "suggest" to the technical staff the object that is worth checking.
Thanks to the exclusion of the two Fulvias, the FIAT cars

Chapter 3 — Family infighting

Cesare Fiorio and Claudio Maglioli pursued development of the F&M in 1970, modifying its front end with a new faired grille and a generous air scoop on the engine cover. These additional touches further lightened the roadster, bringing the weight down to just 640 kg, but certainly did little to improve the overall appearance of the car. In the photo, Sandro Munari at the 1970 Circuito del Mugello, where he finished ninth overall at the wheel of F&M Special 2.

deservedly captured the first eight places in the overall standings, and Alcide Paganelli leaped into the lead of the Italian championship classification. But, perhaps by coincidence, the title that appeared in «Autosprint» now takes on the flavor of a "Mafia warning".

After the misadventures of Lancia in the rallies, news began to circulate — source unknown, but immediately picked up by the Bologna-based weekly — about a probable halt of the Lancia racing team at the end of 1970.

Thus wrote «Marcellino», in his column entitled 'La zanzara': *"Lancia HF's new 1600 roadster prototype debuts as the Mugello circuit. But we have heard that this could be one of the swan songs of the Turin racing team managed by Cesare Fiorio. In fact, as part of the necessary downsizing of the Chivasso company, it seems almost certain that the HF team will cease competitive activity, both rallies and speed events, at year-end, on 31 December 1970. The demobilization is said to be in progress already, as demonstrated last week with the disappearance of the small vans for racing assistance to Lancia customers in the minor rallies and in the sprint regularity events. It is painful news but was to be expected because of the company's problems. Nothing is known yet, however, about future prospects. Transfer of arms and baggage of the Lancia team to the FIAT Groups with greater activity in rallies? The situation is*

Longitudinal section (below) of the 2.4-liter V6 engine of the Dino 246 GT of 1969.

Top section (bottom) of the clutch-gearbox-differential group of the same car.

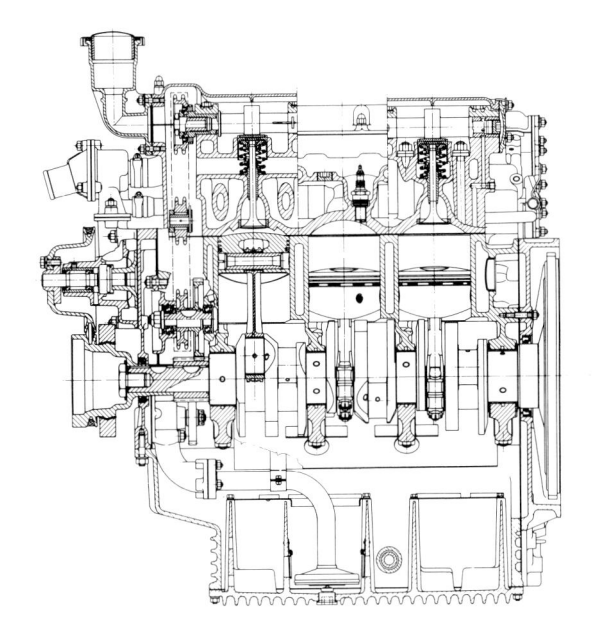

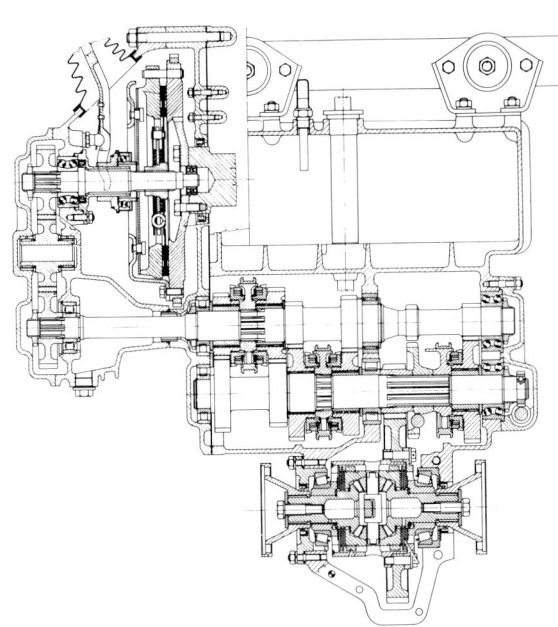

fluid. But perhaps an indication might come from a rumor circulating recently: the entry (not yet confirmed by Paris) of a Dino GT 2400 among the prototypes for the Tour de France. At the wheel Sandro Munari. According to the Cavarzere correspondent of the Bologna-based sports daily, Munari had expressed his enthusiasm over finally finding the road to Ferrari, on this first step, on his ambitions. But nothing is known at Maranello. The Racing Management is totally in the dark. What are we to believe, then? That Cesare Fiorio has bought a Dino Ferrari as the HF Team and is having it race under this banner. Even in this case, there must be some underlying truth. It is no mystery that in certain circles in Turin they are hinting that the young Lancia racing manager could be a candidate for Ferrari racing manager, after the lapse of his candidacy with Dragoni at CSAI".

Dreams and fantasies

The denial came promptly from Turin; the HF Lancia racing team would continue in 1971. The Dino Ferrari was a personal initiative of Sandro Munari and HF was not involved in a program with the Dino Ferrari in 1971. Then, at the end of August, came the news of the registration of the Dino driven by Sandro Munari and Barbasio, both drivers of the Lancia racing team, had been withdrawn.

"The problem must be more 'human' than technical — insinuated Marcello Sabbatini — Let's not forget that Sguazzini, who thus far has supervised the growing rally activity of FIAT, is also in charge of coordinating activities of the so-called Gruppo Marche Associate (at FIAT). We shall see if he gives unto Cesare (Fiorio) that which is not Cesare's (i.e. the Dino for '71)".

Even an interview with the driver by a reporter of «Autosprint» failed to cast light on the obscure aspects of the matter. Munari, in fact, confirmed that he had gone to France with a factory-new Dino to reconnoitre the layout of the Tour. *"The car is still the way it is delivered to a normal buyer — he replied — and therefore not at all "race-modified". We shall have to study a new setup, prepare a series of axle ratios (which are now lacking) and fix all those small items that must be changed to prepare a car for racing, even a poweful, high-performance car".*

Chapter 3 — Family infighting

Munari pleaded "no comment" to questions regarding his possible participation in the Tour with the Dino and the ownership of the car. But it seemed clear that Lancia was attempting to compensate in some way for the modest competitiveness of the Fulvia 1.6 HF against the Alpines and Porsches.

Then «Autosprint» published the imaginative news that the operation had been devised by Pier Ugo Gobbato, Lancia's new general manager and former general manager of Ferrari from May 1965 to November 1966. The program, according to the weekly, called for the participation of two Dinos at the Tour de France, the second one driven by Giorgio Pianta, who had a certain relationship with the HF racing team, competing under the assumed name of "Georg von Baum"; now he had created Italcorse, also entering Autobianchi Primula cars at Montecarlo. Question now on those events, Pianta maintains that he had always been in the dark about them, remembering, in fact, that at the time he was beginning his collaboration with Virgilio Conrero to put the Opens on the track, an effort that later, in 1971, brought him the title in the up to 3000 cc Touring class with the Opel Commodore. Sandro Munari, for his part, recalls that pure-production red Dino assigned to him was owned by Ferrari and had been temporarily loaned for research purposes, to evaluate the behavior of a technical solution of that type (transverse center-rear engine) on the roads where a few special stages of the rally of Montecarlo, as well as the Tour de France, were held. He forcefully denies that Lancia wanted to enter that Dino in a race.

According to the imaginative scoops «Autosprint» at the time, the negative report by Munari after the testing caused the program to be suspended. Munari reportedly wanted a lighter version of the Dino, but the opposition of Sguazzini, often portrayed by «Marcellino» as the chief supporter in FIAT of the battle against Lancia HF, had caused the idea to be postponed. At his press conference during the 1970 Turin Auto Show, Agnelli, gave a better briefing on FIAT's motor racing plans:

"Q. You said that FIAT will participate in road racing. Up to what point and in what way?

A. We are indirectly concerned with competition through Ferrari, which participates in prototype and formula racing. We also participate in road racing through both Lancia and FIAT. Mr. Sguazzini

In 1970 Sandro Munari took a normal Dino 246 GT, a car presented at the 1969 Geneva Auto Show, to the Tour de France layout to evaluate the possibility of using the small Ferrari berlinetta in rally competition, suitably prepared and modified. Although FIAT hastened to categorically deny any use of the Dino in racing, the episode wound up on the auto pages of the day, clearly demonstrating how the Turin-based company's racing team management was feverishly seeking a valid replacement for the Fulvia, outdated and no longer able to cope with an ever-fiercer competition.

will be pleased to give you the proper details.
A. (Sguazzini) As Mr. Agnelli, said, we have a two-pronged program: a Ferrari for the Formula 1 and the cars prototype, then a program that concerns rally competition in Italy and abroad, with both Lancia and FIAT cars, according to the type of race. We can thus choose the cars best suited to the type of competition in each case. This is our program for 1971.
Q. In distributing the activities of the FIAT group, will the road competitions be reserved to Lancia and the circuit events to Ferrari?
A. Both FIAT and Lancia will compete in road events, and Ferrari, of course, in Formula 1 and prototypes".

The words of Sguazzini seem to suggest FIAT and Lancia would not be clashing in road competition but that Lancia or FIAT would participate, according to a mysterious *"according to the type of race"*. No one specified who would be making the decisions (Sguazzini himself?) and with what criterion, given the natural evolution and special adaptations the cars undergo depending on the type of race.

No one could forget that, despite the win in November at the RAC Rally, the season had closed in a disappointing way for Lancia. In the final classification of the Manufacturers' Championship, the HF had finished no better than third, well behind the Porsche and the Alpine, while Alcide Paganelli and Domenico Russo, with their FIAT 124 Spider, had captured the Italian rally title and placed second at the Tour de Belgique, where they had beaten the Fulvia of Sergio Barbasio and Man-

Chapter 3 — Family infighting

Another of the cars the FIAT Group used in rally competition in the late '60s-early '70s was the 124 Spider. The photo shows one crossing the finish-line at Montecarlo in 1971, where it was classified 7th overall with Lindberg-Andreasson.

nucci, while Luciano Trombotto and Zanuccoli, with another 124 Spider had captured the Italian Group 3 title, defeating Giovanni Besozzi and Alessandro Brusati in a Fulvia.

In the annual press conference of Enzo Ferrari before the 1970 Christmas holidays, the problem of the rally Dino for the HF team was broached again:

"Q. What truth is there to the possibility that Sandro Munari will participate in the 1971 rallies with a Dino Ferrari?"
A. In truth, I know very little about rallies. In fact, I don't understand them. For the superhuman fatigue they cause the drivers, forced to drive for days and nights straight. It is a test only valid for the mechanicals of the cars. But we have Mr. Sguazzini here who is more familiar with rally questions.
A. (Sguazzini) A necessary first step is the homologation of the Dino Ferrari. Then we can see how well suited it is to rally competition. Only then will be able to decide whether to participate. Which, I would specify, it will never be in particular initiatives as had been discussed as a possibility for the Lancia HF team. It is different for

the driver, because even Munari himself could be asked to drive it". The awards ceremony for HF Lancia racing team, held in a villa on the banks of the Po trasformed into a *"refined restaurant"*, as Marco Magri, driver and cronista of «Autosprint», recalls, took place in a bitter atmosphere because of failure to achieve the objectives Cesare Fiorio had projected. On that occasion, Pier Ugo Gobbato found an opportunity to "equivocate" on the Dino question *"...up in the air because of certain high-level differences of opinion between FIAT and Lancia"*.

The awards for the *"super assisted"* FIATs, which had bettered the rosiest expectations, were also held during those same final days of December 1970, in a climate of secrecy, almost *"clandestine"*, as «Marcellino» recalled. The corps of drivers had become international, with the addition of Håkan Lindberg, along with Paganelli and Pino Ceccato in the ten most important international rallies, while in those valid for the Italian championship the usual eight crews would be assisted. Notable was the presence of Sguazzini and the absence of the cousins from Lancia, also part of the Gruppo Marche Associate directed by Squazzini, guilty perhaps of having convinced Luca Cordero di Montezemolo, former coéquipier of Cristiano Rattazzi in the FIATs, to change loyalties.

To complete this recounting of the events of 1970, I would add a recent pleasant chat with Pierugo Gobbato in January 2003 in the presence of Enrico Masala; the former Lancia manager, though he clearly recalled the awards ceremony that year, he did not confirm the response reported at the time by the journalist from «Autosprint», stressing that in any case they should have spoken of differences between Lancia and Ferrari, since the Commendatore would never have allowed one of his cars to be used by a team not in the employ of Ferrari. The chief opponent of the Dino program, whom Gobbato did not recall, was not Sguazzini but possibly Enzo Ferrari himself.

Cesare Fiorio, questioned recently, did not recall the detail of the entry at the Tour de France either, while he hastily classified the tests conducted by Munari at the time as normal investigations a company conducts with an eye to the development of new models. The only possibility remaining is that the Bologna-based weekly exaggerated.

Pino Ceccato and Helmut Eisendle drove this FIAT 125 S, entered by the Bassano Corse, in the 24th edition of the Montecarlo Rally, 16-24 January 1970. Entered in group 1, they finished 17th overall and 4th in their group.

A FIAT 125 S of the Squadra Piloti Bardahl of Florence. This team was particularly outstanding into 1968 rally season, in both national and international events, where FIAT entered both 124 saloons and 125 S.

LANCIA **HF**

Chapter 4

Arrival of the Stratos

In spring-summer 1970 Nuccio Bertone — the restless, far-sighted Turinese coachbuilder, veteran of clamorous successes in prior years with the Lamborghini Miura (Geneva 1966), the Alfa Romeo Montreal (Montreal 1967), and the Alfa Romeo Carabo (Paris 1968) — began to ponder the possibility of fathering a new, even more futuristic concept-car, which could accommodate the engine group of the Lancia Fulvia 1.6 HF. That power unit had often been decorated in the field during the 1965-69 competitive seasons and was thus at the maximum level of popularity with the vast audience of racing aficionados as well as the "devotees" in the company. The idea advanced by Bertone was to design a vehicle that would truly represent a break in architectural and stylistic terms with what had been proposed up to then. He no longer considered the wedge shape as the only idea to develop for his new creation, though he had used it to great effect on the Carabo and on that curious, streamlined rear-engine barchetta christened the Runabout at the 1969 Turin Auto Show. That is to say he set out, with Marcello Gandini, his head designer at the time, to find original stimuli, bolder inspiration that departed from simple formal research in the automotive field and projected itself toward broader horizons, detached from the stereotype of the self-propelled vehicle on four wheels. And this creative flight, in which free expression was left to pure fantasy, resulted not in an automobile in the true sense of

Drawn by his personal vocation and passion for racing to high-performance two-seat cars, Nuccio Bertone gained fame in the '60s for numerous creations built on the most prestigious chassis of the day (Aston Martin, Maserati, Ferrari, Iso Rivolta, etc.). At the 1966 Geneva Auto Show, visitors were astonished by the debutante Lamborghini Miura (below left) with transverse mid-engine, a super-car masterfully interpreted by Bertone with an ultra-modern look and extreme elegance. The following year, the creative genius of Bertone expressed itself anew with the Alfa Romeo Montecarlo prototype (below right), which Alfa intended to present at the Universal Exposition of Montreal as a study that *"could satisfy the maximum aspiration achievable by man in automobiles"*. That model later underwent a long, laborious series of modifications that resulted, two years later, in a production car.

Chapter 4 — Arrival of the Stratos

Another concept-car that confirmed Bertone as one of the most versatile, daring coachbuilders was the 1968 Alfa Romeo Carabo, which debuted at the Paris Auto Show in the fall of that year. Built on the chassis of the Alfa Romeo 33/21 Stradale, it represented a courageous challenge for supporters of the wedge profile. The low, flat front end, the large doors opening up and forward by hydropneumatic control, the original overall volume of the car exerted a strong allure on the public and critics.
Bertone revived this extreme wedge shape in 1969 in this original roadster with transverse rear engine, known as the Runabout, a clear reference to the Italian tradition in building powerful, fast inboard racing boats (on the right). Its architectural layout clearly inspired the body design of the FIAT X1/9, which was launched in the winter of 1972: Carrozzeria Bertone produced over 156,000 units up to 1988.

the term but in an "object" that aroused great clamor at the Turin Auto Show in late October 1970. It was christened Stratos, reflecting the space craze at the time (on the eve of the Apollo 14 lunar mission), the same medium in which the Ferrari Modulo of Pininfarina and the unexpected chalk study by Paolo Boano for FIAT were expressed.

Bertone started with a newly conceived floor pan on which he mounted, in a center-rear position, the engine group of a Fulvia 1600 HF they had salvaged, with Alessandria plates and obvious signs of an accident. The steering group and suspensions were designed so that a low, flat closed body could be developed, with revolutionary lines divergent from any known or preconceived scheme. The single-volume "object" that emerged from that study was trapezoidal in shape, finely tapered at the extremes, with four wheels inserted as the only conceptual reference to the current idea of the automobile. At 3.58 m long and just 84 cm tall, that extravagant vehicle vaunted tight, triangular lines that accentuated the overall sculptural value, depriving it of the slightest reference to the conventional canons followed by the other body designers. In extreme synthesis, it looked like the result of pure abstraction. The "Stratolimite", as Nuccio Bertone wanted to call it the first time he saw his new creation, debuted at the Turin Auto Show and made an extraordinary impression. The design of the side windows and the front and rear lighting groups, the deep groove on the side panel which magnified the wedge shape, even the access to the cockpit, which required opening the front end and "walking" to the driver's seat, where the steering column was mobile and jointed: all this served to amaze and

Lancia Stratos

Not even the major carmakers were immune to the extreme wedge trend in design, presenting static models and functioning prototypes of futuristic single-volume models at the various international shows. Outstanding among them was this chalk study by the FIAT Design Center, displayed in the FIAT stand at the 1970 Turin Auto Show. Bertone exhibited another interpretation of the futuristic sports-car theme at that same show, identified by the name Stratos, otherwise called the Stratos Zero or Stratolimite (boundary layer).

even bewilder. Not everyone approved that flight into the future: some felt it was excess for its own sake. Others viewed that car as an imaginative preview of the space vehicles proposed on children's TV programs. In realty, the "Stratolimite" was an extraordinary, courageous exercise in design, masterfully interpreted by the Bertone engineers and craftsmen.

The challenge of the talented Turinese coachbuilder was not launched just to his colleagues, who at the time were displayed large streaks of involution in their creative vein, but was directly primarily at Lancia as a pure provocation. And this is one of the reasons why Bertone, fearing that the factory would take a negative attitude toward such a project, preferred not to reveal his cards by asking Lancia for the mechanical components of the Fulvia to prepare his unconventional prototype.

At Lancia, in effect, the wild venture of the first Stratos aroused no official reaction. At the Auto Turin Show some curiosity was expressed by Cesare Fiorio, who stopped a few times at the Bertone stand, ogling that obscure, enigmatic

Chapter 4 | **Arrival of the Stratos**

One of Bertone's first renderings of the Stratos body (foreground) compared to the 1968 Alfa Romeo Carabo. The original architecture of the car was already evident in these first pencil strokes, reaching an almost absolute abstraction from the conventional concept of an automobile. The cockpit was to be accessed by raising the front section of the car and walking back to sit, in a near-supine position, on the two seats.

automobile, perhaps seeking some competition-related message. The world had to wait until January 1971, when the Stratos — meanwhile painted a brilliant metallic silver in place of the bronze color used for the Turin debut — reappeared on the scene at the Brussels Auto Show, this time exploiting its own resources and exhibiting itself in motion on the Gran' Place of the Belgian capital. It was there that the destiny of that car underwent a drastic metamorphosis. Seeing that strange science-fiction "object" move in traffic among cars that suddenly looked a half-century old projected the Stratos on to the world media, and the resulting clamor also reached the top floors of the Lancia skyscraper in Turin. A few weeks after the

(cont. to page 77)

Lancia Stratos

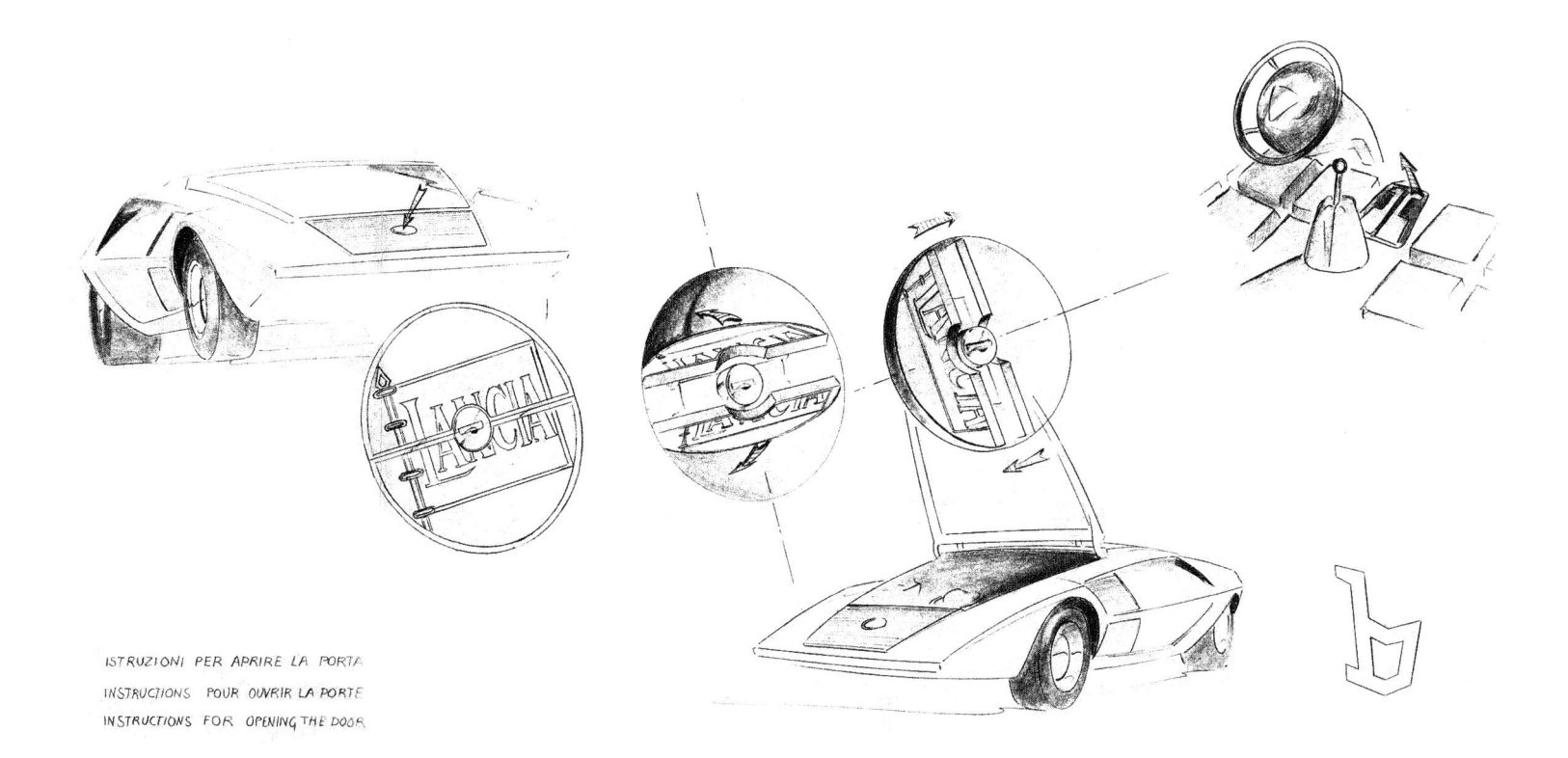

ISTRUZIONI PER APRIRE LA PORTA
INSTRUCTIONS POUR OUVRIR LA PORTE
INSTRUCTIONS FOR OPENING THE DOOR

A few sketches illustrate the Stratos rendering in its final form, with detail of the front-end door opening. Below: photo of the 3-D model of the car in reduced scale (left) and the full-scale wooden mockup on which the beaters formed the body panels for the prototype destined for the Turin Auto Show. Note the reduced dimensions of the car, especially in height (840 mm), on which the engine group of the Lancia Fulvia HF 1.6 liter was rear-mounted.

Chapter 4 | Arrival of the Stratos

The static model of the Stratos based on the initial design renderings. The roof configuration with the arrow-shaped engine vents, had reached its last development stage, while the configuration of the side panels and lateral glazing were further modified before the final version.

Below: two longitudinal sections of the Stratos design by Bertone in 1969-70. The first (upper) shows the final form, the arrangement of the mechanical components and the basic dimensions of the car as they were imagined by the designers. The other image (lower), unlike the other section, shows the placement of the Lancia Fulvia engine and a few structural projections of the bodywork and a different, more inclined placement for the spare tire in a compartment behind the driver.

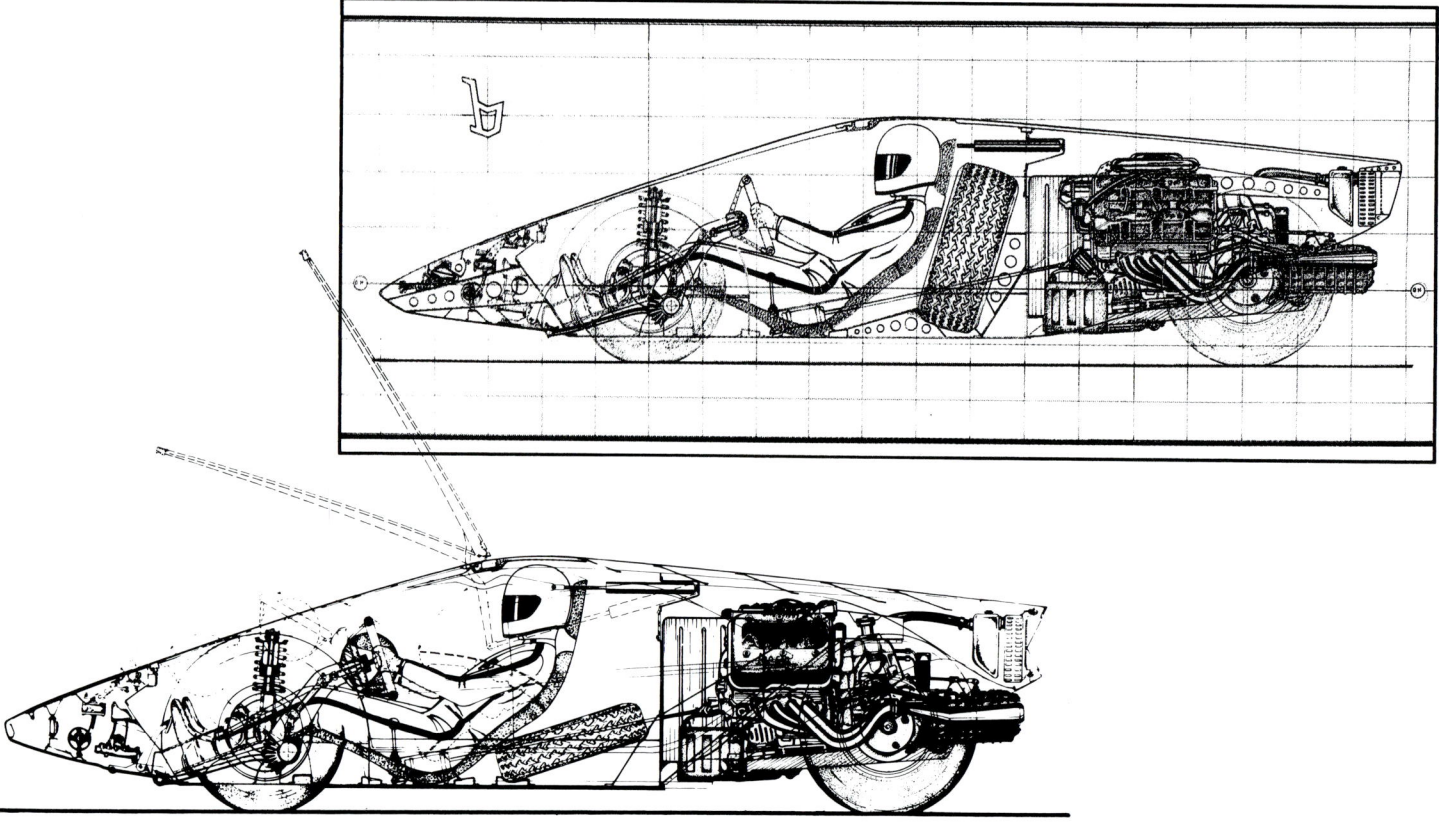

Lancia Stratos

The first photograph of the Stratos prototype just before the Turin Auto Show opened on 18 October 1970 (above). Apart from the large wheels, the shape of the car was totally unrelated to that of others cars of the day, even the most futuristic. The Stratos looked like an abstract sculpture, a pure exercise in coachbuilding art with no pretense of transformation into a functioning prototype. But Nuccio Bertone again astonished everyone a few months later by driving the Stratos himself to the Lancia headquarters to exhibit his latest creation to the company management.

Two more views of the Stratos "all open". The cockpit consisted of two seats in a single block separated by a slight central tunnel on which the gearshift was mounted. The steering column was jointed to permit access to the driver's seat, while the instrument panel was on the driver's left, mounted vertically below the side window. This window was exceedingly small and certainly did not facilitate maneuvers. The "full glass" front view, on the contrary, was almost perfect.

Lancia Stratos

(cont. from page 72)

close of the Belgian Show, Pier Ugo Gobbato, then general manager of the Turin company, told Nuccio Bertone he was curious to see in person that prototype that had appeared on TV and newspapers abroad.

Beppe Panicco, Bertone public relations manager at the time, recalls:

"We left Grugliasco — it was a gray day, not raining but overcast, with a touch of fog — and went to the Lancia racing team. Nuccio Bertone was driving, and a curious episode occurred: we arrived in

View of the Stratos taken with two ladies to put its height (only 840 mm) into perspective. The side window ended along a horizontal structural element that added rigidity and served as a character line to visually lower the side view of the car.

Close-up of the driver's seat of the Stratos (right, above), with the large hemispherical steering wheel hub and the vertical instrument panel on the left. On the right the gearshift lever and, below, a glimpse of the pedal group.

In three-quarter rear view, the Stratos appears in all its streamlined elegance, rich with highly original styling features (right, below). The narrow side window, seemingly set into the lateral moldings, played a geometrical role in total harmony with the futuristic arrowhead shape on the roof, which disguised the presence of the long air intakes over the engine compartment.

Chapter 4 | Arrival of the Stratos

With its two large "lids" open, the Stratos looked even more like a spacecraft, totally unlike any normal cars in circulation. The different sizes of the front and rear tires, as well as the pronounced moldings on the sides that concealed the air scoops for the engine compartment, gave the impression of great power and speed but at the same time were masterfully blended into an extraordinarily well-balanced whole.

Lancia Stratos

Nuccio Bertone shown next to the Stratos in the winter of 1971, when the car, originally a metallic bronze color, had been repainted silver. The talented Turin-based coachbuilder, used to astonishing with his creations, seems to be reflecting intensely on that daring promotional operation that was to give rise in later years to one of the most extraordinary phenomena in Italian autoracing history.

A close-up of the engine rear-mounted on the Bertone concept-car. It was a normal Lancia Fulvia 1.6-liter HF unit recovered from an accident-damaged car. The coachbuilder adopted this makeshift solution to maintain secrecy on the Stratos project.

via San Paolo, at the entrance to the Lancia racing team, and there was, as in all plants, a gatehouse with a barrier. The Stratos is 84 cm tall, the barrier 96. We were stopped in front of the gate and the noise of the Stratos was deafening and summoned Gobbato, Fiorio, Tonti and a few others from the office. Nuccio Bertone said: 'Let's try to pass before they raise the barrier.' He accelerated, we passed under the barrier, and then he opened the door on this sort of strange spacecraft, with Gobbato helping him to alight. From that moment the Stratos was born".

The conceptual formula of the transverse central engine was deemed convincing, and the entire project, though deeply revised and freed of its intrinsic eccentricities, seemed capable of generating another project associated with the possibility of an industrial sequel. In the space of a few months Bertone processed the Stratos into a new coupe, which retained the name of the first but little else, intended expressly for rally competition. This was a challenging task, in which the Turinese coachbuilder expressed his best energies. In place of the Fulvia 1.6 liter group, they began to consider using the 2.4-liter V6 that Ferrari had conceived (with displacement of 2000 cc) for the Formula 2 car of 1967 and had furnished to FIAT to

(cont. to page 82)

Chapter 4 | Arrival of the Stratos

After Bertone's theatrical coup at the 1970 Turin Auto Show with the Stratolimite (a designation dear to him), they began to develop the project for a car based on it but with technical and aesthetic characteristics for series production. At the coachbuilder's design center in Grugliasco, dozens of design rendering were prepared to evaluate their real practical potential on a comparative level.

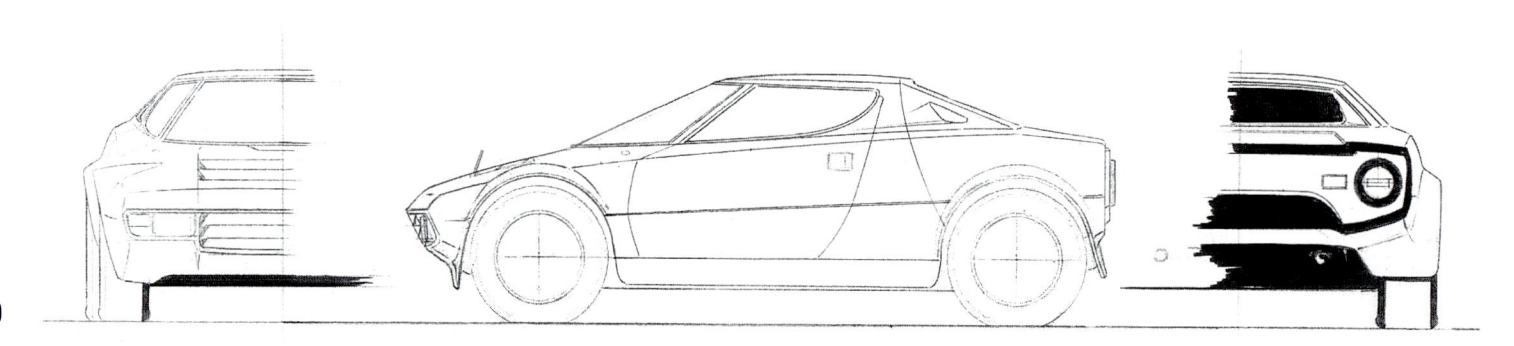

Lancia Stratos

During the summer of 1971, when the latest sketches began to reveal the preferred solution for the Stratos, one on which an industrial project could be based, a clay mockup was built (below), in which the shapes of the car in its definitive form began to emerge: short wheelbase, sharply sloping hood, perfectly blended into the sloping windshield, pronounced wedge-shaped profile, tail section tall and massive enough to accommodate the engine.

Chapter 4 — Arrival of the Stratos

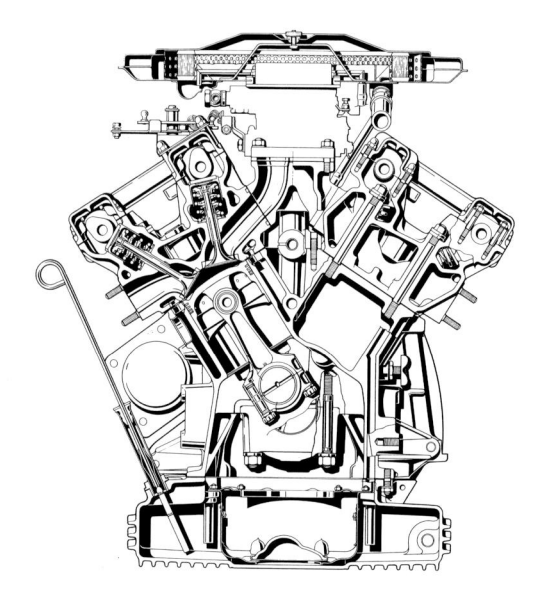

(cont. from page 79)

mount in the Dino 2.4 GT of 1969-72. That was a choice suggested provisionally by Bertone, who wanted to have a new prototype with an adequate engine that could be tested in the shortest time possible. Thus the "Stratolimite" of 1970 became the "Stratos HF", designed expressly for racing, and thus conditioned mechanically and stylistically by its primary intended use. The result was an extremely compact car (3.67 m long, 1.70 wide, 1.08 m tall) endowed with an outstanding personality, though totally different from that expressed by the prototype displayed at the Turin Auto Show a year earlier. The striking features of the new car were its lateral wedge shape and enormous windshield with constant radius, but also the aggressiveness of a true outsider, which seemed to presage that car's victories in competition. The receding line of the narrow lateral glass area lent it a rapacious, almost bellicose look.

Just before the 1971 Turin Auto Show, Bertone issued a new press release that stated:

"On the Stratos HF car, developed by Bertone in conjunction with the Lancia racing department, various engines can be mounted, with displacement ranging from 1600 cc to 2500 cc. The car exhibited at the Show has the engine of another group company, with which road development of the model will be conducted, pending a definitive selection of the engine range with which the car will be marketed, if the outcome of testing is positive".

With these enigmatic lines, «Autosprint» commented, they were attempting to resolve the contrast between the duo Pininfarina-Sguazzini and the team composed of Bertone-Gobba-

Lancia Stratos

Facing page: the Dino 166 F2 single-seater, initially mounting an engine with twin overhead camshafts on each bank and three valves per cylinder (left), debuted at the Race Car Exhibition that opened its doors on 25 February 1967 at the Carlo Biscaretti di Ruffia Automobile Museum in Turin. In the center, the same engine mounted on the 166 F2 but with a four-valve timing system (1968). Top power was 225-230 bhp at 10,600 rpm.
Left, bottom: cross-section of the FIAT Dino engine with 65° between the banks and displacement of 1987 cc. This same fourth generation of the Dino engine includes the 2.4-liter version mounted on the Lancia Stratos, officially credited with 192 bhp at 7000 rpm.

This page: two more renderings of the Stratos in its definitive 1971 version, intended for limited series production.

Chapter 4 | Arrival of the Stratos

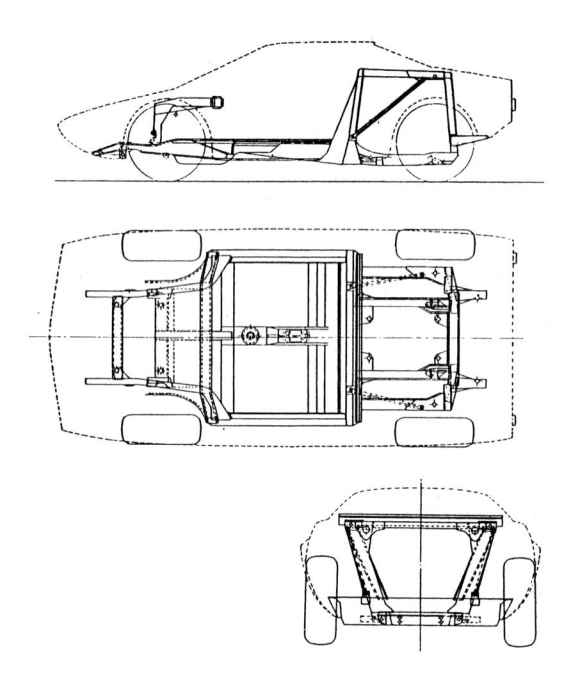

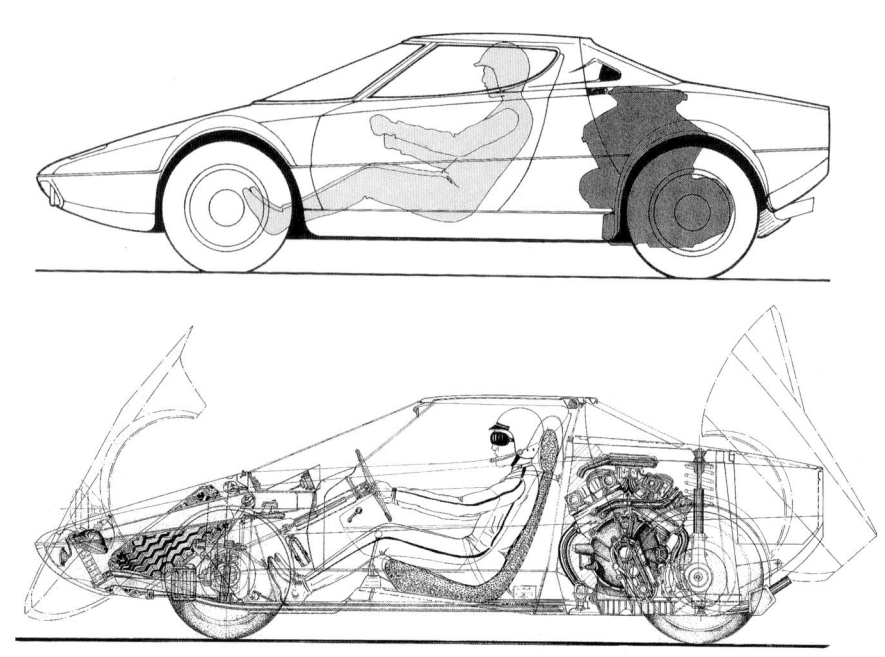

to and Ferrari, supplier of the Dino engine (which, according to a few British commentators, was not the 2400 with cast-iron block but rather the earlier two-liter aluminum 206, no longer in production).

Pier Ugo Gobbato recalled during the oft-cited conference in Milan:

"The engine group of the Fulvia had been mounted on that first Stratos Bertone, but it was obviously ill-suited to the car because it had insufficient horsepower. Nuccio Bertone had reached the Lancia plant with that car, driving it himself. We struggled to pull him out and I had to struggle to get in. I was excited and said to myself: this gentleman, who in essence builds coachwork and wants to try it out even with an unsuitable engine, has given us an idea.

While the original version was presented at the subsequent auto shows, and even test-driven by the specialized press, a version more consonant with practical requirements was taking shape. Bertone had shown formidable intuition, passing from that dream-car to the body of the Stratos with a mental agility that still astonishes me: allow me to say that that car is still modern today.

The original was difficult, not so much due to lack of horsepower as due to the near-horizontal driving position and the minimal ground clearance, which forced the driver to perform impossible contortions

Lancia Stratos

Facing page: the Bertone design office prepared these first technical drawings for building the chassis and bodywork of the Stratos. They already show the transverse mounting of the engine-gearbox group, the basic layout of the suspensions and the new location of the spare tire versus the 1970 prototype. The rear subframe carried the mounts for the McPherson rear suspension group, while on the first units produced it was the same as the front group (two photos below left), with double wishbones and coil springs.

The final design rendering of the Stratos '71, on which the prototype for the Turin Auto Show was based. In formal terms, the car acquired a totally different personality with respect to the previous year. The result was a harmonious, aerodynamic body, low and rounded, with an enormous constant-radius wraparound windshield perfectly blended in to the side windows. The short, clipped tail carried two enormous round lighting groups and a sharp cutout just where the exhaust pipes exit in the middle.

Chapter 4 | Arrival of the Stratos

to reach his position. We quickly reached an agreement with Bertone to create a more practical car.

Bertone had two advantages: first, he had bodied the Lamborghini Miura, which had a central-rear engine, and he had the Ferrari Dino engine group, with which he prepared the FIAT Dino coupes. Using the Ferrari Dino group could be an idea to obtain what we wanted, and Bertone did it, creating the Stratos in its final configuration. I spoke to Ferrari about it, because we had to have those engine groups. Since production was coming to an end on the FIAT Dino coupe by Bertone and roadster by Pininfarina, which used that engine, the tooling that was running out had to be preserved. Ferrari immediately said yes, without particular enthusiasm, but the fact he would be generously paid undoubtedly convinced him that the thing was possible. Bertone was the most enthusiastic of all. He had touched the right switch to ignite all our sensitivities, so we started with that first prototype.

The entire Lancia team began work on the project. I must recall the persons who were involved at that point, apologizing if I forget a few names, but my age is what it is: my memory may be slightly obfuscated. Cesare Fiorio was in charge of the racing department and gave us all the precise indications about what he needed to beat his adversaries. Francesco Di Virgilio, an exquisite person of incredible modesty, who had formerly played a significant role in the D 50 project, ceded to Ferrari as a Formula 1 car. Sergio Camuffo was the technical director. Gianni Tonti was technical manager of the racing department. Claudio Maglioli was the head test-driver of the

The first Stratos of the new generation is photographed in front of Carrozzeria Bertone in October 1971. It already bore the HF emblems and the famed baby elephants that for years had identified the cars of the Lancia Racing Team. The large front and rear wheelhouses indicate that the possibility of mounting oversized tires for better performance in certain types of competition was considered right from the design stage.

Lancia Stratos

Stratos, and Sandro Munari, then piloted this car to victories the world over. In addition to this core group, I cannot overlook Giampaolo Dallara, who also participated in the development of the car, and the late Mike Parkes, who often came to us from Ferrari and lost his life in one of his commutes from Maranello to Turin.

This collaboration, this general involvement, produced an exceptional car, exceptional in part because of the brief time required to produce it and put in on the road.

[…]

This, then, is the history, that may leave the impression that it was an extraordinary adventure without particular obstacles and with a good deal of good fortune. That was not the case. The life of the Stratos was beset with problems, and I am revealing the secrets perhaps for the first time.

The Stratos was born to be a prototype, with characteristics that let it perform well in the competitions and to hold high the Lancia name in the most difficult period of the company's life. I was given carte blanche until the International Federation decided that participation in rallies would be reserved to grand touring cars in Group 4. This meant that production had to total at least 500 identical units, and at this point I found myself on the brink of a precipice. Our idea had been to prepare seven, eight, ten cars per race, but now we would no longer have been able to participate in the rallies that interested us. The commitment was too great, unsustainable with

(cont. to page 90)

The 1971 Stratos, officially attributed to Lancia although it was mostly designed by Bertone, riceived an extraordinary welcome from the press, particularly the automotive press (in the photo the cover of the weekly «L'Automobile» of 21 November 1971), which devoted considerable coverage to the new model.

Right/left: the Lancia drivers – Sandro Munari (left), Amilcare Ballestrieri (center) and Sergio Barbasio – pose next to the same prototype presented at the 1971 Turin Auto show, in an official company press photo.

Chapter 4 | Arrival of the Stratos

Lancia Stratos

Facing page: three top views of the first Stratos, displayed at the 53rd Turin Auto Show (3-4 November 1971), placed on a rotating platform in the Carrozzeria Bertone stand. The car elicited the unanimous consensus of both show visitors and "insiders". The compactness of the body and the design layout, especially conceived for competition, seemed like two original messages in the field of rally cars, usually derived in various forms and measures from mass-produced touring cars.

In an autumn landscape, the red Stratos by Bertone still marks a contrast of strong visual effect in the photography of the day. From all angles the car was judged one of the finest ever produced by the famous Turin-based coachbuilder. It represented a successful touch of innovation in the formal evolution of the Italian design school.

Chapter 4 — Arrival of the Stratos

In contrast with the external lines of the body, so rich in novel elements, the cockpit of the Stratos '71 reflected a more conventional layout, faithful to the canons followed for race-cars in the '60s and '70s. The arrangement of controls was certainly not what is now considered ergonomic and is employed by all the makers of high-performance cars.

Close-up of the double-wishbone rear suspension mounted on the Stratos prototype in early 1972. It was later replaced with a McPherson system with vertical struts.

(cont. from page 87)

just the forces of Lancia, partly because in the meantime a certain squall had emerged in company competition. During that period Lancia was finishing first and FIAT second. This fact was not appreciated, so ... In part because they were paying! In other words, they did everything to convince us to pull out. Pressure was brought to bear on me to abandon the project, but I persisted, partly because I hoped they would understand that in the final analysis this was positive for Lancia and not negative for FIAT.

The production of 500 units was a commitment that I could not guarantee with just the forces of Lancia, in part because in the meantime various obstacles have arisen. I was being pressured to abandon the program and I ran into problems that seemed insurmountable. The first came right from Ferrari. He called me, and I went there to tell him: "Give me 500 engines" and he said: "No, I don't know, I can't ...." "But why?" "But no, forget it". I understood that he, too, had been pressured. I was sorry, because at the outset he had helped me and encouraged me to pursue that project. He said: "You know, we are ending the supply of these groups for the roadsters and coupes of Pininfarina and Bertone, and there is a tooling changeover...". In other words, he was trying to find an excuse linked to production difficulties.

Thus we saw our dreams fade away, because there were no apparent alternatives to that engine group: neither Lancia nor FIAT had anything suitable. We felt we were in a crisis".

The new edition of the Stratos appeared at the Turin Auto Show in November 1971. The monthly «Quattroruote» dedicated an entire color page to it with a few lines of commentary: *"One of the most admired automobiles at the show is this prototype that Bertone is proposing as a rally car; it has a central-rear engine. It was developed in conjunction with the Lancia racing team. It is called the Stratos HF".* In effect, the prototype Stratos HF was provisionally equipped with a V6 Dino engine and double wishbone suspensions in front and rear.

Many months of 1972 went by, however, with no solution to the question of the engine that was deemed the most competitive. In an interview a dozen years ago, Nuccio Bertone recalled that during one of the numerous inconclusive meetings with the Lancia technical staff, he caught the participants by surprise by exclaiming: *"Listen, that engine of yours for the future Lancia Beta or the horizontally-opposed engine of the 2000 HF you have been talking about for so long will never arrive, while the one mounted thus far provisionally has shown it is valid. Why don't you seriously consider it for producing the 500 units necessary to obtain homologation in Group 4?".* That was not a tranquil remark to make in front of those engineers, but it fully reflected the personality of the no-nonsense, decisive man we all knew.

The first two Stratos prepared by the Lancia Racing Team. In the foreground, the car with which Sandro Munari-Mario Mannucci debuted in the Tour de Corse on 3-5 November 1972. The car was forced to retire due to rear suspension problems.

Interior of the assembly line at the Lancia Racing Team, where the official competition cars were assembled.

The first victory of the new Lancia Stratos, not yet homologated and therefore entered in Group 5 reserved to prototypes, came at the Firestone Rally in Spain on 6-8 April 1973. Sandro Munari, recognizable in the photo for the Marlboro windbreaker, won with Mario Mannucci.

A Lancia-Maserati?

During his press conference on the Stratos, Pier Ugo Gobbato recalled:
"We started in November 1970, when the prototype with the Lancia Fulvia engine group was presented. We may call it Prototype Zero, a car that clearly could not be used for the things we required. A year after, in November 1971, Bertone presented the Stratos at the Turin Auto Show with the Ferrari Dino 6-cylinder engine with displacement of 2400 cc. He presented it as a static vehicle, because it had never been tested. But on 26 February 1972 the Stratos made its first laps on the Lancia track at Chivasso, with Claudio Maglioli at the wheel.
The presentation was quite interesting, although a few anomalies in the rear suspension immediately emerged, which Sandro Munari later discovered during the first race. All of 1972, from March to November, was necessary to fine-tune the car. On 4 November, exactly a year from the presentation of the static prototype at the Turin Auto Show, it competed in the Tour de Course, again driven by Munari. It was not a fortunate debut for the Stratos, because anomalies continued to plague the rear suspension, but that day

| Lancia Stratos

marked the beginning of its racing career. I have just read the principal passages of an article written by Piero Casucci that narrates the history of that car. Casucci writes: 'After the testing and promotional phases, the Stratos premiered at the 1972 Tour de Corse but garnered little applause; it failed to finish the race due to suspension trouble.' The Stratos fully satisfied the desires of all — engineers, drivers, co-drivers and mechanics — but initially proved to be a complex, capricious car that was difficult to regulate and control. 'On dirt' he recall, ' it was more or less acceptable and communicated its limits to the driver, but on asphalt it became extremely challenging because of the way it reacted differently in every corner: it had a bit of understeer and a bit of oversteer, and this made life difficult for us. We feared we would never tame it'. But tame it we did. In any case, at the finish line of the Tour de Corse, when Sandro alighted from the car, his face told us that we had serious problems, but we did not give up and pursued the project.

The Rally of the Costa del Sol on 9 December that same year marked the second outing for the Stratos. Munari and Mannucci complained of the same anomaly. The problem was of serious concern, because it derived from the architecture of the suspensions, which, as Fiorio had requested, had to permit changes in ground clearance to fit the type of layout. We finally discovered what the

The C.114 engine-gearbox group engineered at Maserati by Giulio Alfieri to equip the Citroën SM under agreements reached in 1967 between the French and Italian firms. The 90° V6 had initial displacement of 2675 cc, increased in 1974 to 2965 cc. The timing system had four overhead camshafts (two per bank), and the engine was fueled initially by three Weber 42 DCNF carburetors, later replaced by a Bosch indirect fuel-injection system. Maximum power was 180 bhp at 6250 rpm, which could be considerably increased when the engine was used in competition.

The Citroën SM, the top-line four-seat coupe with which the French firm intended to carve a niche in the sports car market. The car was high-tech thanks to a advanced hydro-pneumatic system that controlled the suspensions on all four wheels, the brake system and power-steering. The modern V6 engine declared specific power of 67.3 bhp/liter. Belabored by a long fine-tuning period, it failed to garner broad consensus and was taken out of production in 1975, after 12,290 units have been produced.

Chapter 4 — Arrival of the Stratos

problem was and resolved it through the efforts of Camuffo and his team. The weakness was that, to save money, the stub axles had been built of pressed sheet: they became deformed and the same happened to the mounting of the lower rear suspension arms. The rubber bushings of the arm mounts were too flexible and allowed the toe-in of the wheels to change, causing the car to zig-zag. These defects were quickly eliminated, but it had taken some time to discover what caused them.

The studies on the chassis were conducted first with the help of Francesco Di Virgilio, temporarily transferred from production to the racing department, later replaced by Francesco Faleo, a chassis specialist. When the construction drawings were prepared, we initially considered using upper and lower parallelograms on the four wheels. It was the definitive adoption of the Dino engine that changed things: the impossibility of mounting the engine longitudinally, here again to avoid going over budget, forced us to use inverted lower wishbones and telescopic struts on the rear suspensions.

The car's problems were all resolved, with the collaboration of drivers and mechanics of the racing department, and in 1973 Munari and Mannucci captured their first win with the Stratos at the Firestone Rally. An even more brilliant victory came at the Targa Florio, where the Stratos placed second overall. That was the last year the Targa was a pure speed event, valid for the World Manufacturers' Championship".

Pier Ugo Gobbato continues his presentation:

"Nuccio Bertone encouraged me not to give up [on the Stratos project]; I owe him a great deal, because he assured me that he could meet the commitment to produce 500 cars. This was already something, but the heart was lacking.

I again contacted Enzo Ferrari, that made me understand that he could not handle such a major commitment. So I asked to speak to the boss, Gianni Agnelli in person, as he had called on me several times for the FIAT-Ferrari nuptials and given me the impression that racing appealed to him.

I went to see him on 7 November of '72 and wrote this in my notes: I recounted the vicissitudes of our program, complaining that the negative directives were depriving Lancia of a major opportunity for publicity that we felt was favorable. I said I couldn't understand why I was being denied the possibility of using the engine from Ferrari, which had been part of FIAT since 1969, and asked him to

Lancia Stratos

The 2.7-liter V6 engine initially conceived for the Citroën SM (with displacement upped to 3 liters) was used by Maserati on its Merak coupe (photo), in production from 1972 to 1983. The validity of the Trident design was thus confirmed by the engine's use on a car intended for customers generally devoted to fast driving or even employed in racing. In its most extreme series version, the Merak SS boasted top power of 280 bhp at 6500 rpm and a top speed of 250 kph. The Maserati V6 would therefore have had all its credentials in order as an alternative to the Dino engine for the Stratos.

authorize me to seek other solutions. Agnelli seemed surprised and asked: "What does 'seek other solutions' mean?". I had trouble explaining it, because we were going through a rather unpropitious period.
Under the FIAT-Citroën agreements, Lancia was studying a two-liter car in conjunction with the French firm, which was to supply us the famous centralized hydraulic system it used on its cars. The conversations had always been difficult, because each firm, FIAT and Citroën, was convinced it was better... We went with Camuffo to Paris to test these cars, but the negotiations were difficult, and we were convinced they were not going toward a successful conclusion. Citroën had just acquired Maserati, which produced the Merak, with a 3000-cc V6 engine group. I told Agnelli: "This engine could be mounted on the Stratos". The words were no sooner out of my mouth than I began thinking that after my speech I would be asked to leave not only the office but Lancia as well, and that in his heart Agnelli was thinking: "This guy's crazy!" In effect, a few days later, at the end of November '72, the breakdown of the FIAT-Citroën negotiations was officially announced.
My fears proved to be unfounded: Agnelli listened to me and after a

Chapter 4 | Arrival of the Stratos

The Maserati V6 engine was also used in the early '70s on the Ligier JS2, with which its constructor, French driver Guy Ligier, participated in 26 competitions on track and road in the years 1972-75. The V6 designed by Giulio Alfieri was mounted on a mid-engine GT berlinetta and brought up to a maximum power of 260 bhp with a highly sophisticated preparation. The car later mounted the Ford Cosworth DFV engine, which enabled the pair Lafosse-Chasseuil to finish second at the 24 Hours of Le Mans in 1975 with an average of 190.558 km/h.

bit said: "Give it a try". He knew that things were going poorly, so that "give it a try" was like saying: satisfy yourself, since you won't accomplish anything. But I instantly took him at his word: I went to Modena to meet with Guy Malleret, manager of Citroën-Maserati, to talk with him about our desire to have their engine group. I found him interested, but he told me: "I need to ask my bosses if they agree".

That was near the end of November. The 29th or 30th of that same month the break in relations between Citroën and FIAT was officialized. This once again let the air out of our tires, just when we had found something ... Unexpectedly a few days later, however, toward the end of December, Guy Malleret called me to say: "My people are in agreement, but they would like the request to come from Mr. Agnelli". That was not a clever move. Agnelli had a particular character, and when I reported Citroën's intentions to him, I again thought he was going to ask me to leave. Instead, he took it well and stated: "Sure, they're total idiots!" Moral of the story: everything was on hold. After a few days, however, Maserati said:

Lancia Stratos

"We are willing to give you not only the Maserati Merak 3000-cc 6-cylinder, but we also propose, as an alternative, a more powerful engine, the 4300, mounted on the Quattroporte, for any needs you may have. The thing sounded strange, but in early January I met with Malleret again in Milan to see what process might be followed to obtain the engines.

The news of this meeting hit Maranello like a bomb. Ferrari was always informed of everything that happened with 'those guys', as he called them, those Maserati guys. He called me and said: "I'll give you the engines". I replied: "I'm sorry, but I proceed in a different direction". "No, no, we were joking". Conclusion: from that moment the attitude of FIAT changed, due largely to the intervention of Agnelli but also due to Ferrari's: all the obstacles were overcome and in no time we received assurances that we could count on 500 engines. I believe that this piece of history is being told here for the first time. I don't think I have stepped on anyone's toes, but at my age even toe-stepping is permitted! The truth is that we would have mounted the Maserati engines if FIAT had not dropped its negative attitude.

I don't know whether the car would have been as successful, then, but the fact that the Stratos's record of victories was associated with the Ferrari Dino engine was in a sense compensation for what Lan-

With 800 kg of weight, the Ligier JS2 made its unsuccessful debut at the 1972 Rallye des Ardennes and had to await the 1974 Tour de France to capture its first victory.
The Ligier JS2 is shown here racing in the 1000 Kilometers at Monza on 20 April 1975, piloted by Jean Pierre Jarrier-Jean Pierre Beltoise. On the facing page, it is shown participating unsuccessfully in the "Le Mans Classic" in 2002.

Chapter 4 — Arrival of the Stratos

A young Sandro Munari speaking with a mechanic of the Lancia Racing Team next to a '73 version Stratos. Note the absence of the dynamic air scoop on the roof to feed the engine group.

cia had done for Ferrari, when it ceded the D 50 Formula 1 cars to them in 1955 and Ferrari returned to victory.
Having resolved this problem, we began to work to get the Stratos homologated in Group 4 of the Grand Touring category, which was granted on 1 October 1974. The inspection officials were extremely punctilious: they wanted to see all the cars. We had prepared a plant building at Chivasso just to assemble the car: the 500th unit was finally counted, and all the documentation arrived admitting the cars to Grand Touring of Group 4".

This basically closes the recounting of Pier Ugo Gobbato on the birth of the Stratos. Only two final comments remain. The first is obvious: Gobbato was unable to enjoy the well-deserved success obtained by the Stratos, since he left Lancia in 1976, when the car was still at its competitive zenith, winning the World Rally Championship for the third straight year. Bernard Darniche, second overall with the Ligier JS2 at the 1974 Tour de France behind the twin car of Gerard Larrousse, became European Rally Champion driving the Stratos of French importer Chardonnet, and then repeated his performance in 1977. Secondly, it would have been curious to see the Stratos Maserati at work. When the Ligier JS2s, never homologated, clashed with the Stratos at the 1973 Tour de France, Guy Chasseuil dominated 14 of the special uphill and track stages and only an unlucky puncture of his fuel-tank slowed down the Frenchman's Ligier to the benefit of Munari, who ultimately won. Also in this instance Pier Ugo Gobbato showed excellent instinct, political as well as technical.

Munari's version

Some regarded the granting of the Dino engines by Ferrari as a favored owed, after the Lancia racing team had ceded its material to them in 1955. In truth, the engine had originally been designed in 1956 by Vittorio Jano, design engineer for Lancia for several years following the death of the founder. From a romantic standpoint, it would be nice to consider the gesture by Ferrari as a tribute to Lancia after the tragic death of the skilled engineer (who took his own life in March 1965) and faithful collaborator of the "Drake" since the days the Ferrari

Lancia Stratos

For the 1972 Targa Florio, Ferrari assigned a 312 PB to Arturo Merzario-Sandro Munari, who drove the car to victory in the classic Sicilian race. Munari, as he recalls in his public statements, was the decisive figure who induced Enzo Ferrari to grant the Dino V6 engine to Lancia for mounting on the Stratos. In other words, Lancia permitted its driver to participate in the Targa Florio with a Ferrari and Ferrari lifted the embargo on supplying Dino engine for the Stratos.

team had managed the Alfa Romeo racing cars. But Sandro Munari recently offered a different version of how the agreement to provide the 500 Ferrari engines came about. An article by Sergio Remondino, published recently in the monthly «Rallysprint», suggests that the Commendatore feared competition in the GT market from a Lancia with a Ferrari engine, sold at a lower price than Maranello's corresponding berlinetta. An interview reported by Remondino states:

"Enzo Ferrari — says Munari — wanted me to drive his 312 PB Sports in road races. Ignazio Giunti, who had seen me in action at Mugello with the Lancia Fulvia, wanted me at his side. I was to have raced with him. Then Ignazio died at Buenos Aires in 1971, but Ferrari wanted me anyway and placed me on the scales in the negotiations to grant the Dino V6s for the Stratos. 'If you grant me permission to use Munari in road racing', the diktat of Enzo Ferrari went, more or less, 'I'll give you the engines'. And so it came about: Munari raced for Ferrari (and won the 1972 Targa Florio with Arturo Merzario) and the Stratos was able to obtain the Ferrari engine."

But perhaps the words spoken by Sandro Munari during the conference of Pier Ugo Gobbato were more accurate:

"The Stratos was born with the contribution of all the persons Mr. Gobbato mentioned before. Everyone played his role — the mechanics, engineers, drivers, co-drivers, as well as the 'upper echelon'. The Stratos revolutionized the rally world, it was born thanks to Nuccio Bertone, whom I remember with great pleasure".

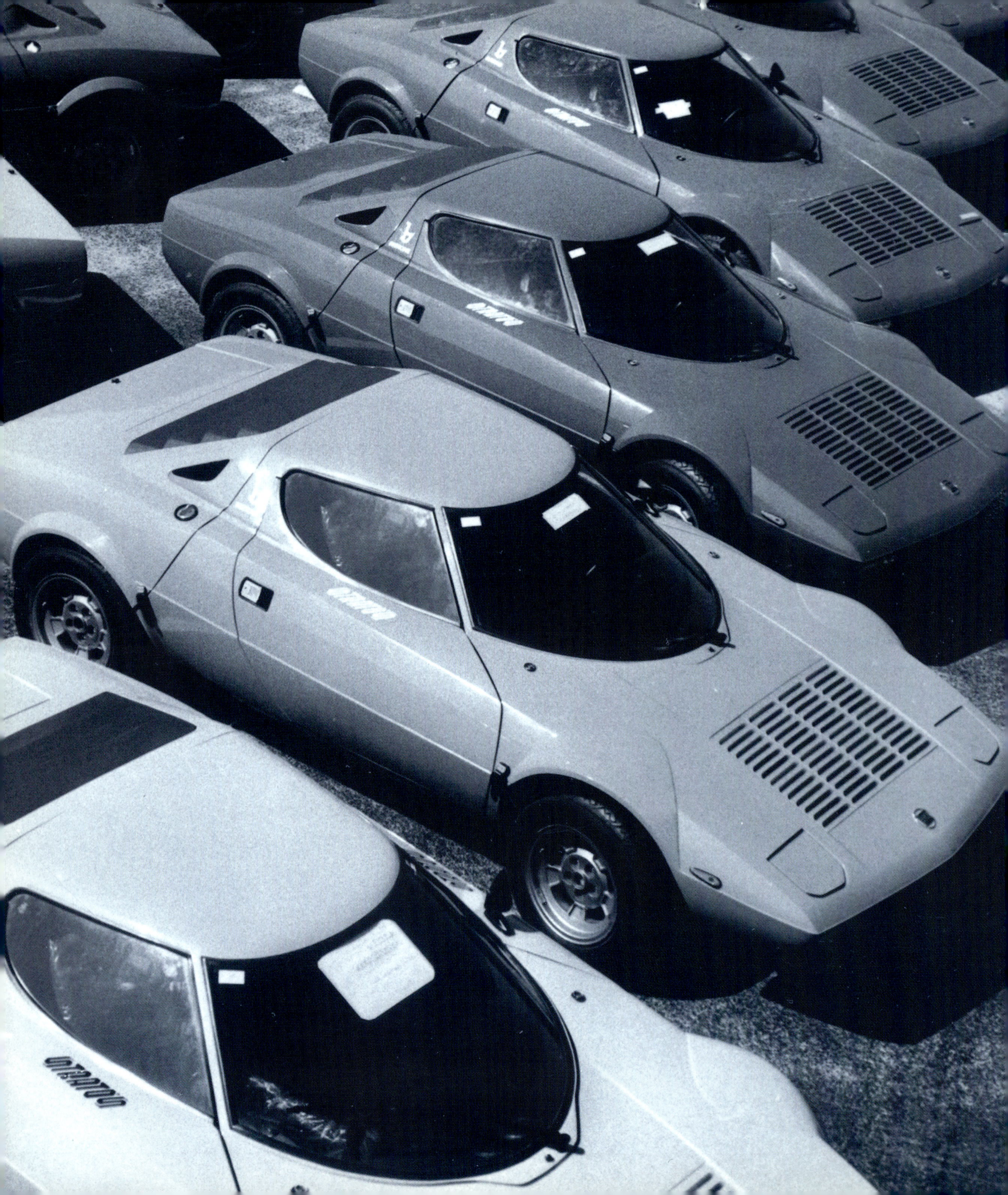

Chapter 5

Separated at home

At the 1971 Brussels Auto Show, Ford had surprised visitors by presenting the GT 70, a central-rear engine sports coupe with a plastic body and a curb weight of only 765 kg. Four engine version were available, two of them designed for competition: the Ford Cosworth BDA and the 3-liter V6 of the Capri. This was the response of Ford's Advanced Vehicle Operation to the Alpines and Porsches racing in the rallies.

Another piece of news shook aficionados in that sad January that had seen Ignazio Giunti burned to death at the wheel of a Ferrari 312 PB during the 1000 Kilometres of Buenos Aires, in a terribile accident caused by the careless actions of Jean Pierre Beltoise and the poor organization at the track. FIAT was to participate in the European Touring Challenge with the 128 under the banner of FIAT France, which had been supplied ten cars to assign to the Ecurie of Switzerland's Georges Filipinetti. The technical director of the operation was to be Mike Parkes, engineer and former driver for Ferrari.

Filipinetti, wealthy administrator for the Aga Khan, had purchased the Formigine factory and all material of Serenissima from Count Giovanni Volpi di Misurata, at the same time dismissing Alf Francis. Of the ten FIATs to be used in the races, seven (only four, according to Trivellato), along with nine engines, were entrusted to Jacopo Trivellato of Vicenza for tuning, while another was finished in the shop of Romeo Ferraris, on Via Ripamonti in Milan.

Only a practical joker could have devised such an outlandish venture: the Challenge, in its brief history, had included a classification for the up to 1300 cc class but never for the up to 1150 cc class. Furthermore, beginning in 1971, the limit of the 1st division, which became the unquestioned monopoly of the Abarth 1000 Sedan, had been lifted from 1000 to 1300 cc precisely to limit the supremacy of the Scorpion cars.

Anyone examining the results of the 1970 races, unless he was in bad faith, would have realized that the FIAT 128 had no possibility on the track of defeating the Alfa Romeo GTA Junior entered by Autodelta. What's more, those sedans would also have irremediably lost to the Abarth 1000 Sedan TCR, if any had been entered, since they belonged to the same divi-

Chapter 5 — Separated at home

The racing venture of the FIAT 128 was not crowned by success, despite the valiant efforts of the Swiss team of Georges Filipinetti, sustained in turn by FIAT. The top photo shows a Filipinetti 128 prepared by Trivellato during an event on the 1971 European Touring calendar at Zandvoort, tailed by Rob Slotemaker in a Hillman Imp. The bottom photo shows another 128 of the same team (driven by Claude Haldi), during a hillclimb at Marchairuz.

sion. This is certainly not a display of mistrust toward highly talented tuners like Ferraris and Trivellato, but the homologation form of the FIAT 128 sedan, still without the five-speed gearbox, left little room for optimism. If, then, its presence on the track was being sponsored to publicize the 128 Rally, soon to be presented to the market, only a healthy dose of masochism could have convinced them to enter it against the GTA Junior, since they could no longer soothe the audience of aficionados with the excuse of smaller displacement.

The car-to-beat in the Touring category in the late '60s was the FIAT Abarth 1000 Berlina, which won several events valid for the Italian Championship and the European Challenge. In the evolved 1970 version, the 1000 Berlina with radial head was credited with top power of 115 bhp and top speed of 190 kph. In 1971 the displacement limit of the Touring 1st Division was raised from 1000 to 1300 cc to quell the supremacy of the Abarths.

The results of the official trials at the 4 Hours of Monza, first race of the Challenge, left no room for doubt. Though well-reputed drivers like Claude Haldi, Charles Ramu-Caccia, Giampiero Moretti, Corrado Manfredini and Jean Vinatier were engaged, only two of the 128s managed to qualify last and next-to-last in the grid, with Moretti and the pair Trivellato-Danieli who had clocked time of 2'08"2 and 2'10"1, respectively, after a major "roasting" of engines that was repeated during the race. The best GTA Junior, driven by Luigi

Chapter 5 — Separated at home

The 1000 TCR engine with radial head mounted on the FIAT Abarth 1000 Berlina garnered many victories in the Group 5 and Group 2 Touring category in the late '60s-early '70s.

Colzani and Ansano Cecchini, had set the best qualifying time of 1'55"5, closely followed by Gianluigi Picchi (1'55"8) and the crew of Luigi Pozzo-Renzo Ruspa in an identical car (1'56"3). Applying the rule of 107% of the best in division, Moretti, the best in the 128, should not even have been allowed to start, since his time was over five seconds slower than the maximum permitted.

In the free trials on Friday, Abarth also showed up with four official 1000 Berlinas, duly registered and entrusted to Arturo Merzario, Johannes Ortner, Giovanni Salvati and Pam (the unforgettable Marsilio Pasotti), and to private driver Pal Joe (the alias of Gianfranco Palazzoli). Merzario was the fastest, with a time of 2'02"9. Abarth's strategy seemed clear: even without applying the maximum qualifying time rule, the FIAT 128s trying with the Abarths in the official practice, would never have been included among the first four cars in the up to 1150 cc class. The officials had allowed this number to start by virtue of a charitable race regulation after the "drum-beating" of the press, amplified by the fact that Filipinetti had entered the semi-official Ferrari 512s and Mike Parkes had been a Ferrari driver and test-driver.

The adjective "charitable" is mandatory, since the organizers had two 4 Hours run for the 1150 cc class: one in the morning for drivers competing in the Italian Championship, which included the classs, and one in the afternoon for Challenge competitors, which included up to 1300 cc class but not the 1150 cc sub-class.

At the official trials on Saturday, the four official Abarths failed to show up, thus freeing up slots in the grid that were occupied by the Abarth of Palazzoli well in front of the two 128s. Marcello Sabbatini, from the pages of «Autosprint», advanced two theories for the defection of the Abarths: either a decision inspired by "mamma FIAT" or the three engines that broke down on Friday and the technical impossibility of approaching the times of the Alfas prepared from the Autodelta.

Carlo Abarth responded in a letter, which Sabbatini published under the headline *"The Prodigal Son"*:

"...Your article attributes a polemic motive to the participation of my cars at the «4 Hours of Monza». I would say that this interpretation is rather self-evident, because every time I participate in a

Lancia Stratos

Philippe Albera and Jacques Coulon alternated at the wheel of the FIAT 128 of the Filipinetti Team during the Six Hours of Paul Ricard, held at the Castellet circuit. That year the Swiss team entered in the race not only the 128 3-door sedan but also the coupe version, in an effort to take the front-wheel-drive car to success. But the on-track results never convinced FIAT to pursue a racing-commercial operation that had already expressed its shortcomings. Within the FIAT Group, the best prospects for excelling in racing were still in the hands of Lancia.

race, I race to win, to beat an adversary, so therefore to polemize with him and demonstrate who is better.
I don't think that even 'mamma FIAT', impartial as all mothers, is interested in her sons' competitive spirit – but if that were so, why should she prefer children that race under the colors of a foreign team to those from her own home? [...]
The day I go to Monza with a 128, and I hope I can satisfy you at the earliest, if I want to continue the tradition of my firm, I will have to lap under two minutes.
Otherwise, I could not expect the tuners and the specialized press to show the respect they have always had for my technical efforts".
Surely Carlo Abarth had many reasons to be chafed. After capturing a number of GT and Touring titles for the parent company, and also brilliantly contributing to the development of the FIAT 2300 S, he had been set aside. And the Direzione Marche Associate, a name more suggestive of aperitifs and spirits than racing cars, according to the jibes of the day by opponents of Squazzini's policies, had forgotten him in favor of Ferrari, FIAT and Lancia. Not even the FIAT rally operation had seen Abarth among the contenders. It had brought first to the limelight the CMG of Attilio Giannini and his sons, who had tuned the first FIAT 124s of Rattazzi and Montezemolo, and then Giannini Automobili, which at the time had the ear and

First page of the FIA (Fédération Internationale de l'Automobile) homologation certificate for the Ferrari Dino 246 GT, issued on 30 September 1972. Homologation became effective on February 1st 1973 and enabled the car to compete in Group 3 events (GTs with production of at least 1,000 units), even though the Ferrari had already participated the two preceding years in a few Group 4 events (GT with production of at least 500 units).

assistance of FIAT. In fact, it had succeeded in homologating in the Touring category first the FIAT Giannini 500 TV Montecarlo then the FIAT Giannini 590 Vallelunga and in 1971 the 650 Modena (the last two in direct competition with the FIAT Abarth 595 and 695). Still with the help of FIAT, they were seeking Touring homologation for the FIAT Giannini 128 NP, for which a five-speed gearbox was also planned.

Then came the farce of Operation 128 with Filipinetti, and FIAT was launching the 128 Rally, which had been developed without involving Abarth. Giving free rein to hypotheses, the error that could be attributed to Carlo Abarth was not having followed, like Giannini, the new FIAT models from the 124 onward, developing versions of them with series bodywork and racier performance but not destined exclusively for competition. The only exception was the Autobianchi A112 Abarth in 1971, a car certainly not intended for racing and whose sport version was attributed to Abarth instead of Giannini, who had offered his services in the fall of 1969.

May best man win

Fortunately, the tension in the FIAT racing environment that had developed in Turin, with tones often exaggerated in the pages of «Autosprint», began to attenuate. The first signal came in the form of a "canard", immediately printed by the Bologna weekly, that in Modena Giuseppe Dondo, since 1969 in the role formerly occupied from 24 November 1966 by Gobbato, had ordered four Ferrari 246 GTs properly tuned according to indications provided the previous year by Munari, two of them intended for Lancia (Munari) and two for FIAT (Alcide Paganelli), so they could oppose the imminent debut of the Ford GT 70.

The Ferrari had, in fact, been homologated in Group 4 beginning 1 January 1971 with form no. 627. This form made interesting reading, since point 23 "Bodywork" states *"steel, light alloy and resin"*, with no detail on the thicknesses or the percentages of materials used, and items 24, 25 and 26, regarding the material of the doors, bonnet and boot lids, simple declare *"light alloy"*. Thus, while maintaining the minimum homolo-

The Dino 246 GT entered by NART (North American Racing Team) in the 24 Hours of Le Mans of 1972 and assigned to Pierre Laffeach and Gilles Doncieux. The car, slightly modified with respect to the series version (a supplementary fuel-tank of 180 liters), finished the race in 17th place overall, after driving 3,602.988 kms at an average of 150.124 kph.

gated weight of the car, 980 kg, it was possible to assemble a 246 GT with an all-aluminum body, doors and lids included, and this was done with at least four chassis (nos. 00518, 00558, 00588 and 00692 GT) of the very first L series (chassis from 00402 to 01116 GT). These models were normally made of steel, with only the front lid of light alloy, and thus not conforming to the racing homologation.

This was one of the many tricks used at the time, which a few years earlier had involved the SEFAC in judicial proceedings under the racing authorities and before the normal courts, for the Ferrari 275 GTB, similarly characterized by an elusive homologation form.

«Autosprint» then published a concise letter from Claude Sage, supervisor of the Filipinetti Team:

"...It is not true that the FIAT management asked its French and Italian branches [and not Swiss?, author's note] *to cease relations with our team and to halt the participation of the FIAT 128 in the European Touring Trophy. Nor, as far as we know, was any initiative taken in that sense by the management of Abarth".*

The fact remains that at the end of May Mike Parkes informed Trivellato and Ferraris that collaboration was ended, following the disappointing results obtained by the 128 in international races up to that point.

Chapter 5 — Separated at home

The rivalry between the FIAT and Lancia teams also seemed to subside. Luciano Trombotto began by helping Amilcare Ballestrieri when the latter's Fulvia ran out of fuel at the Rally of the Adriatic. Cesare Fiorio returned the favor at the Rally 4 Regioni by not acting to slow down Simo Lampinen, first in front of Ballestrieri, and preventing the latter from taking the lead in the Italian Championship classifiction to the detriment of Trombotto, provisional leader up to that point.

In the midsummer conference of the CSAI, the launch of Formula Italia was announced: a single-seat trainer designed and built by Abarth with a ITL 300 million contribution from FIAT. On 15 October, lastly, FIAT officially announced its acquisition of Abarth and the appointment of Gianfranco Sguazzini as sole administrator. The glorious Scorpion firm would abandon the Sport and Sport Prototype categories and concentrate on the tuning of a FIAT rally car and a few models derived from series production. With the extruding of Carlo Abarth, a rational solution was also found to the gradual proliferation of racing teams within FIAT. The Lancia problem remained along with the rivalry that opposed Sguazzini to Gobbato in defense of the structures they had been called to manage.

Another cold shower came during Agnelli's press conference at the 1971 Turin Auto Show '71. In fact, he first provided the generic response:

"In the rally field, we feel that competition between the marques of the FIAT group is the most sporting solution and what the public expects. So in this field, each is autonomous and free to participate in the most appropriate formula with car models linked to those in production".

And then, to the specific question from journalist Ceccarelli: *"What are the prospects for the Stratos HF?"*, Agnelli responded: *"Oh yes, that Bertone prototype... but no use of cars of this type: ... prototypes are not used in rallies, and the Stratos HF will have no sequel".*

Due perhaps to a delayed reaction on the part of the press office, neither the question or the embarrassing answer were reflected in the stenographer's record of the conference. But it was now public knowledge that the new weapon of FIAT, increasingly focused on racing, was to be a car with the body of the FIAT 124 Spider by Pininfarina, latest model to be pro-

Lancia Stratos

At the 10th International Rally of San Martino di Castrozza in 1973, the crew Barbasio-Macaluso partecipated with this FIAT 124 Abarth, finishing eighth in 4 hours 48'09".

The FIAT 124 Spiders were assiduous competitors at the Montecarlo Rally for some years. The one driven by Trombotto-Enrico is shown here during a service stop to change brake pads during the 40th edition of that wintertime competition.

moted in the markets, an engine derived from that of the new FIAT 132, soon to be presented, and all the chassis modifications Abarth would judge appropriate. The car, therefore, would not differ in appearance from the *"production"* car, as Sguazzini had ably suggested to Agnelli in his response.

Amid the interminable duel between Sguazzini and Gobbato, fought without particular regard for the rules of etiquette, it was proposed that Sandro Munari could be taken to a well-deserved victory in the European Rally Championship for drivers, a classification led by Poland's Sobieslaw Zasada with the official BMW 2002, by a thin margin over the Italian.

This was one of the negative results of the creation in 1968 of the International Rally Manufacturers' Championship, which gradually sapped importance from the traditional European Rally Championship for Drivers, initiated in 1953.

The first was based on the results obtained in the general classification in ten events to be held in various countries — from Montecarlo to Sweden, from the East African Safari to Sanremo and the RAC Rally — in which only cars of Groups 1 (series touring) and 4 (special grand touring) were admitted. The events were to have a minimum total distance of 3,000 km, including at least 1,000 of common road sections and 200 km of special stages, where one kilometer of special stages is

Chapter 5 — Separated at home

In 1972 Abarth on Corso Marche in Turin began preparing the FIAT 124 Spider 1600s racing in the European Rally Championship. Barbasio-Macaluso raced with one of these cars at the 1973 Medio Adriatico Rally.

regarded as equal to five kms of road section. For a race to be valid, there had to be at least 50 starters, and the points attributed were identical to those of the World Championship for Manufacturers (from 1st to 10th with this point breakdown: 20 – 15 – 12 – 10 – 8 – 6 – 4 – 3 – 2 - 1).

The less demanding Drivers' Championship was based on the results obtained in around 30 European rallies, often overlapping with the international manufacturers events, and consisting of several events valid for a given country, with a minimum length of 1,000 kms and at least five special stages of at least 100 kms each. The points assigned were the same as in the international championship for manufacturers, but only the six best results counted for each driver for purposes of the final classification, with no more than two races in any one country. A race was considered valid if at least 40 competitiors participated and, if the regulations of the particular race permitted, Sport Prototype cars of Group 5 were also admitted to the start. Because of the overlapping of the events valid for the two championships, Zasada was leading the Drivers' Championship with the BMW, a car that had certainly not excelled in the more challenging Manufacturers Championship.

Given the modest results achieved in the international season, limited to the final victory of the Fulvia 1.6 HF of Munari-Mannucci in the little-known Mitropa Cup, the Direzione Marche Associate entered, first in Austria, the FIAT 124 Spiders of Alcide Paganelli, Lindberg and Ceccato, for the sole purpose

Lancia Stratos

The crew Verini-Torriani finished fifth at San Martino of Castrozza 1973, also with a FIAT 124 Abarth. The Rally was won by an "exponent" of the FIAT Group: Sandro Munari and Mario Mannucci in a Lancia Fulvia HF.

of preceding Zasada and causing him to lose points. Thus, given the residual hopes hanging on the results of the Tour de Belgique, where Sport Prototype cars were also admitted, Munari was assigned a FIAT Abarth 2000. His objective was to seek the overall victory, given the particular characteristics of the race, with all the stages and legs on asphalt, some of them even on a circuit. Daniele Audetto was entered with a Fulvia 1.6 HF, which Munari would use in case of snow, and Amilcare Ballestrieri with an Alfa Romeo GTAM, the only Italian car that could challenge Zasada in Group 2. Unfortunately, the abundant rain found its way under Munari's distributor cap, forcing him to retire, despite the help of several foreign competitors, particularly Darniche and Henry with the official Alpines.

Nevertheless, this choral Italian participation in favor of FIAT group victories also confirmed the idea that, given the existing regulations, it was useless to commit suicide in the continental title while depriving themselves of a car like the Stratos HF, which could compete well in the foreign rallies where Sport Prototypes were allowed. The response of Agnelli at the press conference of the Turin Show, already forgotten in the stenographer's record, was about to fall permanently into oblivion, also the ultimate destination of the feared Ford GT 70 after a couple of rallies in France, all with disappointing results.

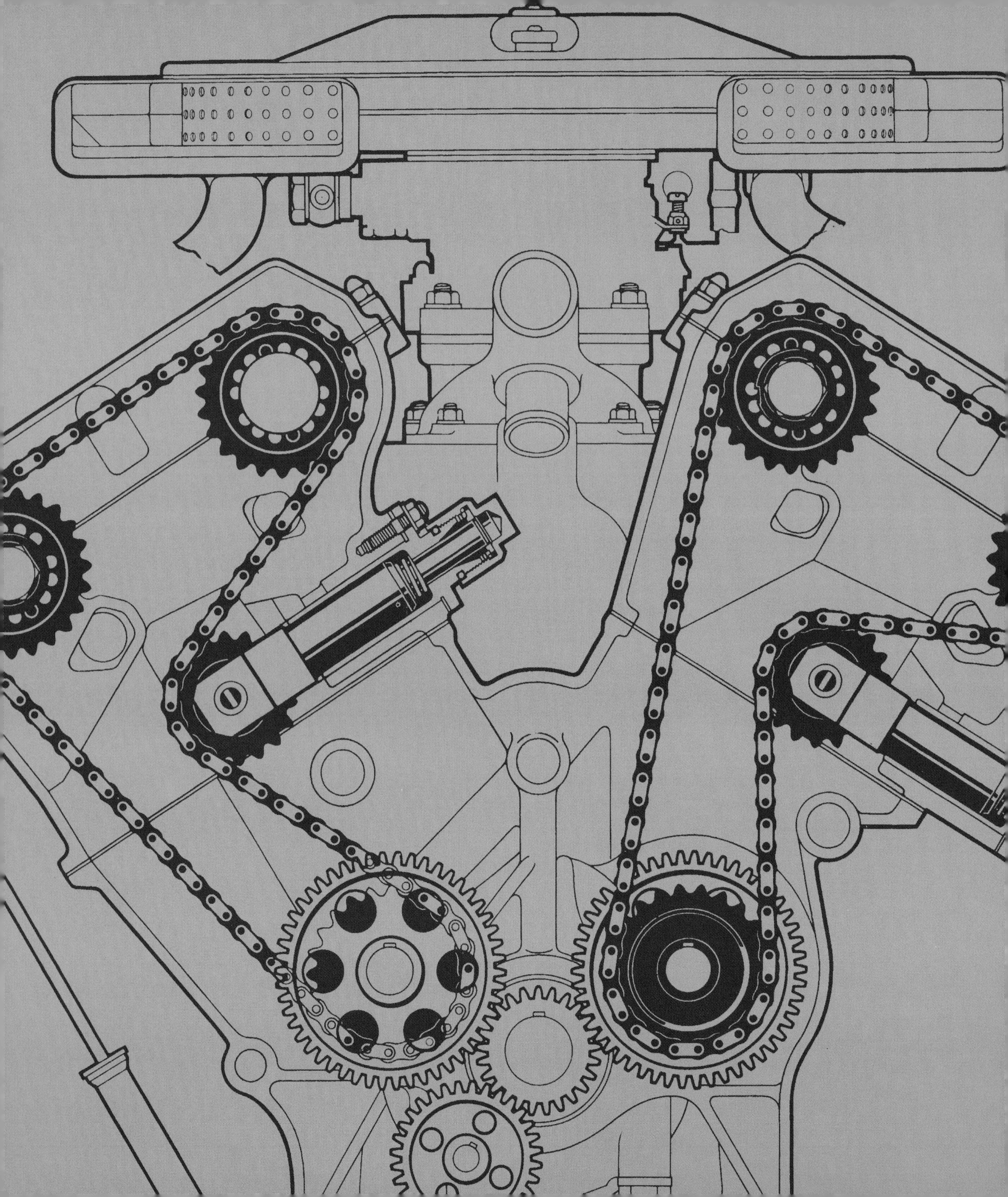

Chapter 6

An engine in search of a master

While the Stratos HF situation was still on hold, changes in the sporting regulations for the FIA championships did not escape the more attentive observers. First of all, beginning in 1973, the International Rally Championship for Manufacturers was to become the World Championship for Manufacturers, with much greater visibility and reserved to cars of category A, defined in FIA Appendix J as homologated automobiles belonging to Groups 1 to 4, thus reserved to series production cars. After 1970 homologation was granted when a car exceeded minimum annual production that varied from 5,000 units (Group 1 or production Touring) to 1,000 units (Group 2 or Touring Group 3, designated Series Grand Touring). For Group 4 or Grand Touring (often called Special Grand Touring in Italy), the minimum was set at 500 identical cars built in 24 consecutive months.

Homologation was granted after the FIA had ascertained that the required number of identical cars had been produced, and it lapsed five years after series production of the model had permanently ceased. Production was considered ended when annual output became less than 10% of the required minimum for the respective group. In the case of a Group 4 car, therefore, its production was declared over from the standpoint of the sporting regulations beginning in the year when less than 50 units were built.

Then in 1972 the European Trophy for GT cars was to be held, sponsored with 30,000 dollars from Camel cigarettes, a considerable sum considering the 14,000 dollars allocated to the organizers of the European Touring Championship. The new championship was also held under the auspices of the FIA and, like the Touring Championship, included a calendar of endurance races reserved just to cars belonging to Groups 3 and 4. This was a turning point in motor racing. Considering the growing costs of preparation and participation in an international championship, technical sponsors were gradually being replaced by others from different product categories. The first to come forward was the British cigarette Gold Leaf, which in 1968 had sponsored the F1 and Sport efforts of the

During the '70s the massive participation of cigarette manufacturers as sponsors of autoracing in the various specialties drastically altered the competitive panorama and environment.
Lancia also joined the general movement and, beginning in 1972, its cars were entered for racing with the gaudy red-and-white livery that replicated the Marlboro cigarette package.
The photo shows an official Fulvia Rally 1.6 HF of the Racing Team close to one of the first Stratos prepared by the Lancia Racing Team, still mounting the snorkel for funneling air to the 6-cylinder engine, later eliminated on the definitive version.

Chapter 6   An engine in search of a master

The massive involvement of tobacco sponsors began in 1968 with an initiative of Lotus, which took the start of the Monaco GP (26 May) with its 49-B Ford Cosworths painted red and gold, the colors of Gold Leaf cigarettes. The event aroused clamor in Formula 1 circles and, as a result, led to the gradual abandonment of national colors on the race-cars. Only Ferrari remained faithful to the traditional Italian red.

Lotus Team, with the cars painted in their colors red and gold. This was followed by Martini&Rossi, whose logo appeared on the Porsche 906 of Jöst-Bitter at the Nürburgring 1000 Kilometres that year.

The example of Gold Leaf was followed in 1972 by their competitor Marlboro, which had begun by sponsoring the BRM in F1 and then, that same year, Lancia Corse. The Stratos of Munari-Mannucci therefore debuted at the 1972 Tour de Corse in the classic red-and-white livery that clearly recalled the cigarette packaging.

Many things had happened prior to those November days in Corsica. While Ford had abandoned the GT 70 project, due not only to chassis defects but also to the 500-unit production requirement enter it in the first World Championship for Manufacturers the following year, another dangerous rival had entered rally competition, joining the Alpines and Porsches: the French Ligier JS 2.

This was a mid-engine sports coupe that Guy Ligier had begun producing in small series with the Maserati engine Giulio Alfieri had designed for the Citroën SM. It premiered at the end of March 1972 at the Rallye des Ardennes, retiring, and on 16 April was at the start of the Criterium Alpin without much luck, later attempting the adventure of the 24 Hours of Le Mans with three units entered. Although the victories did not begin arriv-

Martini also sought to promote its brand name with the international public by sponsoring a few autoracing teams in the late '60s. It made a triumphal debut at the Nürburgring 1000 Kilometres , where the Martini logo appeared next to Shell's on the Porsche 906. That first approach was later formalized in an agreement of December 1970 with the German carmaker that lasted until 1972. The Martini Racing-Porsche binomial was recomposed in 1973 and continued to be present in racing until 1980, year in which Martini "eloped" with Lancia.

ing until 1973, when Maserati furnished Ligier the 3-liter engine of the Merak, equipped with special four-valve cylinder heads, the story of this car, or at least its engine, was intertwined with that of the Stratos.

What I have recounted in the preceding pages might suggest that Enzo Ferrari haughtily rejected any form of collaboration with other Italian carmakers and that his actions were motivated solely by feelings of all-out rivalry and petty utilitarianism. Many will also conclude that the FIAT-Ferrari nuptials, of which Pier Ugo Gobbato was a principal author, was born of a desire on the part of Ferrari to participate with a competitive car in the European F2 Championship, than the most important promotional category toward F1.

The championship, instituted in 1967, was reserved to single-seaters mounting engines derived from those of production cars, homologated for racing at least in the GT category and thus with production of at least 500 units. Ferrari, which said it had a suitable engine, the Dino V6 in fact, was unable to satisfy the minimum production requirement and therefore, due in part to the shaky financial situation caused by its racing commitments in the Sport-Prototype and GT categories, was forced to seek assistance from FIAT.

This fact was significant. From the racing standpoint, this meant the return of an Italian engine to the promotional for-

Chapter 6   An engine in search of a master

One of the first Stratos assembled in 1974, with which Ballestrieri-Maiga contended the Rally of Sicily (finishing first) and later the 4 Stagioni and Alpi Orientali Rallies. Compared to earlier versions, note the different composition of the aluminum hood, with an additional row of dynamic air intakes.

mula, dominated in 1964-66 (when the allowed displacement was only one liter) for the first two years by the Ford Cosworth SCAs derived from the Ford Anglia block and then by the four-cylinder Hondas. In economic-commercial terms, it represented the achievement of synergies, which Ferrari had probably been secretly seeking since the Fifties, when he built the 854, the so-called Ferrarina, produced by modifying a FIAT 1100 bodied by Pinin Farina and mounting a four-cylinder engine developed and built at Maranello.

The "Ferrarina" case (1959-1963)

Jean-Pierre Gabriel, in his book *"Dino. The Other Ferraris"*, writes:
"From a distance of so many years, one still wonders what convinced Ferrari to build a car with such a small engine. At Maranello they have always spoken of it reluctantly and with a touch of embarrassment, as though they wished to erase the memory. The 854 was never sold, not even as a prototype. In fact, it was disposed of along with other scrap from the shop. In recent years Carlo Chiti revealed that Ferrari was very attached to that car and wanted to name it for his son Dino, but had ruled out the possibility of producing it in his

The 4-cylinder 854 engine mounted on the so-called "Ferrarina" became an event of national scope in 1959, while rumors spread that Ferrari was preparing the prototype of a small sports car with less than one liter of displacement. With 849 cc, single overhead camshaft timing system and a compression ratio of 7.5:1, that engine generated 68 bhp at 7000 rpm. For initial testing, it was mounted on a small two-seat coupe with body derived from the one Pinin Farina was building at the time for the FIAT 1200 (photo bottom with Enzo Ferrari at the wheel).

plant, with the excuse that he lacked the proper equipment. An arms manufacturer from Bologna then expressed an interest, wishing to place his machine-gun emblem on the grille, an excellent opportunity for a new nickname and the malicious observation that in reality the car's exhaust noise closely resembled the firing of an automatic weapon. But nothing came of it. There was also talk of Innocenti and the German carmaker Glas, later absorbed by BMW, as possible purchasers of a manufacturing license. In effect, the 854 could have been added to the Goggomobil-Isar range of 1960-61, but these rumors were never confirmed either.

On the other hand, it is impossible to imagine that Ferrari designed the 854 for the sole purpose of selling its engine to a few Italian manufacturers, as O.S.C.A. had successfully done by selling to FIAT the manufacturing license for the 1500-cc 4-cylinder competition engine derivative. The use of a FIAT chassis and a Pinin Farina body seemed to rule out the assumption that Ferrari had any secondary intentions with regard to FIAT.

So why did Ferrari decide to reveal in 1959 the existence of his 850-cc four-cylinder, soon increased to 973 cc with the adoption of a new crankshaft? And why was the same block bored out to 1032 cc for 91 bhp SAE with two 38 mm Weber carburetors, horsepower that, according to the manufacturer, was afterwards increased to 98 bhp with two 40 mm Weber carburetors?

Were these simply studies conducted on an experimental basis, a project that could soon have been employed in Formula 2 racing, where the regulations from 1960 to 1966 called for 1000 cc engines, using the 854 to replace the Dino 156? Or was it a reaction of wounded pride on the part of Ferrari, who wanted to establish the superiority of his creations over those of all competitors in all segments? Or, another possibility, was it a discreet invitation to FIAT to purchase the engines from Ferrari, whose racing activity it had been "unofficially" supporting since 1954? All these hypotheses are valid, especially the last one. One thing is certain: Ferrari had not undertaken these studies free of charge or for pure amusement. His intention was undoubtedly to sell the manufacturing license for the small car or its engine.

He only needed to find a truly interested buyer".

Whatever Ferrari's mysterious objectives, it is a well-known fact that he personally contacted Bertone to put a body on the prototype, and the result was exhibited at the 1961 Turin Auto

Chapter 6   An engine in search of a master

From the 854 a second engine was derived with displacement of 973 cc, single overhead camshaft and dual two-barrel carburetors (85 bhp). The third version, with displacement increased to 1032 cc (98 bhp) was the one mounted on the Mille coupe with body by Bertone, displayed at the 1961 Turin show.

Turin Auto Show, November 1962: Nuccio Bertone (center) with Oronzo De Nora (right) and son Niccolò at the christening of the ASA 1000 GT coupe, whose engine was derived from that of the "Ferrarina" of three years before. Then the ambitious project stalled and was never pursued.

Show in the coachbuilder's stand with the anonymous emblem "Mille" on the hood. Bertone built a second prototype, exhibited at the 1962 Show, with just a few slight modifications to the body and bearing the emblem of the project buyer, that ASA company which had been established in Milan in April 1962 by Oronzo De Nora, the wealthy industrialist in chemicals.

Bertone's affair with ASA was a brief one, as everyone knows, because at the end of 1963 the coachbuilder decided to sell all the rights to the Milan firm, in light of the serious delays hindering the start of series production.

The Innocenti 186 GT

The case of collaboration between Ferrari and Bertone, before the so-called "Mille", had been limited to three cars: a convertible on the 166 Inter chassis in 1950, a 250 GT in 1959 and, two years later, another 250 GT, which the coachbuilder was to drive as his personal car.

The relationship did not dissolve, however, despite the close relations established between Ferrari and Pininfarina. In fact, it resulted in a 186 GT prototype that was to be produced by Innocenti of Milan, another new firm that was appearing on the horizon of the domestic market, manufacturing automobiles under license from BMC, as it gradually converted from the wilting motorcycle and scooter segment.

Lancia Stratos

The Dino engine had a long career but also missed a few opportunities. The contact between Maranello and Innocenti of Milan sprouted under the auspices of Nuccio Bertone, who bodied the 186 GT coupe (in the photo), provisional designation of the new 4-seat sports car Innocenti was planning to launch in the mid-60s. The first-generation Dino 60° V6 engine (1788 cc) was mounted on the prototype. Due to internal problems at Innocenti, development on the project mired down and was then abandoned at the end of 1964.

For Innocenti, Ferrari chose a Dino engine of the second generation, i.e. that SOHC unit with 60° between the cylinder banks, which derived directly from the 2-liter engine of the 1959 Sport 196 S. Only the stroke had been reduced with respect to the competition model from 71 mm to 64 mm (retaining the bore of 77 mm), dropping the total displacement from 1983 cc to 1788 cc.

Development on this new Ferrari project in conjunction with Bertone was halted at the end of 1964. Jean-Pierre Gabriel recounts that:

"Innocenti would declare that it had abandoned the program «for fear of seeing the marque's image obfuscated by a product not sufficiently perfected...». In reality, it is a widely held opinion that it was financial difficulties that blocked the production and the hopes of Ferrari. The death of Fernando Innocenti in 1966 made the company's situation even more precarious. It was entering a difficult period, culminating in 1972 with the absorption of the automotive sector by British Leyland".

An agreement of cooperation between FIAT and Ferrari was signed, in effect, on March 1, and the press release spoke clearly of the production of a small series of a convertible mounting a Ferrari V6 engine of 1600 or 2000 cc, which had to be series-produced before the end of 1966, in time for racing homologation and subsequent use (the engine) in F2.

Chapter 6 An engine in search of a master

One event that raised commotion in the autoracing world was FIAT's decision in 1966 to launch a high-level sports car and to mount a Ferrari-designed V6 engine on it. It was the fourth-generation Dino with 65° between the banks and a four-OHC timing system, initial displacement of 1987 cc and top power of 160 bhp at 7500 rpm. The FIAT Dino (the Spider with body by Pininfarina in the photo below) debuted at the 1966 Turin Auto Show but met with obstacles because of its cantankerous engine and inadequate rear end suspension, in a car with top speeds above 200 kph. In 1969 an independent-wheel rear axle was introduced, but the commercial fate of that model was already sealed.

The FIAT Dino

Thus was born the FIAT Dino, with a new two-liter DOHC supersquare Dino engine produced at Maranello and bodied in Turin by Bertone (coupe version) and by Pininfarina (roadster). With this operation, FIAT was blocking entry into the market of the new Innocenti 186 GT, in a segment where the FIAT 2300 S was already laboring against the Alfa Romeo 2600 Sprint. At the same time, it lent a significant hand to Ferrari, which was being paid for the engines, and certainly did not displease Bertone with the large order for bodywork. According to the record, Bertone produced 3,670 bodies for the 2000 Coupe during 1967-69 and 2,398 for the 2400 version from 1969 to 1973. Pininfarina's production was smaller, with 1,163 of the 2000 Spiders and only 420 of the 2400 version. In total, therefore, Ferrari apparently built at least 7,651 Dino road engines over a span of five years, a considerable number for the Maranello factory, plus the assembly of the Dino beginning in 1969, when it was displaced from Turin to make room for the assembly lines of the FIAT 130. Ferrari's annual production had always been well below 1,000 cars/year (more precisely, 654 automobiles in 1964 and 740 the following year) but, thanks to the new investments associated with the FIAT Dino program, and the consequent 50% increase in staffing, the output of cars with the Ferrari trademark reached 629 in 1969 and 928 in 1970.

The decision to suspend production of the FIAT Dino was therefore an unpleasant surprise for Bertone. As Gobbato recollects, such reasoning probably lay behind the industrial promotion at Lancia and Bertone of a model with the engine already used in the FIAT Dino, a car that was lauded for the refinement of its engine but heavily criticized for the modest layout of other components. The sales campaign was heavily influenced by this criticism, so that over 75% of the production of the FIAT Dino 2000 was sold in the domestic market, which also absorbed over 50% of the models with the 2400 engine. Whether Gianni Agnelli statement that *"When Ferrari wins, Olivetti sells more typewriters around the world!"* FIAT Dino's life was certainly not supported by victories of Cavallino.

Lancia Stratos

One of the few 2-liter FIAT Dinos with competitive aims was Piero Botalla's, tuned by Samuele Boggiali (shown in the courtyard of the latter's shop). The car was homologated to race in Group 3 on 1 April 1967, and the engine, in conformity with the regulations, retained virtually its original characteristics. It participated in a few races in 1967-68 but was immediately overshadowed by the Porsche 911 S, which had been homologated on November 1st 1966.

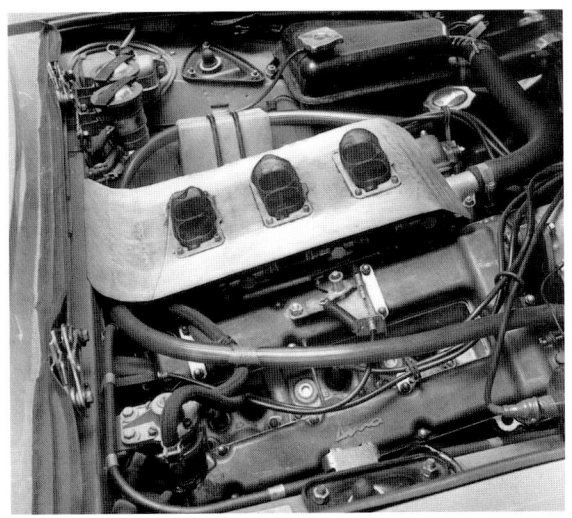

CAMPIONE DEL MONDO
Alitalia
S. MUNARI-S. MAIGA
10
R. PINTO-A. BERNACCHINI
8
LANCIA
Alitalia
LANCIA

Chapter 7

The Stratos HF and the races

Thus far we have analyzed the oft-converging stories of the protagonists associated with the birth of the Stratos: on the one hand the difficulties of Lancia, with the enviable racing past that it could no longer defend with current production; on the other Ferrari, which its founder wanted to keep at the summit of motor sports at all costs; and, lastly, the desire of certain people at FIAT who had rediscovered in competition a valid instrument of commercial publicity, almost 50 years after the company's official withdrawal from racing. The attitude of the Turin-based colossus toward racing is not as contradictory as it might appear at first glance, and it is totally obvious that the market had undergone a natural transformation in five decades. At the end of the Twenties the public, but also the government, was asking national industry to produce an "economy" car for all families under the aegis of a protectionist policy. In the late Sixties the phenomenon of free trade policy and the expansion strategies of the major international groups had already spread, and a carmaker's results in racing competition could once again be a weapon for outrunning the foreign competition.

The Stratos HF was sired for the sole purpose of dazzling the collective imagination, through its total supremacy in rally competition, and its history demonstrates this.

Its origins, in fact, were singular. It is recounted that its general design specifications derived from a survey conducted by Cesare Fiorio among the drivers, co-drivers and service mechanics of the Lancia racing team about the ideal characteristics a "winning" car had to possess in any type of rally. This procedure would represent a true innovation in the specific world of this specialty, as driver Sandro Munari recounted:

"The «revolution» brought by the Stratos was first of all technical: until the early Seventies, the cars used in rally racing usually came from series production. They were modified a little, bolstered in a few areas, and then sent out to race.
The Fulvia was an example of this: an exceptional car though it was not born for competition. It offered little opportunity for technical

The color range with which the Lancia Stratos was offered to the market in its catalogue.

Chapter 7 | The Stratos HF and the races

Lancia Stratos

Facing page: two views of the Lancia Stratos in the 1974 normal production version. Black louvers were mounted on the rear window, stressing the extreme compactness of the car and its primary vocations of speed and competition.

The Stratos shot with only the body section corresponding to the center cell, clearly showing the front and rear subframes with the two suspension groups: double wishbones and coil springs in front, McPherson groups with vertical strut in the rear, preferable for regulating the vertical bounce and for mounting various sized tires.

change: it had a transverse leaf spring in front and a rigid rear axle, so there was very little that could be modified, except the shocks and springs. Or a leaf could be added when it had to be raised to have a car capable of racing over the roughest terrain, like the Safari and similar events.
The Stratos, on the other hand, was conceived expressly for competition, with independent-wheel suspensions, with a McPherson system in the rear, and, for the first time in rallies, an aerodynamic study. It required controls and some technical assistance, but it was well suited to any situation and road condition".
Engineer Giampaolo Dallara also remembered it in an interview granted to the magazine «Ruoteclassiche» in 1987, where the Stratos was being compared to the Dino 246 GT:
"In technical terms, a direct comparison between the Stratos and the 246 GT (one is better than the other) is impossible. A parallel comparison is required. The two cars had the engine in common, the

Chapter 7 | The Stratos HF and the races

The instrument cluster on the production Lancia Stratos, unlike the one mounted on the prototypes, had a different, aesthetically more conventional layout, with two large round instruments (tachimeter and speedometer) and five smaller ones (water temperature, oil pressure, oil temperature, amperometer, fuel level). At the base of the instrument panel was a series of switches for auxilliary services.

The Stratos engine group was mounted transversely in the center, in the space left by the two massive side members of the rear subframe (photo on the right). In this close-up note the upper mounting of the McPherson suspension struts.
The double wishbones of the front suspensions, the steering componensts and the radiators with cooling fans were mounted on the front subframe (photo below).

Facing page: cover of the weekly «Autosprint» (issue no. 28 of 1017 July 1972), which reported on the testing of the Lancia Stratos at Chivasso track near Turin.
The scant Lancia literature on the Stratos includes the use and maintenance manual, of little use to owners of the car due to its modest content concerning the structural details of the mechanical components.

Dino 60° V-6, only slightly different in the tuning and exhaust design. For the rest, the two cars were different, because one, the Stratos, had been conceived as a racing animal, a thoroughbred, while the other was for fast road driving (even though the Dino engine lent it a victorious ascendancy on the track). It must be said that both achieved their parallel objectives perfectly.
Let's start with the Stratos. This car was born of a singular convergence between an ideal model of rear-engine rally car, which Lancia

racing department director Cesare Fiorio had clearly in mind, and a Stratos 0 prototype that coachbuilder Bertone had meanwhile prepared on his own on Lancia mechanicals. The chassis of the Stratos was commissioned to Bertone with technical specifications clearly aimed at competition. The wheelbase was short (16 centimeters shorter than the 246 GT, so the car would be as agile as possible on the tortuous layouts typical of rallies, particularly the Tour de Corse). The weight of the Lancia was concentrated 63.1% on the rear drive wheels (versus 57.7% on the Dino), to provide maximum traction. The McPherson rear suspensions were chosen for their rapid adaptability to the various racing terrains. The gearbox was modified so that the final drive ratio could be quickly replaced (in about 20 minutes). The chassis was designed as a self-supporting steel structure (the cockpit is practically incorporated in a tube section) to give the greatest rigidity with the least weight (200 kg lighter than the Dino). The car was developed and fine-tuned in relation to the racing tires mounted. Less attention was paid to development with road tires, since production was limited to a few hundred units. As a result, the normal version sold to customers was notoriously delicate to drive.

The opposite was true for the Dino 246GT. The classic Ferrari chassis was formed of round and elliptical tubing with the addition of a partial structure of steel plate, which contributed significantly to overall rigidity. The wheelbase was longer, the weight greater. The suspensions, all A-arms, were perfectly and exclusively developed for road tires. Compared to the Stratos it was more comfortable, less noisy, and didn't require the normal driver to have professional reflexes and skills".

The Stratos that Dallara was talking about was the final version, achieved after long trials conducted by Claudio Maglioli during 1972 on the Chivasso track with the prototype that had been shown at the 1971 Turin Auto Show. Enrico Benzing had the opportunity to test-drive that Stratos, and his report appeared in the July 1972 issue of «Autosprint» under the title "How Easy It Is to Drive the Stratos". It is interesting to reread that piece, because it reveals how much the car changed during its fine-tuning phase, and how clearly the Lancia people foresaw the technical-structural development it required right from the outset. The well-known racing journalist wrote the following:

Chapter 7 | The Stratos HF and the races

This photo of the Stratos with doors and lids open, drawn from the public catalogue, shows how small the cockpit was, dominated by the enormous wraparound windshield whose pillars were positioned well back. The movable body parts were built of aluminum in the first two units but then formed of fiberglass.

The 2400-cc V6 with two valves per cylinder. Recognizable in the photo are Daniele Audetto (center) and chief mechanic Gotti.

"A truly exciting, unforgettable experience, believe me: not so much for the weight/power ratio, as I had encountered lower values, as for the original ride this car was endowed with. Short wheelbase of 2.16 meters (the Ferrari 'Dino' had a wheelbase of 2.34 meters), with maximum weight concentration internally, for a car with a total length of just 3.67 meters (4.150 m for the Dino), with tracks of 1.4 meters and center of gravity that distributed the weight 42% on the front axle and 58% on the rear. The suspension and steering geometries are important: the entry of the car into corners is even

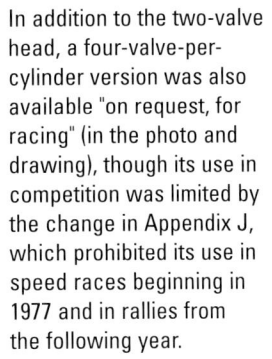

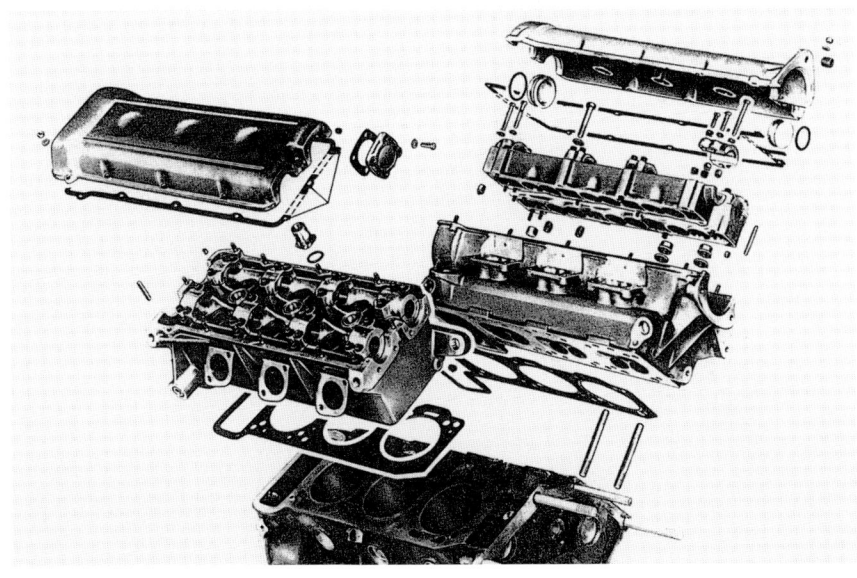

In addition to the two-valve head, a four-valve-per-cylinder version was also available "on request, for racing" (in the photo and drawing), though its use in competition was limited by the change in Appendix J, which prohibited its use in speed races beginning in 1977 and in rallies from the following year.

surprising (we're speaking of tight corners), with a gradual stiffening that truly impressed us. Small bar angles (the steering ratio is about 1:2.5 at full lock) produce strong progression on the inside wheel, permitting rapid, precise corrections, in order to have wide margins of driving utilization of all the components deriving from the drift angles of the tires.
[…] The fact is that this Stratos has a more than surprising readiness and precision of cornering (we would have liked to try a few wide corners as well) and is astonishingly easy to handle, even at the limits, considering that it mounts Pirelli Super Sport 5.00-9.60-14 tires, pending the arrival of the 'racing' version, and transmits something like 200 bhp in a car weighing over 800 kg. In fact, for the time being, in this phase of completion and definition, the car mounts a rather normal transverse 'Dino' V6 engine of 92.5 x 60 mm (2,418 cc) with three dual-barrel carburetors and slight timing and manifold adjustments that lift power from 195 bhp to 220 bhp, at 7,400 rpm rather than 7,600, to have greater cornering power. A more powerful version is planned for the near future, with 260-270 bhp, indirect fuel injection, presumably at the same engine speed, with further gains for the torque and mean effective pressure curves, proportional quantities.
The adaptation of the engine to rally requirements also involved many other changes, such as shifting the alternator to a high accessible position on the left, taking drive from the camshaft (intake) of

Chapter 7   The Stratos HF and the races

Nuccio Bertone looking proudly at his production Stratos, photographed in 1974 in front of the coachbuilder's Grugliasco plant.

The production Stratos, shown next to the concept-car presented at the 1970 Turin Auto Show, showed few analogies with the latter. But it drew its concept, if not its form, from that predecessor.

the front cylinder bank, and changes to ensure more perfect fuel feed (carburetor reservoirs) even in the tightest corners, with high centrifugal force. For now, the car has the series gearbox, […]. But it is clear that a new gearbox will be prepared for the type of racing to which the car is intended, to have much shorter, closer gearing (will they move to front meshing?) and a series of gears for fast changing of the total reduction from the external housing. […]. For now, the top speeds are of no interest, since fine-tuning and utilization will proceed in close succession; and as the speed increases (with 270 bhp we calculate at least 260 kph with these dimensions), the aerodynamic characteristics of the car will also require correction.
[…]
Now the car weighs almost 900 kg, but it will drop to around 800 kg with the two lids of plastic and a different rear sub-frame, with the objective of three kg/bhp. There is also a bit of revolution in the suspensions, now with inverted double wishbones, front and rear, and in the rear the vertical member uses the steering pickup for a small toe-in correction strut; later there will be a McPherson layout in the rear with rather similar geometries that will offer the advantage of increasing space, with a view to other engines to test and ease of corrections. In fact, the suspensions of a rally car must accommodate rapid changes in height (at least 3 cm), with various mounts, according to the terrain involved".

At the 1974 Turin Auto Show the production Stratos was displayed in the Lancia stand in its definitive version intended for sale. Elements distinguishing it from previous editions included the aerodynamic appendages added to the top of the roof and the large one on the trailing edge of the engine cover. Latches were added on the sides for the safety closure of the front and rear lids.

Its victories…

In autoracing, the most important titles are the FIA world titles. They have a relatively recent history, however, since the first to be instituted after that of Formula 1 in 1950 was the European Rally Championship reserved just to drivers, in 1953, along with the World Manufacturers' Championship for sports cars. The continental rally title was long dominated by foreign drivers and cars, and it was not until 1969 that the title was captured by Sweden's Harry Källström driving a car of Italian construction: the Lancia Fulvia 1.6 HF. Not until 1972 did an all-Italian victory come, with Raffaele Pinto, of Como, who won driving the FIAT 124 Spider.

It should be noted, however, that this delayed victory was caused in part by the lack of national interest in this specialty (the first Italian championship, in fact, dated from 1961), and by the institution in 1968 of the European Constructors' Championship. Its designation was changed in 1970 to the International Manufacturers' Championship, which obviously attracted the interest of a greater number of official teams.

In 1974, thanks to the homologation of the Stratos on 1 October and its three victories at the Rally of Sanremo, at Rideau Lakes in Canada and in Corsica, the Lancia captured the International Manufacturers' title, also due to solid finishes by the Fulvia and the Beta coupe in other valid races. The Stratos enabled the Turin-based company to recapture the world title

| Chapter 7 | The Stratos HF and the races |

Also in 1973, Jean-Claude Andruet was engaged to conduct fine-tuning work on the Stratos, still in need of refinements especially on the rear suspensions and Dino 2.4-liter engine. Top: the French driver on the track at Casale Monferrato during a test session.

After the disappointing initial performance of the Stratos in the first two rallies entered in 1972, where it proved difficult to tune and suffered rear suspension problems, 1973 was its first true racing season. Assigned to Munari-Mannucci and Andruet-"Biche", the Stratos took no time to display its qualities, with a highly respectable record at year-end: three victories in the European championship at the Firestone Rally (with the car shown in these two photos in the courtyard and interior of the Lancia Racing Department on Via Caraglio), at the Tour de l'Aisne and at the Tour de France, in addition to second place in the Targa Florio.

again in 1975 and 1976 with four victories in each year. Its predominance seemed total, especially in 1976, when the car took the first three places at Montecarlo and the first four at the Rally of Sanremo
The team of Munari-Maiga was the first to set the record that year of three overall world rally victories in the same season, also claiming the Italian overall Rally Championship. Bernard Darniche confirmed the monopoly of the Stratos prepared by Claudio Maglioli with victories in both the European and French championships, while "Tony" Fassina and Mauro Mannini won the Italian national rally title with a car tuned in Padua by Giuliano Michelotto.

Lancia Stratos

The 1974 rally season began on 2 February with the 24 Hours of Chamonix, raced entirely on frozen roads, offering the opportunity to compare the new Stratos of Munari-Andruet with timeless Fulvia HF of Ballestrieri-Lampinen. The latter car won the event, ahead of the other Lancia which was forced to lap too many slower cars during the crucial phases of the race. The Stratos soon revealed its unquestioned qualities on the icy roads, and one month later the Ronde Neige et Glace was captured by Andruet-"Biche".
The photo shown here was taken during tire and tuning tests on the car prior to that edition of the 24 Hours of Chamonix.

Chapter 7 — The Stratos HF and the races

Finally homologated in Group 4 on 1 October 1974, the Stratos seized its first victory in a rally valid for the World Manufacturers' title at Sanremo (bottom left); the Stratos was piloted to victory again by Munari-Mannucci, who with that win brought Lancia back into contention for the title: three races from the end, Lancia had caught up to the FIAT 124 Spiders, under increasing pressure from the Stratos. This trend was confirmed in the remaining events of 1974, with Munari first again with Mannucci at Rideau Lakes and third with Sodano at the RAC (bottom right). At the conclusion of an excellent season, Andruet-"Biche" also captured the final championship event at the Tour de Corse, handing Lancia its first world rally title with the Stratos.

Sandro Munari also partecipated with the Stratos at the 1973 Tour de France, traditional event consisting of a series of road trials linked to other on various French circuits, such as Clermont Ferrand, Le Mans and Le Castellet, to which the image left/right refers. For the Stratos the 1973 Tour was an extraordinary test bench, and one of Munari's most important victories.

Lancia Stratos

Underscoring the car's absolute superiority of the moment off the road, Austria's Franz Wurz, father of F1 driver Alexander, won the European rallycross title, just instituted by the FIA, at the wheel of a Stratos prepared in Turin by Almo Bosato. His bench test of the engine on this car gauged the performance of that power-plant. The register of the famed Turin-based tuner indicates that the series engine was braked at 7,000 rpm generating 180.21 bhp, while the maximum torque was 21.75 kgm at 4,000 rpm, values well below those declared by the company (190 bhp at 7,000 rpm and 23 kgm at 4,000 rpm).

In the period 1974-76 Lancia, like the other companies, had enjoyed a special period of deregulation in the technical rules, since beginning in 1970 it was sufficient to present just 100 units of a particular model to obtain racing homologation. It had therefore been possible to enrich the technical papers of the Stratos with four-valve cylinder head, various front and rear lids and various details of the suspensions. The freedom

In 1975, Alitalia airlines took over from Marlboro as the main sponsor on the Stratos cars, which thus gained a new white and green livery, retained until 1977. In this regard, Piero Casucci wryly observed in his book on the Stratos:

"*It was easy to say that the Stratos had stopped smoking and therefore began to fly*", which it confirmed indeed from the opening race of the 1975 season, the Montecarlo Rally.

Chapter 7   The Stratos HF and the races

The 43rd edition of the Montecarlo Rally (1975) took place under extremely adverse weather conditions, with fog and icy roads for almost the entire race, placing a heavy burden on men and machinery. Lancia entered three official Stratos and, thanks to the extraordinary support of Pirelli, which provided the cars with six different types of tire specially developed for the race, it won that rally with a crew composed of Munari-Sodano.

The Stratos was much less at home on the rough terrain and long dirt sections typical of the Acropolis, surfaces it often showed an aversion to. This photo shows the car of Waldegaard-Thorszelius during the 1975 edition, where it was blocked by electrical system problems. The event was won by Röhrl-Berger in an Opel Ascona.

| Lancia Stratos

The mechanics of the Lancia Racing Department completing tuning on the cars for the 1975 Montecarlo Rally, where three official Stratos were entered with Andruet-"Biche", Munari-Mannucci and Pinto-Bernacchini.

On this last car, shown in the photo, they adjusted the McPherson rear suspension and the supplementary lighting groups, below. Its race was rudely interrupted by a spinout, caused by a sheet of ice.

for modifications permitted by Appendix J then in force had permitted the engine in its maximum rally evolution with the four-valve head, used in 1976, to surpass 280 bhp, while maintaining good elasticity. The engines equipped with indirect fuel injection boasted some 40 bhp more.

Unfortunately for the racing career of the Stratos, a few unfavorable coincidences came along. Its production was declared concluded, from the racing standpoint, so its life in Group 4 would permanently lapse on 31 December 1982, and in the meantime no alteration of the homologation papers would be permitted. On 1 January 1976 Appendix J was changed so that the use of those items like cylinder heads and gearboxes homologated exploiting the 100-unit exclusion was no longer

Chapter 7   The Stratos HF and the races

In addition to confirming its supremacy in the world manufacturers' championship, the Lancia Stratos also won the European title in 1976 with Darniche-Mahé and the Italian title with "Tony" Fassina and Mauro Mannini, shown in the photo during a dirt segment at the Isola d'Elba that year.
The Stratos of "Tony" was tuned by Giuliano Michelotto of Padua and raced under the colors of the Jolly Club.

The excellent results of the Stratos in the 1975 World Rally Championship were confirmed in the following season, right from the opening race, the Montecarlo Rally, where the Lancias captured the first three places in the overall classification with Sandro Munari, Bjorn Waldegaard and Bernard Darniche, in that order. After that great exploit, the performance of the car — shown here in the non-title Rally of Morocco — remained high throughout the season: three more victories at the rallies of Portugal and Sanremo and the Tour de Corse procured for Lancia its second consecutive world title.

Lancia Stratos

A sequence of rare photos document a series of Stratos "nudes" inside the Lancia Racing Department in 1976, during the preparation phase, conducted under the supervision of Sandro Munari himself (photo on the left). The structure of the Stratos without bodywork illustrates how essential and compact the design was, with the 2.4-liter Dino engine as its true point of force. Bottom: next to the official "Alitalia" car, the Stratos Turbo still sponsored by "Marlboro", driven by Carlo Facetti and Piero Sodano during the 1976 Giro d'Italia.

permitted in speed racing beginning with the 1977 season. In rallies this restriction was postponed until 1 January 1978.
The obvious difficulties were aggravated by the fact that engineer Pier Ugo Gobbato, *"without ever having written a letter of resignation"* as he likes to recall, learned through the press that his resignation had been regretfully accepted by the FIAT management. The removal of this manager from the front office at Lancia facilitated certain decisions to focus everything in the rallies on the new FIAT 131 Abarth, which was created with four-valve heads and many other items designed for competition as standard equipment, though the body was derived from a production sedan, as dictated by the Boardroom.
Thus the 1977 title was won by the more conventional FIAT 131 Abarth, which with five victories in five events captured the World Manufacturers' title. It preceded the equally traditional Ford Escort RS 1800 Mk2, which claimed four victories against a single win obtained by the Stratos, driven to first place in the Montecarlo Rally again by Sandro Munari. He won the fledgling FIA Drivers' Cup, however, and once again the Italian overall rally title. The European Championship went

Chapter 7 — The Stratos HF and the races

Topping off the triumphal 1976 season for the Stratos, the French pair Darniche-Mahé also captured the European Championship with a car prepared by Claudio Maglioli. Top: the French crew during a special night stage at the 1976 Montecarlo Rally, where they finished third overall.

An unusual context for the Stratos was the rallycross championship, in which it participated in 1976 driven by Franz Wurz, father of Formula 1 driver Alexander Wurz, also winning the European title in that category.
The car was prepared by Almo Bosato of Turin.

During the 1976 season, the Scuderia Grifone entered a few Stratos in the European Championship, one of them assigned to the crew of "Tony"-Mannini, shown in the photo top right during the Quattro Regioni Rally that year.

again to Bernard Darniche still driving the blue Stratos of Chardonnet, again prepared by Maglioli, while Mauro Pregliasco and Vittorio Reisoli won the Italian Championship reserved to the international rallies.

The situation did not change in 1978: the FIAT 131 Abarth continued to dominate, with five victories in the 11 championship rallies, only one of which went to Lancia with the victory of Alén-Kivimäki at Sanremo. The Finn, alternating at the wheels of the Stratos and FIAT 131 Abarth, also captured the FIA Drivers' Cup.

This was the tangible result of the creation in December 1977 within the FIAT group of EASA (Ente Attività Sportiva Automobilistica) — briefly known as DASA, where the term "Ente" had been replaced by "Direzione" — with the task of defending and coordinating the racing activity of FIAT and Lancia. Cesare Fiorio was called to manage it, while Audetto became the racing manager of the unified team. For the rallies, it was decided to focus on the World Manufacturers' title with the 131. The Lancia program was downsized with the objective of

Lancia Stratos

In 1977 and 1978 the Stratos had to confront increasing competition from the Ford Escorts and the new FIAT-Abarth 131s (which purloined the "Alitalia" sponsorship from Lancia), capable of winning ten races and two world titles in two seasons. In 1978, abandoned by sponsor Alitalia, the Stratos displayed the red-and-black livery imposed by Pirelli, long a partner of Lancia in the rally events. Munari-Sodano raced in the Montecarlo Rally but failed to conclude the race due to engine failure.

This Stratos also participated in the 1978 Montecarlo Rally, driven by a female crew composed of Michelle Mouton and Françoise Conconi, who finished seventh overall.

Chapter 7   The Stratos HF and the races

Directly following the creation in December 1977 of a special section within FIAT to manage all the group's racing acitivity, with Cesare Fiorio as director, the roles of the FIAT 131 Abarth and the Lancia Stratos were redefined to avoid continued direct clashes: the former was employed in the World Championship, the latter in the European Championship, where it again demonstrated all its competitiveness with Tony Carello and Maurizio Perissinot, who also won that title in 1978. In the photo, the Italian crew is portrayed at the victorious Rally of the Costa Brava that year.

In 1982 the postal service of the Principality of Monaco issued a stamp dedicated to the rally held at Monte-Carlo every year since 1911: the Stratos, which had garnered four victories on those roads ('75, '76, '77 and '79), was selected as the principal subject.

the European title, in preparation for the World Sport Prototype Championship, where it participated with the Beta Montecarlo beginning in 1979. This brought an end to the dichotomy that had characterized ten years of racing activity for the two marques within the FIAT group.

The objective was fully reached in 1978 with victory in the European Championship by Tony Carello and Maurizio Perissinot with the official Stratos, sponsored by Pirelli, which thus also captured the Italian overall title. The international rally title was claimed by the team of Vudafieri-Mannini, which had changed tuners from Michelotto to Maglioli. There were also victories by Andy Bentza in the European Rallycross Championship for the second division (reserved to cars in groups 3 and 4), not yet recognized by the FIA, Darniche in the French national rally championship, and Siroco in the Greek championship.

With Lancia now competing primarily in speed with the Beta Montecarlo, everyone though the adventure of the Stratos at the international level was finished. But in 1979 there was a reaction of pride with three victories out of 12 events valid for the World Manufacturers' title. Bernard Darniche, still driving the Maglioli Stratos, won at Montecarlo and at the Tour de Corse, while "Tony" Fassina triumphed at Sanremo paired with Mannini driving a car also prepared by Maglioli, thus winning the Italian title per the international rallies. With fifth place,

Lancia Stratos

Brothers Andrea and Luca Betti racing in the 4th Rally of San Marino. They were not fortunate in that race, but at season's end won the Italian rally title, winning six of the 20 events on the championship calendar, driving a Stratos prepared by Claudio Maglioli.

Among the various Stratos used in the 1980 Italian Championship was the one entered by the Jolly Club and driven by Cunico-Meggiolan, shown in the bottom photo at the Rally del Ciocco (26-28 June), where it placed third.

then, obtained by Alén at the R.A.C. Rally, Lancia unexpectedly captured fourth place that year in the final classification of the World Manufacturers' Championship.

Again in 1979 Jorge de Bragation won the Spanish rally championship, repeating again in 1981. It was up to Andrea and Luca Betti to win the Italian national rally title in 1980 with the car formerly driven by Vudafieri, while the following year that championship was captured by Pierfelice Filippi with Giampaolo De Mela driving a Stratos prepared da Piero Gobbi, but that had long sat in the workshop of Bosato in Turin.

Also in 1981 Darniche also captured the last victory of the

Chapter 7   The Stratos HF and the races

In the early '80s the use of the Stratos was still massive, with the Lancias always protagonists in the hands of private teams and drivers, in both the European and Italian Championships. Fabrizio Tabaton, shown (top) at the 1982 Colline di Romagna Rally, where it finished first, competed in numerous events with the "Olio FIAT" Stratos.

The last international rally in which the Stratos competed before its homologation expired at the end of 1982 was the Rally of Monza, not valid for any title. This charming photo taken in the woods close to the banked track portrays the car of Giancarlo Biasuzzi tuned by the driver.

Stratos in a world rally event by winning the Tour de Corse again. This was the 17th victory in a FIA Championship race, thus equalling the record of consecutive victories of the FIAT 131 Abarth and establishing itself as the winningest car in world rally competition during its racing activity.

The famed cars of the new Group B were at the doors, with their turbos and four-wheel drive. But the Lancia with the new 037, developed by Sergio Limone and Gianni Tonti since 1978, had been preparing secretly to regain top world ranking in 1983.

Lancia Stratos

The three Lancia Stratos that competed in the 1975 Safari included this one driven by Munari and navigator Drews, selected by the "Dragon" because he was familiar with the local languages. The Lancia was prepared for the event with a significant marshalling of forces, with two aircraft providing assistance to the cars at any point along the course. But victory once again escaped Lancia, not through the fault of the team but the serious limitations of the Pirelli tires, which proved ill-suited to the stresses of the race layout. Munari-Drews had to settle for second place behind the Peugeot 504 of Andersson-Hertz.

...and its allergies

The all-purpose nature of the Stratos in the rallies did not appear just in three rallies valid for the world title: the RAC, the Acropolis and the Safari. Regarding this last race, Sandro Munari recalled in the oft-mentioned press conference:
"the Stratos was born with predominantly road characteristics, better suited to paved surfaces: the suspensions had little bounce, so in rather special circumstances like dirt roads, especially those of the past, we had to anticipate the possibility of problems. We entered our first Safari in '75; the car still had the two-valve engine, and I recall insisting that we go compete in the Safari. I was coming under some heavy fire from the press, and the entire organization--the Lancia racing department and even top management—was being criticized for competing in a race with a car they said was not up to the task.
I must say that, though I never won a Safari with the Stratos, I am still pleased we competed and am convinced that the car could have won, that nothing stood in the way of that possibility: it was a truly exceptional car.
[...]
Now we are used to seeing racing teams that move like those in Formula 1: helicopters, cars, vans, mechanics and the lot. Once, however, we had much tighter budgets and used to go race overseas by renting cars locally, doing a bit of reconnoitering. Only the first time

Chapter 7 — The Stratos HF and the races

The Lancia Stratos participated in the Safari for the first time in 1975, since the year before it was still awaiting FIA homologation. Compared to the "normal" version, the Lancia Stratos Safari was equipped with a supplementary steel-tubing structure with metal grating to protect the headlamps and an additional headlamp located on the right side, probably to assist the navigator in reading his notes. Modifications were also made to the rear suspension, with an increased excursion to adapt it to the heavy stresses of the course.

we went with the Stratos we took the backup car to see at least what was happening and what there was to be done. But we didn't drive the whole course, just some rather limited tests.

The car that we used for the tests, besides Waldegaard's and mine, was then loaned to a local driver, son of Vic Preston. It was a sort of barter, because we had used their logistics base, i.e. garage and other, and decided to make this gesture as compensation. Since the son of Preston raced only in Kenya and was not a professional driver, we gave him the backup car used for the tests.

In those days, in 1975, 70 or 80 cars were entered in the Safari; the roads were not like today's nor was the length of the race! Now there are 1800-2000 kilometers and what's more they don't drive at night. The cars then had to have an electrical system that could withstand lots of stresses, and there were often problems with the alternator, especially when they had to use the instruments necessary for better vision: the wipers, extra headlamps,... lots of problems arose at night.

The cars had to be much more complete, just as the drivers had to be more complete, since they remained for days in the car, in daylight and at night. The length of the Safari at the time was, I think, around 6,000 kilometers, so just finishing the race was a great achievement. I want to stress that, if the Stratos participated today in the Safari, I think it could still hold its own, all the more so if it had four-wheel drive!

Lancia Stratos

Things did not improve at the Safari the following year, demonstrating that the Stratos project had not been developed for racing of this type. Munari, paried with Maiga on that occasion, and Waldegaard-Thorszelius were both forced to retire due to engine failure (the former) and a broken oil pump (the latter).
The only Stratos to finish the African marathon was the one driven by Preston-Lyall, with a modest 12th place.

In 1975 eleven cars reached the finish-line: I finished second, Waldegaard third and Vic Preston eleventh: three Stratoses started, three Stratoses finished. Preston had never driven the car before, was not a professional driver, had received the car just before the start. The newspapers wrote: "The Lancia with Munari loses the Safari!" This was the conclusion and the satisfaction I received from the press! I must recognize, however, that at the time we were so strong everywhere that when we came in second it was like losing the Safari!
Now I'll tell you what happened to me at that Safari. During the race I had an accident, a crash with another competitor, without particular consequences. At 500 km from the finish I was in the lead. 500 Km seemed like a lot, but out of 6000 it is rather acceptable distance, so the objective was to consolidate the result achieved to that point.
Up to then, we had had mostly problems with the tires, which were Pirellis. Probably the tire had not been developed properly for that type of car and those conditions, with the speed, the lateral forces, the rocks. The sidewalls were fairly robust. It was our misfortune that 50 km from the end of the stage we had three flats in succession: we had two spares, couldn't carry more, one was even on the roof. When we had the third flat, we had a 56-minute lead over the second car in the classification and were, as I said, 50 kms from the end of the stage, where the assistance service was.

Chapter 7   The Stratos HF and the races

Another race ill-suited to the Stratos was certainly the Acropolis, where the Lancia car never expressed its full potential, often halted by technical failures.
Three cars participated in the 1976 edition: one of them was driven by Pregliasco-Garzoglio, forced to retire with clutch problems.

Facing page: the Lancia Stratos shown in the classic backdrop of the Safari rally.

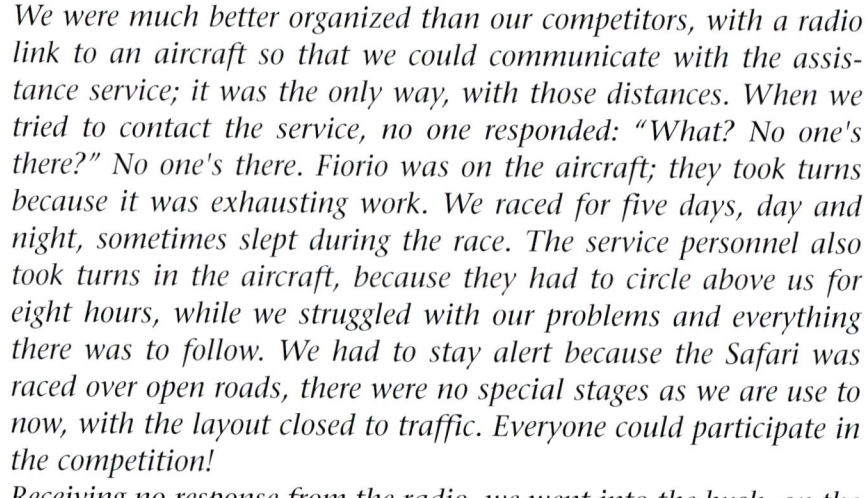

We were much better organized than our competitors, with a radio link to an aircraft so that we could communicate with the assistance service; it was the only way, with those distances. When we tried to contact the service, no one responded: "What? No one's there?" No one's there. Fiorio was on the aircraft; they took turns because it was exhausting work. We raced for five days, day and night, sometimes slept during the race. The service personnel also took turns in the aircraft, because they had to circle above us for eight hours, while we struggled with our problems and everything there was to follow. We had to stay alert because the Safari was raced over open roads, there were no special stages as we are use to now, with the layout closed to traffic. Everyone could participate in the competition!

Receiving no response from the radio, we went into the bush, on the dirt roads, as best we could. I had a local navigator, Lofty Drews, skilled also from the mechanical standpoint. Since the last tire to puncture was in the rear, we said: "Well, let's mount the front wheel in back, until we reach the national highway". To lighten the front end, Lofty sat in the back so as raise the right front wheel. Finally we reached the National, which was only lightly traveled. It was already five in the evening, and after several attempts Lofty was able to hitch a ride to reach the service area, which was 14 more km ahead. In the meantime I proceeded at a snail's pace. Finally the service arrived and changed the tire. They changed the tire, we arrived at the control, and at the end we lost the race by 22 minutes, a race that was already in the bag.

We still didn't understand why the aircraft hadn't responded. At dusk, that twin-engine couldn't land on the various strips scattered here and there along the layout, normally used by single-engines; they had landed at Nairobi before darkness fell. So the Stratos, in my view, was capable of winning even races like the Safari".

If we start from the F2 Championship, which had been the cause of the FIAT-Ferrari nuptials, exploited then by Lancia, we shall recall that after a disastrous debut they tried again in 1975, assigning to Ernesto Brambilla a few Stratos four-valve engines with fuel injection to adapt to the F2. The results were not forthcoming, even though the Project Four Racing team of Ron Dennis had mounted them on a few semi-official Marches, winners with other engines. They were assigned to drivers of the caliber of Jochen Mass, Eddie Cheever and Jilles Vil-

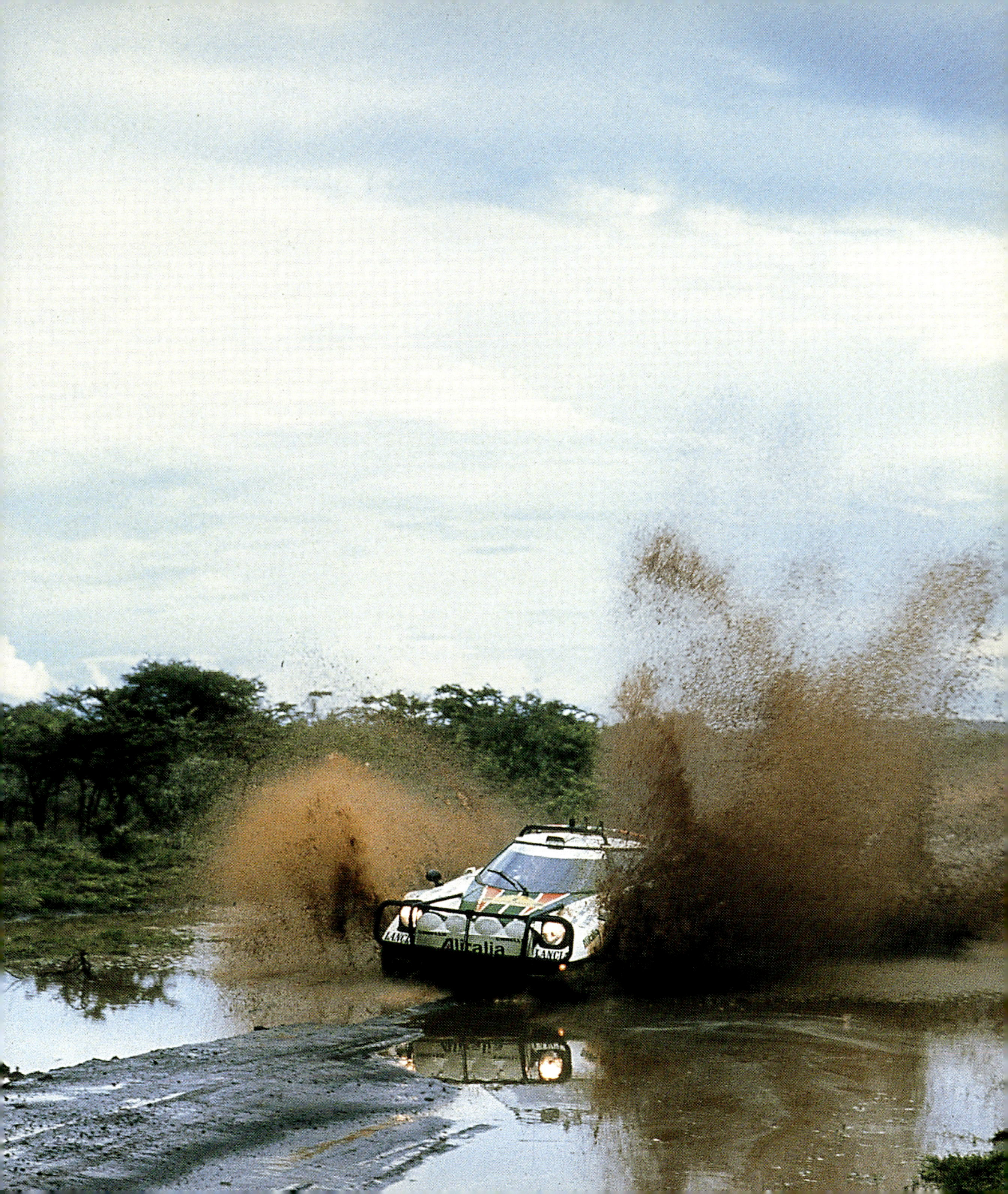
Alitalia

Chapter 7 The Stratos HF and the races

In 1975 Ernesto Brambilla mounted a four-valve injected engine of the Lancia Stratos on a March F2, but the operation brought no noteworthy racing results and was soon abandoned.

leneuve. After breaking off relations with the team of Ron Dennis, who then became the manager of McLaren, one engine was mounted on the old March 732 of Vittorio Brambilla, who in August obtained a modest 11th and last place two laps behind the March 762 with BMW engine driven by Hans-Joachim Stuck. It was then discovered that the main problems of that single-seater were linked to the old concept of the engine and the lack of a dry sump, which for one thing uselessly raised the center of gravity and penalized handling regardless of the chassis used, They realized this the following year when Ferrari, thanks to the contribution of CSAI and FIAT Oil, began to furnish engines to the Italian teams of Trivellato (Chevron chassis) and to the Everest team (Ralt chassis).

And yet Brambilla had also exploited all the experience acquired by the Facettis in the Marlboro speed Stratos that in 1975 had participated without fortune in the FIA European GT Championship. In fact, he had just inserted liners in the cylinder of the Lancia four-valve engine with Kugelfischer indirect injection, reducing the bore from the original 92.5 mm to 84 mm, thus getting under the two-liter mandatory displacement limit. Then in 1977 one of the engines was marinized for use on an inboard catamaran built in the boatyard of Angelo and Renato Molinari.

A rendering by Carrozzeria Bertone, probably in 1974, shows a version of the Stratos for circuit racing, rather similar to the car actually used that year by Facetti-Brambilla in the World Manufacturers' Championship.

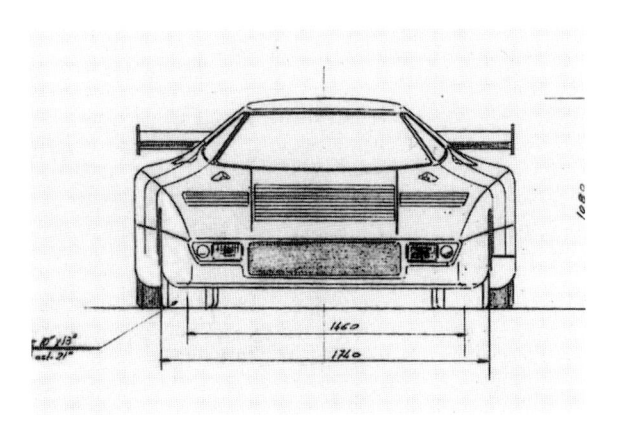

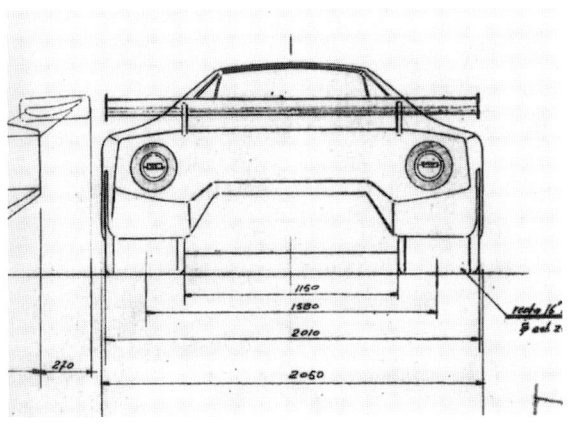

The principal characteristic favorable in the rallies, the small polar moment of inertia, which made the Stratos extremely agile in tight corners, proved counterproductive in the fast curves on the circuits. To remedy this they increased the wheelbase of a car racing among the prototypes, but this measure was not applicable to Group 4, as not permitted by Appendix J.

The Stratos in the GT Championships

The encouraging results of 1974 in road speed races prompted the idea of entering the four-valve Stratos in the European GT Championship, instituted in 1972 and in effect reserved to drivers of Porsches, given the absence of other truly competitive cars. In fact, the car had won that year at the Targa Florio, no longer valid for the FIA championships, with the team of Ballestrieri-Larrousse preceding the German-tuned Porsche RSR of Restivo-Apache, while the private Facetti Stratos of Emilio Paleari and Mauro Pregliasco had placed fourth. The race of the other official four-valve Stratos driven by Sandro Munari and Jean-Claude Andruet was unfortunate, halted by a fire while refueling at the Cerda pit. It was unable to repeat the performance of the previous year, when it placed second overall behind the Porsche Carrera RSR of the Martini Racing team driven by Dutchman Gijs van Lennep and Herbert Müller.
Confirmation of basic equality with the Porsches in road competition came in 1975 at the Tour Auto. The two-valve Stratos tuned by test-driver Claudio Maglioli for French importer Chardonnet and assigned to Andruet and Biche came in third overall behind two Ligier JS 2s, preceding the German rivals.
Given the good level of reliability Carlo Facetti, thanks to sponsor Marlboro, registered for the FIA Championship with a four-valve Stratos, presented to the press as having 320 bhp for 890 kg of weight. With the adoption of new Lockheed disc brakes, the hope was to be competitive on the track with the Porsche RSRs, which on paper started with a 600 cc advantage. The Stratos debuted in the European Championship at the Bevilacqua Cup in Imola on 13 April 1975. The race was of brief duration, however, as Carlo Facetti was immediately halt-

(cont. to page 154)

Chapter 7 The Stratos HF and the races

Immediately after the 1974 Tour de France, the Stratos underwent a check-up at the Lancia Racing Department: the nearest one, without the front lid cover and with the profile frame exposed, was the car of Andruet-"Biche", which finished third in the French race, while in the center is the car driven by Munari-Mannucci, retired due to engine problems.

One of the most important results garnered by the Stratos in 1974 was the win at the Targa Florio. Gérard Larrousse and Amilcare Ballestrieri, shown crossing the finish-line, covered the eight laps of the small Madonie circuit in 4 hours 35'2" at an average of 125.653 kph, ahead of the Porsche 911 Carrera RSR of Raffaele Restivo and Alfonso Merendino and Abarth Osella of Giovanni Boeris and Achille Soria.

Lancia Stratos

In 1975 Carlo Facetti wanted to test the qualities of the Stratos on the circuit and, with the support of sponsor Marlboro, entered a four-valve Stratos in the FIA Championship, where the strongest adversary was the Porsche RSR. After two unsuccessful attempts, the Bevilacqua Cup at Imola and the race at Zeltweg in Austria, both concluded with retirements, the reliability and performance of this Stratos, whose development was followed personally by Mike Parkes (in the top photo, standing next to the car) improved significantly, enabling Carlo Facetti to earn some good placements, including a third at the Intereuropa Cup in Monza (abetted by the retirement of the Porsches).

Chapter 7   The Stratos HF and the races

(cont. from page 151)

ed by gearbox problems, which previously in trials had caused him to "go off" at the Acque Minerali corner. The problem was later said to relate to overheating of the gearbox fluid, due in part to its position and the lack of a dry-sump lubrication system mentioned earlier.

Facetti entered the race at Zeltweg for the second event on the championship calendar, but after six laps encountered brake problems, caused perhaps by improper operation of the suspension struts. Although officially Lancia had no direct commitment with engineer Mike Parkes, Parkes personally followed the development of the speed car, which seemed to improve in reliability, managing to cross the finish-line at both Norisring (ninth) and Hockenheim (twelfth).

At the 1975 Euro Life Cup, held at Misano on 1 August 1975, Carlo Facetti again entered with the Lancia Stratos Marlboro. In the official trials he almost took the pole, classifying just one tenth behind the Porsche Carrera RSR three-liter of Tim Schenken. The race lasted less than two laps, however, since Facetti was forced to retire by the usual breakage of the rear hubs, which plagued the car especially in the track version, since it was much more powerful.

The Stratos reappeared at the Intereuropa Cup (6 Hours of Monza) on 28 September, assigned to Carlo Facetti and Vittorio Brambilla. In the trials, the faster speeds permitted by the Monza track even increased the gap from the faster Porsche RSRs, which also had engines with 600 cc more than the Stratos HF. Facetti qualified with seventh fastest time (1'47"08), over two second from John Fitzpatrick. The suicidal driving of the faster Porsches led to their retirement, and the Stratos took the checkered flag in third position, even though a timekeeper error relegated it to fourth, enabling Carlo Facetti to capture 14th position in the final rankings of the FIA Championship out of 47 classified.

For 1976 sponsor Marlboro was shunted to the Manufacturers' Championship, where it was to support the Turbo assigned to Carlo Facetti and Vittorio Brambilla. Lancia dealer Mocauto of Milan and publisher Rino Fabbri Editore shouldered the expense of participating in the GT Championship with a new four-valve Stratos prepared by the Facettis. The Stratos had to

Claudio Magnani was protagonist of the Italian GT Speed Championship. Driving the Facetti Stratos formerly of Rino Fabbri, he won the CSAI Cup for Group 4 cars up to 2500 cc in 1977 and 1978.

Before going to Claudio Magnani, the Stratos had been raced by Gianfranco Ricci, often paired with Carlo Facetti. At the 6 Hours of Mugello in 1976, valid for the World Manufacturers' Championship, the pair was forced to withdraw at lap 81.

Lancia Stratos

Particularly outstanding among the drivers for University Motors of Genoa was Leo Pittoni, shown here next to the Stratos he drove in the Valli Piacentine Rally of 1978. The previous year Pittoni, paired with Bertocchi, participated in the Montecarlo Rally (bottom) with a Jolly Club Lancia prepared by Claudio Maglioli.

The Stratos was always at home on the Madonie course at the Targa Florio, not coincidentally very similar to a rally layout. In 1976 Gianfranco Ricci, paired with Carlo Facetti, captured second place overall in the Sicilian classic, no longer valid for international titles.

contend not only with the Porsche Carrera RSRs of the previous year but also the new 934 RSRs with a turbocharged engine equivalent to 4190 cc of displacement (actual displacement of 2993 cc times the coefficient of 1.4 then in use).

Gianfranco Ricci's performance was above all expectations, and he finished ninth overall in the final classification of the Championship, preceded by eight Porsche 934 RSRs. But let us not forget his victory in the Italian overall championship for Group 4 and the fact that he, paired with Renzo Zorzi aboard a Gr.4 Stratos, brought Lancia the only three points earned in the Constructors' Championship of 1976, with eighth place overall at the 6 Hours of Vallelunga.

At the end of 1976, as mentioned earlier, the FIA enacted a directive that prevented the use of many technical extensions homologated before 31 December 1975, so the Stratos was forced to race on the track without the four-valve head and with the series gearbox with synchronizers. Just for rallies, this requirement went into effect at the end of 1977.

The following year, it was again the Facetti Stratos of Rino Fabbri, driven now by Emilio Paleari and Anna Cambiaghi, that enabled Lancia to assemble three more points, the only ones

(cont. to page 158)

Chapter 7   The Stratos HF and the races

A reunion after almost 30 years. Top: brothers Giuliano (left) and Carlo Facetti, tuners of the fastest circuit Stratos, posing proudly next to the car formerly of Rino Fabbri. The key figures on that team got together a few years ago and posed next to the same car. Left to right: Piero Mocarelli, Claudio Magnani, Gianfranco Ricci and Giovannino Fabbri.

Lancia Stratos

Gianfranco Ricci's former Lancia Stratos was carefully restored by the Facetti brothers, who returned the car to its original condition both internally and mechanically: the two-valve V6 injection engine developed by the Facettis in the configuration with which the car raced with Claudio Magnani in the mid-70s.

Chapter 7 | The Stratos HF and the races

At the third event on the 1978 Italian Speed Championship calendar, held at Pergusa, Claudio Magnani competed with his Stratos and won the race. He is shown here overtaking the Alpine 1600 of Sergio Rombolotti.

In 1980 Magnani returned to racing with the nickname "Mac", again winning his class in the CSAI Cup. In the photo, "Mac"s Stratos with white livery leads the other Stratos prepared by Facetti and driven by Francesco Capuzzo during the Nappi Trophy at Vallelunga on 2 November 1980.
The two contenders finished the season with equal point totals, but the title went to "Mac" again based on total victories.

(cont. from page 155)
in the Manufacturers' Championship, with a fair eighth place in the overall classification and fifth in the GT rankings.
The car was gradually losing competitiveness in track speed races, and its use was restricted to Italy with national drivers at the wheel. The only foreigner to use in a race outside Italy was Anatoly Arutunoff, an American of Russian origin, who drove it in the IMSA events without particular success.
The Italians included Claudio Magnani, winner of the CSAI Cup reserved to the up-to-2500 cc Group 4 class in 1977, 1978

Lancia Stratos

With this Lancia Stratos Francesco Capuzzo participated in the Italian Speed Championship from 1977 to 1982, winning a few races and capturing the Group 4 title in 1981. This car's competitive career ended the following season.

Magione, 20 May 1979: wheel-to-wheel race between the Stratos of Francesco Capuzzo, on the outside, and Antonio Runfola on the inside with the car prepared by Giani. Capuzzo finished the race third, while the race was won by Giovanni Alberti, Italian champion at season's end.

Chapter 7   **The Stratos HF and the races**

The drivers competing at the wheel of the Stratos in the late '70-early '80s included Luciano Dal Ben, protagonist in the Italian Championship during that period. These photos show him at the Targa Florio (right) and the Coppa Città di Asiago (left).

and 1980 with the former-Rino-Fabbri Stratos, alternating with Giovanni Alberti in 1979, both driving a Stratos tuned by Facetti. The no. 2 in the Championship classifications in these four years was Francesco Capuzzo, driving an identical car formerly of Emilio Paleari. In 1981 he succeeded in taking home the Italian Group 4 trophy in the up-to-2500 cc class, preceding Cortes and "Mac". Last but not least, Germano Nataloni, of Viterbo had always raced since the Fifties, driving Lancias tuned by Gioacchino Vari, and won a few timed hillclimbs.

The Stratos Turbo

The presence of the naturally-aspirated Lancia Stratos HF was not particularly significant, primarily because of the displacement gap with the Porsches, even with the improved gearbox and suspensions that enhanced the reliability of the rally version. The Turbo version proved incapable of providing satisfactory performance and has remained merely a curiosity for Lancia connoisseurs.

The lack of horsepower with respect to the Porsches, in fact, convinced Carlo Facetti and engineer Mike Parkes, with the consulting of specialist Michael May, to adopt turbocharging to increase the horsepower of the track car, partly with a view

Lancia Stratos

to participation in the World Manufacturers' Championship, to which Group 5 cars (also called "silhouettes") were admitted. Development of the turbo engine had begun in 1974 with the modification of a two-valve carburetor racing engine on which a turbocharger was mounted upstream to operate just on the intake side. It debuted at the Rally of Sicily with the Stratos assigned to the team of Andruet-"Biche". The French driver's comments, reported in the press, were quite explicit:
"I won't drive this car again, because it is too powerful. When I step on the accelerator I get a strong blow to the back and the rear of the car fishtails. In this trial I spun around a couple of times. It cannot be driven serenely". The car then reappeared at the Tour Auto, where it had retired with Munari at the wheel, but its performance against the Ligier was compromised by an accidental fall from the transport trailer. The overall victory at year-end in the Tour of Italy rekindled hopes for 1976.

The subsequent season was disastrous for the Turbo version. The car caught fire a first time at Mugello during the free trials and could therefore not take the start of the 6 Hours. In the next event, at Vallelunga, it was the gearbox that broke down, than at Zeltweg the car caught fire again. A small satisfaction came in June at the 24 Hours of Le Mans, with the 20th place of the pairing Christine Dacremont-Lella Lombardi in the old Stratos Turbo of Chardonnet, which then had to retire with Andruet at the Tour Auto in September. Lastly came the breeze at the Tour of Italy, with the retirement of Pinto in the carburetor Turbo and the victory of Facetti with the injection Turbo.

The Stratos that won the 1974 Giro d'Italia with the crew Andruet-"Biche", sporting the Marlboro livery at the time, again participated in the Giro in 1975, with wheelbase lengthened by 12 cm, driven by Munari-Mannucci. It finished sixth. The same car competed in the 24 Hours of Le Mans in 1976 with the distaff pair of Christine-Dacremont and Lella Lombardi, finishing in 20th place.

Chapter 7 The Stratos HF and the races

Carlo Facetti-Vittorio Brambilla were protagonists at the 6 Hours of Vallelunga in 1976: after clocking the third best qualifying time with 1'17"29, a gearbox failure on lap 185 forced them to retire, after long holding on to second place behind the Porsche 935 of winners Jacky Ickx and Jochen Mass.

In this regard, Sandro Munari recalls:
"Sensing the need to compete in track races, like the Tour de France, which was raced on all the French circuits — we won this race with the Stratos the first time we entered it in '74 — we attempted to develop a more powerful engine. Before reaching the four-valve, Gianni Tonti and Mike Parkes had begun to work on the turbo, using a KKK unit that suffered problems not only of reliability, but especially turbo lag.
The car was difficult to drive: in acceleration, there were response lags to power demands, and in deceleration, when you took your foot off the accelerator the turbine continued to turn, so you had to brake a few hundred meters beforehand or accelerate beforehand. Thanks to the skill of the technicians, and then Gianni Tonti, racing department manager, and with the information that we drivers provided on the behavior of the engine, we understood that two turbines had to be mounted, if we wished to race with the turbo. This was before the fad of turbos in Formula 1 began, before Renault started using two turbines. All this information was passed on to Ferrari, before it began using turbos on its cars".
It should be noted in this regard that in 1976 André de Cortanze, designer of the Alpine, had built the A 500, an F1 with a V6 turbo engine derived from the naturally-aspirated unit of the F2 car that was dominating the FIA Championship with Jean Pierre Jabouille.
The press gave ample coverage to the long testing that was being conducted, so first Alfa Romeo, then Ferrari, followed the path beaten by the French: building F1 engines using F2 units and exploiting the technical regulations, which imposed a mul-

Lancia Stratos

The Stratos Turbo of Piero Facetti and Carlo Sodano on the circuit during the victorious 1976 Tour of Italy.

tiplier of two for the displacement of turbocharged engines, while the maximum displacement remained at 3000 cc.

In November 1980 Toleman also drew on the experience acquired by Lancia with turbocharged engines and installed the Beta Montecarlo engine on its F1 car. Then, for political reasons of the FIAT group, it was forced to fall back on the Brian Hart four-cylinder, similar in concept but not as reliable. Thus Ayrton Senna debuted in F1 in 1984 with a British engine.

Given the success of the Brazilian driver, it would have been nice to close the Stratos fable with a note that the followers of Gianni Lancia, those engineers who had enabled our berlinetta to rule the rally world for three years, had also succeeded in returning the marque to the maximum category of racing, powering with their engine the single-seater for the person who was to become one of the greatest race drivers of all times.

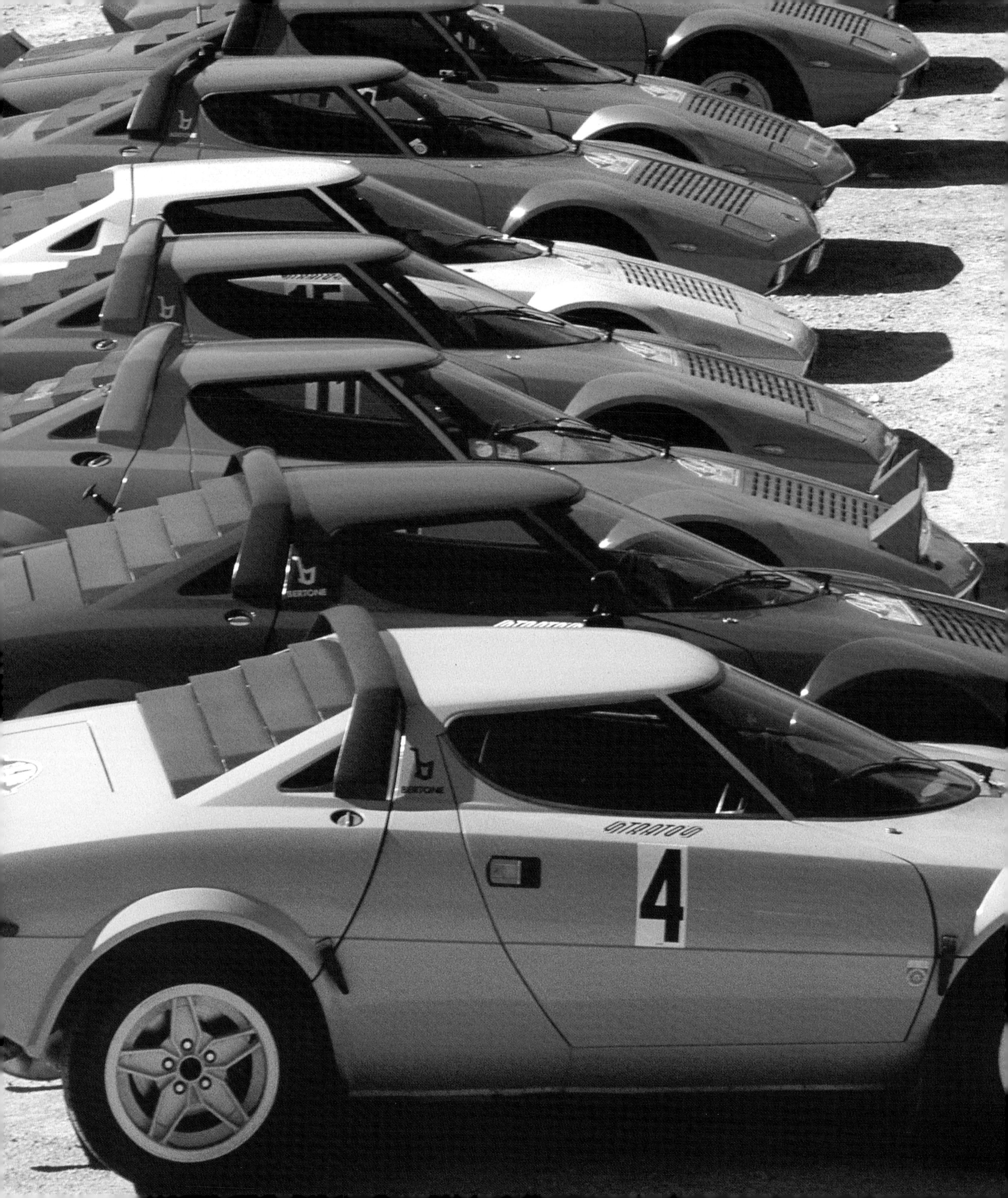
BERTONE
4

Stratos facts and figures

Bodyshell production	**166**
Car production	**179**
The homologation form	**180**
A few road tests	**190**
Results	**191**

Bodyshell production

List of exterior-interior colors and respective matchups, in the sequence in which the bodyshells were readied at Carrozzeria Bertone

From production order register 1240 of Carrozzeria Bertone of Grugliasco related to the Lancia Stratos, specifications have been extracted concerning the interiors of the Stratos bodyshells associated with the exterior paint colors. The list of Stratos bodyshell numbers, also derived from historical documents of the Carrozzeria, provides information on the upholstery according to the exterior colors but does not follow the chronological sequence of production. It seems certain that part of the finished bodyshells remained for some time in storage at Bertone, waiting to be delivered in lots to Lancia, which in turn did not proceed immediately with assembly of the mechanical components.

In other cases, the bodyshells were completed in subsequent periods and then delivered to Lancia even months after the original production date. Of the 502 bodyshells assembled at Grugliasco, two were produced in 1973, 183 in 1974, and 277 in 1975, while for 40 of them the documentation of Bertone furnishes no definite delivery date.

The four assembly sheets for cars completed at Lancia (reproduced on page 179) also indicate that the mechanical components were not mounted on the bodyshells produced by Bertone according to the numerical sequence attributed to them by the coachbuilder. Unfortunately, the body numbers attributed by the Lancia documents to many units of the Stratos do not reflect the numerical sequence shown in the register of Carrozzeria Bertone, resulting in chronological discrepancies between the dates the bodyshell was produced and the date the car was completed. Carrozzeria Bertone, in any case, produced from 101 bodyshells to a maximum of 141 by 1 October 1974, the date the Stratos received FIA homologation, for which the minimum prescribed number of 500 finished cars should have been reached.

EXTERIOR COLOR	INTERIOR COLORS				
	"Marvik" dashboard	Seatbacks *"mock leather"*	Door panels *"flocked"*	Carpets and firewall *saval*	Seat covers *"alcantara"*
Red-orange 2-464-171	Black 161	Black 90	Black	Red 05	Havana
Fly Yellow 2-469-019	Black 161	Black 90	Black	Gold 06	Blue
Light green 2-465-070	Black 161	Black 90	Black	Kenya 02	Havana
Blue 2-466-190 (ton. 2312)	Black 161	Black 90	Black	Sereno 15	Havana
Light-blue 2-466-440 (ton. 2310)	Black 161	Black 90	Black	Sereno 15	Black

BODYSHELL		SEAT COLOR	EXTERIOR COLOR	CARPETING
1	2/4/74	Black	Acrylic red-orange 2-464-171	Red 05
2	31/1/75 Returned for transformation Germany shipped 22/12/75	Black	Acrylic red-orange 2-464-171	Red 05
3	31/10/73	Black	Acrylic red-orange 2-464-171	Red 05
4	22/3/74	Black	Acrylic red-orange 2-464-171	Red 05
5	21/11/73	Black	Acrylic red-orange 2-464-171	Red 05
6	26/4/74	Black	Acrylic red-orange 2-464-171	Red 05
7	22/4/74 and 4/4/75	Black	Acrylic red-orange 2-464-171	Red 05
8	29/4/74 Returned for transformation Germany	Black	Acrylic red-orange 2-464-171	Red 05
9	8/4/74	Black	Acrylic red-orange 2-464-171	Red 05
10	11/1/74	Black	Acrylic red-orange 2-464-171	Red 05
11	27/3/74	Black	Acrylic red-orange 2-464-171	Red 05
12	2/9/74	Black	Acrylic red-orange 2-464-171	Red 05
13	27/3/74	Black	Acrylic red-orange 2-464-171	Red 05
14	2/4/74	Black	Acrylic red-orange 2-464-171	Red 05
15	10/5/75	Havana	Acrylic red-orange 2-464-171	Red 05
16	7/1/75 Returned for transformation Germany	Black	Acrylic red-orange 2-464-171	Red 05
17	16/4/74	Black	Acrylic red-orange 2-464-171	Red 05
18	5/6/74	Black	Acrylic red-orange 2-464-171	Red 05
19	27/2/75 Swiss version	Black	Acrylic red-orange 2-464-171	Red 05
20	Shipped in March with doors, without lids, with black seats for seatbelt testing acr. 464-171	Black	Acrylic red-orange 2-464-171	Red 05
21	4/3/74 Returned for transformation Switzerland	Black	Metal. dark blue (special)	Red 05
22	26/2/75 Dutch version	Black	Red-orange ac 2-464-171	Red 05
23	29/1/75 Dutch version	Black	Acrylic red-orange 2-464-171	Red 05
24	29/1/75 Dutch version	Black	Acrylic red-orange 2-464-171	Red 05
25	10/10/75 Returned for transformation Germany	Havana	Acrylic red-orange 2-464-171	Red 05
26	30/11/74 and 24/4/75	Havana	Acrylic red-orange 2-464-171	Red 05
27	29/1/75	Havana	Acrylic red-orange 2-464-171	Red 05
28	12/6/75	Havana	Acrylic red-orange 2-464-171	Red 05
29	3/4/75 Dutch Version	Havana	Acrylic red-orange 2-464-171	Red 05
30	28/8/74	Havana	Acrylic red-orange 2-464-171	Red 05
31	26/8/74	Havana	Red-orange 2-464-171	Red 05
32	7/5/74 and 4/9/74	Havana	Red-orange 2-464-171	Red 05
33	28/8/74	Havana	Red-orange 2-464-171	Red 05
34	2/9/74	Havana	Red-orange 2-464-171	Red 05
35	28/8/74	Havana	Red-orange 2-464-171	Red 05
36	10/2/75	Havana	Red-orange 2-464-171	Red 05
37	4/9/74	Havana	Red-orange 2-464-171	Red 05
38		Havana	Red-orange 2-464-171	Red 05
39	28/5/74	Havana	Red-orange 2-464-171	Red 05
40		Havana	Red-orange 2-464-171	Red 05
41	10/2/75	Havana	Red-orange 2-464-171	Red 05

BODYSHELL		SEAT COLOR	EXTERIOR COLOR	CARPETING
42	17/1/75	Havana	Red-orange 2-464-171	Red 05
43		Havana	Red-orange 2-464-171	Red 05
44	4/9/74	Havana	Red-orange 2-464-171	Red 05
45	21/2/75	Havana	Red-orange 2-464-171	Red 05
46	30/8/74	Havana	Red-orange 2-464-171	Red 05
47	14/2/75	Havana	Red-orange 2-464-171	Red 05
48	14/2/75	Havana	Red-orange 2-464-171	Red 05
49		Havana	Red-orange 2-464-171	Red 05
50	17/1/75	Havana	Red-orange 2-464-171	Red 05
51	14/2/75	Blue	Fly yellow 2-469-019	Gold
52	4/3/75	Blue	Fly yellow 2-469-019	Gold
53	3/4/75	Blue	Fly yellow 2-469-019	Gold
54	29/1/75	Blue	Fly yellow 2-469-019	Gold
55	4/4/75	Blue	Fly yellow 2-469-019	Gold
56	30/6/75 Returned for transformation Germany	Blue	Fly yellow 2-469-019	Gold
57	27/5/75	Blue	Fly yellow 2-469-019	Gold
58	German version 5/6/75	Blue	Fly yellow 2-469-019	Gold
59	10/2/75	Blue	Fly yellow 2-469-019	Gold
60	10/2/75	Blue	Fly yellow 2-469-019	Gold
61	17/1/75	Blue	Fly yellow 2-469-019	Gold
62		Blue	Fly yellow 2-469-019	Gold
63	14/7/75	Havana	Light green 2-465-070	Kenya
64	11/4/75	Havana	Light green 2-465-070	Kenya
65	31/1/75	Havana	Light green 2-465-070	Kenya
66	21/2/75	Havana	Light green 2-465-070	Kenya
67	17/7/75	Havana	Light green 2-465-070	Kenya
68	4/9/74	Havana	Light green 2-465-070	Kenya
69	12/8/75	Havana	Light green 2-465-070	Kenya
70	26/11/75	Havana	Light green 2-465-070	Kenya
71	26/6/75	Havana	Light green 2-465-070	Kenya
72	2/9/74	Havana	Light green 2-465-070	Kenya
73	German version 16/5/75	Havana	Light green 2-465-070	Kenya
74	31/1/75	Kenya	Light green 2-465-070	Red
75	29/1/75	Havana	Light green 2-465-070	Kenya
76	14/4/75	Havana	Acrylic blue 2-466-190	Sereno
77	3/4/75	Havana	Acrylic blue 2-466-190	Sereno
78	29/1/75	Havana	Acrylic blue 2-466-190	Sereno
79		Havana	Acrylic blue 2-466-190	Sereno
80	11/3/75	Havana	Acrylic blue 2-466-190	Sereno
81	10/2/75	Havana	Acrylic blue 2-466-190	Sereno
82	3/3/75 Cockpit painted, including doors, partially upholstered, part of the 18 at Lancia	Havana	Acrylic blue 2-466-190	Sereno
83	3/3/75 Cockpit painted, including doors, partially upholstered, part of the 18 at Lancia	Havana	Acrylic blue 2-466-190	Sereno

BODYSHELL		SEAT COLOR	EXTERIOR COLOR	CARPETING
84	18/4/75	Havana	Acrylic blue 2-466-190	Sereno
85	13/5/75	Havana	Acrylic blue 2-466-190	Sereno
86	9/6/75	Havana	Acrylic blue 2-466-190	Sereno
87	10/10/75	Havana	Acrylic blue 2-466-190	Sereno
88	German version 12/5/75	Black	Light blue 2-466-440	Sereno
89	31/1/75	Black	Light blue 2-466-440	Sereno
90	23/7/75	Black	Light blue 2-466-440	Sereno
91	German version 22/5/75	Black	Light blue 2-466-440	Sereno
92	4/6/74	Black	Light blue 2-466-440	Sereno
93	7/3/75	Black	Light blue 2-466-440	Sereno
94	14/2/75	Black	Light blue 2-466-440	Sereno
95	28/2/75	Black	Light blue 2-466-440	Sereno
96	German version 28/5/75	Black	Light blue 2-466-440	Sereno
97	9/6/75	Black	Light blue 2-466-440	Sereno
98	4/9/74	Black	Light blue 2-466-440	Sereno
99	18/4/75	Black	Light blue 2-466-440	Sereno
100	31/1/75	Black	Light blue 2-466-440	Sereno
101	16/5/75	Havana	Red-orange 2-464-171	Red
102	15/5/75	Havana	Red-orange 2-464-171	Red
103	18/4/75	Havana	Red-orange 2-464-171	Red
104	18/4/75	Havana	Red-orange 2-464-171	Red
105	German version 5/5/75	Havana	Red-orange 2-464-171	Red
106		Havana	Red-orange 2-464-171	Red
107	German version 3/6/75	Havana	Red-orange 2-464-171	Red
108	German version 22/5/75	Havana	Red-orange 2-464-171	Red
109	10/10/75 Returned for transformation Germany-shipped 9/12/75	Havana	Red-orange 2-464-171	Red
110	Returned for transformation Germany	Havana	Red-orange 2-464-171	Red
111	German version 5/5/75	Havana	Red-orange 2-464-171	Red
112	3/3/75 Cockpit painted with doors, partially upholstered, part of the 18 at Lancia, complete unfitted shells and not painted	Havana	Red-orange 2-464-171	Red
113	15/5/75	Havana	Red-orange 2-464-171	Red
114	Returned for transformation Germany	Havana	Red-orange 2-464-171	Red
115	17/1/75	Havana	Red-orange 2-464-171	Red
116	26/6/75	Havana	Red-orange 2-464-171	Red
117	9/5/75	Havana	Red-orange 2-464-171	Red
118	12/5/75	Havana	Red-orange 2-464-171	Red
119	24/4/75	Havana	Red-orange 2-464-171	Red
120	26/5/75	Havana	Red-orange 2-464-171	Red
121	10/10/75 Returned for transformation Germany-shipped 9/12/75	Havana	Red-orange 2-464-171	Red
122	9/5/75	Havana	Red-orange 2-464-171	Red
123	7/1/75	Havana	Red-orange 2-464-171	Red
124	Dutch version 3/4/75-Returned for	Havana	Red-orange 2-464-171	Red

BODYSHELL	SEAT COLOR	EXTERIOR COLOR	CARPETING
transformation Switzerland			
125 19/5/75	Havana	Red-orange 2-464-171	Red
126 28/10/74	Havana	Red-orange 2-464-171	Red
127 8/4/75	Havana	Red-orange 2-464-171	Red
128 German version 26/5/75	Havana	Red-orange 2-464-171	Red
129 10/2/75	Havana	Red-orange 2-464-171	Red
130 10/10/75 Returned for transformation Germany	Havana	Red-orange 2-464-171	Red
131 13/3/75	Havana	Red-orange 2-464-171	Red
132 3/3/75 Cockpit painted with doors, partially upholstered, part of the 18 at Lancia, complete with unfitted shells and not painted	Havana	Red-orange 2-464-171	Red
133 14/2/75	Havana	Red-orange 2-464-171	Red
134 Swiss version 26/2/75	Havana	Red-orange 2-464-171	Red
135	Havana	Red-orange 2-464-171	Red
136 22/5/75	Havana	Red-orange 2-464-171	Red
137 30/6/75	Havana	Red-orange 2-464-171	Red
138 10/10/75 Returned for transformation Germany	Havana	Red-orange 2-464-171	Red
139 10/10/75 Returned for transformation Germany	Havana	Red-orange 2-464-171	Red
140	Havana	Red-orange 2-464-171	Red
141 26/7/74	Havana	Red-orange 2-464-171	Red
142 5/5/75	Havana	Red-orange 2-464-171	Red
143 28/2/75	Havana	Red-orange 2-464-171	Red
144 Returned for transformation Germany	Havana	Red-orange 2-464-171	Red
145 24/4/75	Havana	Red-orange 2-464-171	Red
146 3/3/75 Cockpit painted with doors, partially upholstered, part of the 18 at Lancia, complete with unfitted shells and not painted	Havana	Red-orange 2-464-171	Red
147 21/2/75	Havana	Red-orange 2-464-171	Red
148	Havana	Red-orange 2-464-171	Red
149 10/10/75 Returned for transformation Germany- shipped Germany 19/11/75	Havana	Red-orange 2-464-171	Red
150 20/6/75	Havana	Red-orange 2-464-171	Red
151 Dutch version 7/4/75	Havana	Red-orange 2-464-171	Red
152 9/6/75	Havana	Red-orange 2-464-171	Red
153 31/4/75	Havana	Red-orange 2-464-171	Red
154 16/6/75	Havana	Red-orange 2-464-171	Red
155 Returned for transformation Germany	Havana	Red-orange 2-464-171	Red
156 10/2/75	Blue	Yellow 2-464-171	Gold
157 6/2/75	Blue	Yellow 2-464-171	Gold
158 10/9/74	Blue	Yellow 2-464-171	Gold
159 German version 15/5/75	Blue	Yellow 2-464-171	Gold
160 9/6/75	Blue	Yellow 2-464-171	Gold
161 23/5/75	Blue	Yellow 2-464-171	Gold
162 14/4/75	Blue	Yellow 2-464-171	Gold

BODYSHELL		SEAT COLOR	EXTERIOR COLOR	CARPETING
163	9/6/75	Blue	Yellow 2-464-171	Gold
164	18/3/75	Blue	Yellow 2-464-171	Gold
165	9/6/75	Blue	Yellow 2-464-171	Gold
166	10/2/75	Blue	Yellow 2-464-171	Gold
167	24/10/75	Havana	Light green 2-465-070	Kenya
168	16/6/75	Havana	Light green 2-465-070	Kenya
169	14/2/75	Havana	Light green 2-465-070	Kenya
170	16/6/75	Havana	Light green 2-465-070	Kenya
171	German version 22/5/75	Havana	Light green 2-465-070	Kenya
172	9/6/75	Havana	Light green 2-465-070	Kenya
173	4/3/75	Havana	Light green 2-465-070	Kenya
174	16/6/75	Havana	Light green 2-465-070	Kenya
175	23/5/75	Havana	Light green 2-465-070	Kenya
176		Havana	Light green 2-465-070	Kenya
177	24/4/75	Havana	Light green 2-465-070	Kenya
178		Havana	Blue 2-466-190	Sereno
179	5/3/75	Havana	Blue 2-466-190	Sereno
180	9/6/75	Havana	Blue 2-466-190	Sereno
181	15/7/75	Havana	Blue 2-466-190	Sereno
182	9/6/75	Havana	Blue 2-466-190	Sereno
183		Havana	Blue 2-466-190	Sereno
184	16/6/75	Havana	Blue 2-466-190	Sereno
185	1/7/75	Havana	Blue 2-466-190	Sereno
186	20/6/75	Havana	Blue 2-466-190	Sereno
187	15/7/74	Havana	Blue 2-466-190	Sereno
188	12/5/75	Havana	Blue 2-466-190	Sereno
189		Black	Light blue 2-466-440	Sereno
190	1/7/75	Black	Light blue 2-466-440	Sereno
191	10/2/75	Black	Light blue 2-466-440	Sereno
192	4/9/74	Black	Light blue 2-466-440	Sereno
193	5/3/75	Black	Light blue 2-466-440	Sereno
194	16/6/75	Black	Light blue 2-466-440	Sereno
195		Black	Light blue 2-466-440	Sereno
196	18/4/75	Black	Light blue 2-466-440	Sereno
197	4/9/74	Black	Light blue 2-466-440	Sereno
198	19/6/75	Black	Light blue 2-466-440	Sereno
199	27/5/75	Black	Light blue 2-466-440	Sereno
200	2/7/74	Havana	Red 2-464-171	Red
201	28/5/75	Havana	Red-orange 2-464-171	Red
202	28/6/74	Havana	Red-orange 2-464-171	Red
203	Returned for transformation Germany	Havana	Red-orange 2-464-171	Red
204	28/6/74	Havana	Red-orange 2-464-171	Red
205	4/9/74	Havana	Red-orange 2-464-171	Red
206	8/7/74	Havana	Red-orange 2-464-171	Red

BODYSHELL	SEAT COLOR	EXTERIOR COLOR	CARPETING
207 20/6/75	Havana	Red-orange 2-464-171	Red
208 24/6/74	Havana	Red-orange 2-464-171	Red
209 14/9/75	Havana	Red-orange 2-464-171	Red
210 10/10/75 Returned for transformation Germany	Havana	Red-orange 2-464-171	Red
211 1/7/75	Havana	Red-orange 2-464-171	Red
212 22/5/75	Havana	Red-orange 2-464-171	Red
213 27/11/75 Returned for transformation Switzerland	Havana	Red-orange 2-464-171	Red
214 25/6/74	Havana	Red-orange 2-464-171	Red
215 17/1/75	Havana	Red-orange 2-464-171	Red
216 18/4/75	Havana	Red-orange 2-464-171	Red
217 30/8/74	Havana	Red-orange 2-464-171	Red
218 30/8/74	Havana	Red-orange 2-464-171	Red
219 26/7/74	Havana	Red-orange 2-464-171	Red
220 22/5/75	Havana	Red-orange 2-464-171	Red
221 15/5/75	Havana	Red-orange 2-464-171	Red
222 30/6/75	Havana	Red-orange 2-464-171	Red
223 24/7/74	Havana	Red-orange 2-464-171	Red
224 10/4/74	Havana	Red-orange 2-464-171	Red
225 9/7/74	Havana	Red 2-464-171	Red
226 15/5/75	Havana	Red 2-464-171	Red
227 9/7/74	Havana	Red 2-464-171	Red
228 20/6/75	Havana	Red 2-464-171	Red
229 5/7/74	Havana	Red 2-464-171	Red
230 7/1/75	Havana	Red 2-464-171	Red
231 9/6/75	Havana	Red 2-464-171	Red
232 26/7/74	Havana	Red 2-464-171	Red
233 11/4/75	Havana	Red 2-464-171	Red
234 2/9/75 Prototype Germany	Havana	Red 2-464-171	Red
235 12/6/75	Havana	Red 2-464-171	Red
236 29/1/75	Havana	Red 2-464-171	Red
237 14/2/75	Havana	Red 2-464-171	Red
238 5/6/75	Havana	Red 2-464-171	Red
239 26/2/75	Havana	Red 2-464-171	Red
240 17/4/75	Havana	Red 2-464-171	Red
241	Havana	Red 2-464-171	Red
242 17/4/75	Havana	Red 2-464-171	Red
243 19/6/75	Havana	Red 2-464-171	Red
244 28/8/74	Havana	Red 2-464-171	Red
245 19/5/75	Havana	Red 2-464-171	Red
246 14/7/75	Havana	Red 2-464-171	Red
247 10/10/75 Returned for transformation Germany- shipped 22/12/75	Havana	Red 2-464-171	Red
248 22/7/74	Havana	Red 2-464-171	Red
249 16/6/75	Havana	Red 2-464-171	Red

BODYSHELL		SEAT COLOR	EXTERIOR COLOR	CARPETING
250		Havana	Red 2-464-171	Red
251	21/2/75	Havana	Red 2-464-171	Red
252		Havana	Red 2-464-171	Red
253		Havana	Red 2-464-171	Red
254	10/2/75	Havana	Red 2-464-171	Red
255	26/2/75	Havana	Red 2-464-171	Red
256	3/6/75	Blue	Yellow 2-469-019	Gold
257	5/3/75	Blue	Yellow 2-469-019	Gold
258	22/12/75 Returned for transformation Germany	Blue	Yellow 2-469-019	Gold
259	29/1/75	Blue	Yellow 2-469-019	Gold
260		Blue	Yellow 2-469-019	Gold
261	3/6/75	Blue	Yellow 2-469-019	Gold
262	4/9/74	Blue	Yellow 2-469-019	Gold
263	11/4/75	Blue	Yellow 2-469-019	Gold
264	16/6/75	Blue	Yellow 2-469-019	Gold
265	22/7/74	Blue	Yellow 2-469-019	Gold
266	5/6/75	Blue	Yellow 2-469-019	Gold
267		Blue	Yellow 2-469-019	Gold
268		Havana	Light green 2-465-070	Kenya
269	9/5/75	Havana	Light green 2-465-070	Kenya
270	28/4/75	Havana	Light green 2-465-070	Kenya
271	9/5/75	Havana	Light green 2-465-070	Kenya
272	14/7/75	Havana	Light green 2-465-070	Kenya
273		Havana	Light green 2-465-070	Kenya
274	9/5/75	Havana	Light green 2-465-070	Kenya
275	7/4/75	Havana	Light green 2-465-070	Kenya
276	7/1/75	Havana	Light green 2-465-070	Kenya
277		Havana	Light green 2-465-070	Kenya
278	5/6/75	Havana	Light green 2-465-070	Kenya
279	4/9/74	Havana	Blue 2-466-190	Sereno
280	7/4/75	Havana	Blue 2-466-190	Sereno
281	30/4/75	Havana	Blue 2-466-190	Sereno
282	16/6/75	Havana	Blue 2-466-190	Sereno
283	9/5/75	Havana	Blue 2-466-190	Sereno
284	24/4/75	Havana	Blue 2-466-190	Sereno
285	Paris Auto Show 3/9/74	Black	Yellow 2-469-019	Red
286	28/8/74	Havana	Blue 2-466-190	Sereno
287		Havana	Blue 2-466-190	Sereno
288	17/4/75	Havana	Blue 2-466-190	Sereno
289		Havana	Blue 2-466-190	Sereno
290	18/7/74	Black	Light blue	Sereno
291	28/5/75	Black	Light blue 2-466-440	Sereno
292	22/8/74	Black	Light blue 2-466-440	Sereno
293	5/9/74	Black	Light blue 2-466-440	Sereno

BODYSHELL	SEAT COLOR	EXTERIOR COLOR	CARPETING
294 23/5/75	Black	Light blue 2-466-440	Sereno
295 9/12/75	Black	Light blue 2-466-440	Sereno
296 9/6/75	Black	Light blue 2-466-440	Sereno
297 10/9/74	Black	Light blue 2-466-440	Sereno
298 19/7/74	Black	Light blue 2-466-440	Sereno
299 16/5/75	Black	Light blue 2-466-440	Sereno
300	Black	Light blue 2-466-440	Sereno
301 5/6/75	Havana	Acrylic red 2-464-171	Red 05
302 24/7/74	Havana	Acrylic red 2-464-171	Red 05
303 31/1/75	Havana	Acrylic red 2-464-171	Red 05
304 31/1/75	Havana	Acrylic red 2-464-171	Red 05
305 28/2/75	Havana	Acrylic red 2-464-171	Red 05
306	Havana	Acrylic red 2-464-171	Red 05
307 21/2/75	Havana	Acrylic red 2-464-171	Red 05
308 22/9/74	Havana	Acrylic red 2-464-171	Red 05
309 26/7/74	Havana	Acrylic red 2-464-171	Red 05
310 22/7/74	Havana	Acrylic red 2-464-171	Red 05
311 26/7/74	Havana	Acrylic red 2-464-171	Red 05
312 12/5/75	Havana	Acrylic red 2-464-171	Red 05
313 22/8/74	Havana	Acrylic red 2-464-171	Red 05
314 26/7/74	Havana	Acrylic red 2-464-171	Red 05
315	Havana	Acrylic red 2-464-171	Red 05
316 19/5/75	Havana	Acrylic red 2-464-171	Red 05
317 28/8/74	Havana	Acrylic red 2-464-171	Red 05
318 26/8/74	Havana	Acrylic red 2-464-171	Red 05
319	Havana	Acrylic red 2-464-171	Red 05
320 22/8/74	Havana	Acrylic red 2-464-171	Red 05
321 26/8/74	Havana	Acrylic red 2-464-171	Red 05
322 22/8/74	Havana	Acrylic red 2-464-171	Red 05
323 Returned for transformation Germany	Havana	Acrylic red 2-464-171	Red 05
324 30/8/74	Havana	Acrylic red 2-464-171	Red 05
325 30/6/75	Havana	Acrylic red 2-464-171	Red 05
326 9/6/75	Havana	Acrylic red 2-464-171	Red 05
327 30/5/74	Havana	Acrylic red 2-464-171	Red 05
328	Havana	Acrylic red 2-464-171	Red 05
329 26/8/74	Havana	Acrylic red 2-464-171	Red 05
330 28/8/74	Havana	Acrylic red 2-464-171	Red 05
331 30/8/74	Havana	Acrylic red 2-464-171	Red 05
332 10/2/75	Havana	Acrylic red 2-464-171	Red 05
333 30/8/74	Havana	Acrylic red 2-464-171	Red 05
334 21/4/75	Havana	Acrylic red 2-464-171	Red 05
335 2/9/74	Havana	Acrylic red 2-464-171	Red 05
336 30/8/74	Havana	Acrylic red 2-464-171	Red 05
337 27/711/75 Returned for transformation Switzerland	Havana	Acrylic red 2-464-171	Red 05

BODYSHELL	SEAT COLOR	EXTERIOR COLOR	CARPETING
338 30/8/74	Havana	Acrylic red 2-464-171	Red 05
339 12/9/74 Returned for transformation Germany	Havana	Acrylic red 2-464-171	Red 05
340 7/1/75	Havana	Acrylic red 2-464-171	Red 05
341 10/9/74	Havana	Acrylic red 2-464-171	Red 05
342 12/9/74	Havana	Acrylic red 2-464-171	Red 05
343 10/10/75 Returned for transformation Germany	Havana	Acrylic red 2-464-171	Red 05
344 5/9/74	Havana	Acrylic red 2-464-171	Red 05
345 16/9/74	Havana	Acrylic red 2-464-171	Red 05
346 10/9/74	Havana	Acrylic red 2-464-171	Red 05
347 16/9/74	Havana	Acrylic red 2-464-171	Red 05
348 12/9/74	Havana	Acrylic red 2-464-171	Red 05
349 16/9/74	Havana	Acrylic red 2-464-171	Red 05
350 23/9/75	Havana	Acrylic red 2-464-171	Red 05
351 16/9/74	Havana	Acrylic red 2-464-171	Red 05
352 5/9/74 and 14/7/75	Havana	Acrylic red 2-464-171	Red 05
353 16/9/74	Havana	Acrylic red 2-464-171	Red 05
354 24/10/74	Havana	Acrylic red 2-464-171	Red 05
355 10/9/74	Havana	Acrylic red 2-464-171	Red 05
356 21/10/74	Blue	Yellow 2-469-019	Gold
357 14/10/74	Blue	Yellow 2-469-019	Gold
358 24/9/74	Blue	Yellow 2-469-019	Gold
359 18/11/74	Blue	Yellow 2-469-019	Gold
360 27/9/74	Blue	Yellow 2-469-019	Gold
361 23/9/74	Blue	Yellow 2-469-019	Gold
362 27/9/74	Blue	Yellow 2-469-019	Gold
363 14/10/74	Blue	Yellow 2-469-019	Gold
364 8/10/74	Blue	Yellow 2-469-019	Gold
365 19/10/74	Blue	Yellow 2-469-019	Gold
366 30/8/74	Blue	Yellow 2-469-019	Gold
367 14/10/74	Havana	Light green 2-465-070	Kenya
368 21/10/74	Havana	Light green 2-465-070	Kenya
369 28/10/74	Havana	Light green 2-465-070	Kenya
370 14/10/74	Havana	Light green 2-465-070	Kenya
371 14/10/74	Havana	Light green 2-465-070	Kenya
372 14/10/74	Havana	Light green 2-465-070	Kenya
373 21/10/74	Havana	Light green 2-465-070	Kenya
374 14/10/74	Havana	Light green 2-465-070	Kenya
375 21/10/74	Havana	Light green 2-465-070	Kenya
376 14/10/74	Havana	Light green 2-465-070	Kenya
377 14/10/74	Havana	Light green 2-465-070	Kenya
378 21/10/74	Havana	Acrylic blue 2-466-190	Sereno
379 12/11/74	Havana	Acrylic blue 2-466-190	Sereno
380 25/11/74	Havana	Acrylic blue 2-466-190	Sereno
381	Havana	Acrylic blue 2-466-190	Sereno

BODYSHELL	SEAT COLOR	EXTERIOR COLOR	CARPETING
382 18/11/74	Havana	Acrylic blue 2-466-190	Sereno
383 26/11/75	Havana	Acrylic blue 2-466-190	Sereno
384 12/11/74	Havana	Acrylic blue 2-466-190	Sereno
385 5/12/74	Havana	Acrylic blue 2-466-190	Sereno
386 21/7/75	Havana	Acrylic blue 2-466-190	Sereno
387 12/12/74	Havana	Acrylic blue 2-466-190	Sereno
388 10/2/75	Havana	Acrylic blue 2-466-190	Red 05
389 18/11/74	Havana	Light blue 2-466-440	Red
390 31/10/74	Black	Light blue 2-466-440	Sereno
391 31/10/74	Black	Light blue 2-466-440	Sereno
392 31/10/74	Black	Light blue 2-466-440	Sereno
393 28/10/74	Black	Light blue 2-466-440	Sereno
394 21/10/74	Black	Light blue 2-466-440	Sereno
395 25/11/74	Black	Light blue 2-466-440	Sereno
396 25/11/74	Black	Light blue 2-466-440	Sereno
397 21/10/74	Black	Light blue 2-466-440	Sereno
398 24/10/74	Black	Light blue 2-466-440	Sereno
399 19/11/74	Black	Light blue 2-466-440	Sereno
400 31/10/74	Black	Light blue 2-466-440	Sereno
401 24/10/74	Havana	Red-orange 2-464-171	Red
402 24/10/74	Havana	Red-orange 2-464-171	Red
403 24/10/74	Havana	Red-orange 2-464-171	Red
404 31/10/74	Havana	Red-orange 2-464-171	Red
405 12/11/74	Havana	Red-orange 2-464-171	Red
406 28/10/74	Havana	Red-orange 2-464-171	Red
407 19/11/74	Havana	Red-orange 2-464-171	Red
408 28/10/74	Havana	Red-orange 2-464-171	Red
409 24/10/74	Havana	Red-orange 2-464-171	Red
410 Swiss version 20/2/75	Havana	Red-orange 2-464-171	Red
411 18/11/74	Blue	Acrylic yellow 2-469-019	Gold 06
412 29/11/74	Blue	Acrylic yellow 2-469-019	Gold 06
413 18/11/74	Blue	Acrylic yellow 2-469-019	Gold 06
414 29/11/74	Blue	Acrylic yellow 2-469-019	Gold 06
415 18/11/74	Blue	Acrylic yellow 2-469-019	Gold 06
416 12/11/74	Blue	Acrylic yellow 2-469-019	Gold 06
417 24/10/74	Blue	Acrylic yellow 2-469-019	Gold 06
418 19/11/74	Blue	Acrylic yellow 2-469-019	Gold 06
419 25/11/74	Blue	Acrylic yellow 2-469-019	Gold 06
420 25/11/74	Blue	Acrylic yellow 2-469-019	Gold 06
421 Dutch version 20/2/75-Returned for transformation Switzerland	Havana	Light green 2-465-070	Kenya
422 19/11/74	Havana	Light green 2-465-070	Kenya
423 25/11/74	Havana	Light green 2-465-070	Kenya
424 6/12/74	Havana	Light green 2-465-070	Kenya

BODYSHELL		SEAT COLOR	EXTERIOR COLOR	CARPETING
425	20/2/75	Havana	Light green 2-465-070	Kenya
426	25/11/74	Havana	Light green 2-465-070	Kenya
427	25/11/74	Havana	Light green 2-465-070	Kenya
428	16/1/75	Havana	Light green 2-465-070	Kenya
429	25/11/74	Havana	Light green 2-465-070	Kenya
430	Swiss version 20/2/75	Havana	Light green 2-465-070	Kenya
431	29/11/74	Havana	Acrylic blue 2-466-190	Sereno 05
432	25/11/74	Havana	Acrylic blue 2-466-190	Sereno 05
433	29/11/74	Havana	Acrylic blue 2-466-190	Sereno 05
434	7/4/75	Havana	Acrylic blue 2-466-190	Sereno 05
435	29/11/75	Havana	Acrylic blue 2-466-190	Sereno 05
436	28/11/74	Havana	Acrylic blue 2-466-190	Sereno 05
437	7/4/75	Havana	Acrylic blue 2-466-190	Sereno 05
438	6/2/75	Havana	Acrylic blue 2-466-190	Sereno 05
439	29/1/75	Havana	Acrylic blue 2-466-190	Sereno 05
440	31/1/75	Havana	Acrylic blue 2-466-190	Sereno 05
441	16/3/75	Black	Light blue 2-466-440	Sereno
442	Shipped in March with doors, without lids and with black seats for seatbelt testing	Black	Light blue 2-466-440	Sereno 015
443	31/10/74	Black	Light blue 2-466-440	Sereno
444	31/10/74	Black	Light blue 2-466-440	Sereno
445	Dutch version 13/3/75	Black	Light blue 2-466-440	Sereno 015
446	28/10/74	Black	Light blue 2-466-440	Sereno
447	4/2/75	Black	Light blue 2-466-440	Sereno
448	5/3/75	Black	Light blue 2-466-440	Sereno
449	29/11/74	Black	Light blue 2-466-440	Sereno
450	5/12/74	Black	Light blue 2-466-440	Sereno
451	14/2/75	Blue	Yellow 2-469-019	Gold
452	29/11/74	Blue	Yellow 2-469-019	Gold
453	Dutch version 11/3/75	Blue	Yellow 2-469-019	Gold 06
454	11/12/74	Blue	Yellow 2-469-019	Gold
455	11/12/74	Blue	Yellow 2-469-019	Gold
456	16/1/75	Blue	Yellow 2-469-019	Gold
457	27/2/75	Blue	Yellow 2-469-019	Gold
458	6/12/74	Blue	Yellow 2-469-019	Gold
459	11/12/74	Blue	Yellow 2-469-019	Gold
460	11/12/74	Blue	Yellow 2-469-019	Gold
461	9/1/75	Havana	Light green 2-465-070	Kenya
462	21/1/75	Havana	Light green 2-465-070	Kenya
463	11/12/74	Havana	Light green 2-465-070	Kenya
464	6/12/74	Havana	Light green 2-465-070	Kenya
465	29/1/75	Havana	Light green 465-070-02	Kenya
466	6/12/74	Havana	Light green 2-465-070	Kenya
467	11/12/74	Havana	Light green 2-465-070	Kenya

BODYSHELL	SEAT COLOR	EXTERIOR COLOR	CARPETING
468 Dutch version 7/3/75	Havana	Light green 2-465-070	Kenya 02
469 9/1/75	Havana	Light green 2-465-070	Kenya
470 16/1/75	Havana	Light green 2-465-070	Kenya
471 9/1/75	Havana	Acrylic blue 2-466-190	Sereno
472 29/1/75	Havana	Acrylic blue 2-466-190	Sereno
473 16/1/75	Havana	Acrylic blue 2-466-190	Sereno
474 11/4/75	Havana	Acrylic blue 2-466-190	Sereno
475 6/2/75	Havana	Acrylic blue 2-466-190	Sereno
476 31/1/75	Havana	Acrylic blue 2-466-190	Sereno
477 29/1/75	Havana	Acrylic blue 2-466-190	Sereno
478 27/2/75	Havana	Acrylic blue 2-466-190	Sereno
479 21/1/75	Havana	Acrylic blue 2-466-190	Sereno
480 9/1/75	Havana	Acrylic blue 2-466-190	Sereno
481 31/1/75	Black	Acrylic blue 2-466-190	Sereno
482 27/2/75	Havana	Acrylic blue 2-466-190	Sereno
483 5/3/75	Havana	Acrylic blue 2-466-190	Sereno
484 Dutch version 11/3/75-Returned for transformation Switzerland - shipped 22/12	Havana	Acrylic blue 2-466-190	Sereno
485	Havana	Acrylic blue 2-466-190	Sereno
486 Swiss version 30/1/75	Havana	Acrylic blue 2-466-190	Sereno
487 27/2/75	Havana	Acrylic blue 2-466-190	Sereno
488 4/2/75	Havana	Acrylic blue 2-466-190	Sereno
489 27/2/75	Havana	Acrylic blue 2-466-190	Sereno
490 5/3/75	Havana	Acrylic blue 2-466-190	Sereno
491 13/3/75	Blue	Fly yellow 2-469-019	Gold
492 Dutch version 13/3/75-Returned for transformation Switzerland - shipped 9/12/75	Blue	Fly yellow 2-469-019	Gold 06
493 Swiss version 6/2/75	Blue	Fly yellow 2-469-019	Gold 06
494 14/2/75	Blue	Fly yellow 2-469-019	Gold
495 27/2/75	Blue	Fly yellow 2-469-019	Gold
496 27/2/75	Havana	Acrylic red 2-464-171	Red 05
497 13/3/75	Havana	Acrylic red Acr. 2-464-171	Red 05
498 11/4/75	Havana	Acrylic red 2-464-171	Red 05
499 5/3/75	Havana	Acrylic red 2-464-171	Red 05
500 27/2/75	Havana	Acrylic red 2-464-171	Red 05
501 Swiss version 6/2/75	Black	Light blue 2-466-440	Sereno 015
502 Swiss version 16/2/75	Havana	Acrylic red 2-464-171	Red 05

Car production

Car production: as an example, the first four assembly sheets for Stratos cars completed at Lancia

Homologation form

A few comments to assist in interpreting the data. Article 251 of Appendix J to the International Sporting Regulations, of which we provide the version carried in the FIA Yearbook of 1974, provides the following definitions:

Title I
Classification of the cars
Article 251.-Categories and Groups. The cars used in competition shall be divided up into the following categories and groups:
Category A: Homologated production cars (the number in parentheses indicates the minimum number of cars produced in 12 consecutive months):
-Group 1 : Series Touring Cars (5000).
-Group 2 : Special Touring Cars (1000).
-Group 3 : Series Grand Touring Cars (1000).
-Group 4 : Special Grand Touring Cars (500).
-Group 5 : Sports Cars (25).
...

Title II
Definitions and general prescriptions
Article 252.-Definitions.
a) Homologated production cars: cars for which the series production of a certain number of identical cars has been verified (see that item) within a determined period of time and intended for normal sale to the public (see that item). This period of time is 12 consecutive months. Verification of the minimum series permits the Automobile Club in the country of production to request homologation (see that item) from the FIA.
...
d) Identical: identical cars are those belonging to the same production series and which have the same bodywork (outside and inside), same mechanical components and same chassis (even though this chassis may be an integral part of the bodywork in case of a unitized construction). The "mechanical" parts include all those necessary to the propulsion, suspension, guidance and braking, as well as all the accessories, mobile or otherwise, that are necessary to normal functioning (such as electrical accessories). Chassis is intended to mean the overall structure of the car that anchors the mechanical parts to the bodywork, including all the parts unitized with that structure found below the horizontal plane passing through the wheel hubs.
e) Minimum production: the production minimum, which varies according to the car group considered, is intended to refer to "identical" cars whose construction is completely terminated within the period of 12 consecutive months.
f) Normal sale: Means the distribution of cars to individual purchasers through the normal commercial channels of the manufacturer.
g) Homologation: is the official certification made by the FIA that a minimum number of cars of a specific model has been made on series-production terms to justify classification in groups 1, 2, 3, 4 or 5 of these regulations. Application for homologation shall be submitted to the FIA by the ASN (Association Sportive Nationale) of the country in which the vehicle is manufactured and shall include the presentation of a homologation form. It must be established in accordance with the special regulations called "Regulations for homologation", laid down by the FIA, and each manufacturer desiring to have their car model(s) homologated must undertake to observe its prescriptions. Homologation will only be granted for models still in production at 1 January 1968 or whose construction began after that date. The homologation of a series-produced model lapses four years after the definitive termination of series production of the model in question. The homologation of a model can only be valid for a single group. Consequently, if a model homologated in one group is transferred to a second group, the first homologation is nullified.
h) Homologation form: All cars recognized by the FIA will be the subject of a descriptive form called homologation form, on which shall be entered all data enabling identification of the said model. For this purpose, all the ASNs shall use only the homologation forms, as well as the homologation extension forms ("normal evolution" or "variants") established by the FIA.
...

Title VI
Special Grand Touring Cars (former Group 3)
Article 264.-Definition: two-seat cars constructed in small series that may be subject to modifications intended to adapt them specifically for racing competition. This group also includes cars derived from those homologated in Group 3 (series GTs) whose modifications exceed the limits authorized for Group 3.
Art.265.- Minimum production and number of seats: Special Grand Touring cars must have been produced in a minimum number of 500 units and have at least two seats.
Art.266.- Permitted modifications: the same as for Group 2- Special Touring Cars (see Article 260).

We are not repeating the lengthy Article 260, which in fact permitted reboring of the engine to the limit of displacement to which the car belongs, i.e. in the case of the Stratos up to 2500 cc. Intake and exhaust manifolds were unrestricted, as were the fuel system and gearbox, though the number of gear ratios could not be altered. Wheels and rims were also unrestricted, provided that at least one-third of their circumference was covered by the fenders. "Aesthetically acceptable" fender extensions could be homologated, without production minimums, "provided they did not increase the width of the fenders more than 5 cm on each side". The result was that the racing Stratos could therefore be significantly different from the one described in the basic form, which is shown on the following pages.

AUTOMOBILE CLUB D'ITALIA
COMMISSIONE SPORTIVA AUTOMOBILISTICA ITALIANA
FEDERATION INTERNATIONALE DE L'AUTOMOBILE

Omologazione F.I.A. N° 640
Omologazione C.S.A.I. N°
Gruppo IV
Vetture GRAN TURISMO

Scheda di Omologazione
secondo l'allegato J al Codice Sportivo Internazionale

Casa costruttrice: LANCIA - BERTONE   Modello: STRATOS HF
N° di serie: autotelaio 829.AR.0   Costruttore: LANCIA
motore 829.A.000   Costruttore: LANCIA
Cilindrata motore: 2418 cm³   147,5 cu.in
La costruzione del modello descritto nella presente scheda è iniziata il 1 LUGLIO 19 72 e la serie minima di 500 esemplari identici e conformi alle caratteristiche qui riportate, è stata raggiunta il 31 LUGLIO 1974 19
Omologazione valida dal 1.10.1974 Lista

• Foto A

Il modello descritto su questa scheda è stato oggetto delle seguenti estensioni d'omologazione:

VARIANTI | EVOLUZIONI NORMALI DEL TIPO
Data | Omolog. N° | Lista | Data | Omolog. N° | Lista

Timbro e firma della C.S.A.I.   Timbro e firma della F.I.A.

Casa costruttrice: LANCIA   modello: STRATOS HF   Omologazione F.I.A. N°

IMPORTANTE — Per le voci sottolineate è obbligatoria l'indicazione in due sistemi di misura, di cui uno deve essere il sistema metrico (vedere tabella di conversione a fondo pagina).

DIMENSIONI E CAPACITÀ:

* 1. Passo .... 2180 mm   85,5 in
* 2. Carreggiata anteriore (¹) .. 1430 mm   56,3 in
* 3. Carreggiata posteriore (¹) .. 1460 mm   57,5 in

4. Lunghezza totale della vettura .. 3710 mm   in
5. Larghezza totale della vettura .. 1760 mm   in
6. Altezza totale della vettura (vuoto) 1110 mm   in
* 7. Capacità serbatoio benzina (compresa riserva) 80 litri   21 gals US   gals GB
8. Numero di posti .. 2
* 9. Peso totale vettura in ordine di marcia, con acqua, olio, ruota di scorta, accessori e finiture indicate nella presente scheda, senza carburante ed attrezzi 880 kg   lbs   cwt

Peso F.I.A. 888 kg

(¹) Indicare in una figura la distanza da terra corrispondente alle carreggiate anteriore e posteriore, riferita a due parti non modificabili della struttura della vettura. I valori delle distanze da terra sono richiesti solo per il controllo delle carreggiate e non interessano la qualifica della vettura.
Riportare a pag. 10 le diverse carreggiate nel caso di impiego di cerchioni con larghezza maggiore da quelli di base.

TABELLA DI CONVERSIONE

1 in (pollice)	= 25,4 mm	1 qt US (1/4 di gallone US)	= 0,9464 lt
1 ft (piede)	= 30,4794 cm	1 qt GB (1/4 di gallone GB)	= 0,568 lt
1 sq.in (pollice²)	= 6,452 cm²	1 gal GB (gallone GB)	= 4,546 lt
1 cu.in (pollice³)	= 16,387 cm³	1 gal US (gallone US)	= 3,785 lt
1 lb (libbra)	= 453,593 g	1 cwt (1/20 di long ton)	= 50,802 kg

Timbro e firma della C.S.A.I.

Casa costruttrice: LANCIA   modello: STRATOS HF   Omologazione F.I.A. N°

AUTOTELAIO E CARROZZERIA (foto A, B e C):

* 20. Tipo di struttura: con telaio indipendente / monoscocca
* 21. Struttura monoscocca: materiale ACCIAIO - VETRORESINA
  Struttura con telaio indipendente:
  * 22. Materiale telaio
  * 23. Materiale carrozzeria
* 24. Numero porte: 2   materiale VETRORESINA
* 25. Materiale cofano motore VETRORESINA
* 26. Materiale cofano portabagagli VETRORESINA
27. Materiale lunotto posteriore Plexiglas
28. Materiale parabrezza CRISTALLO
29. Materiale vetri porte posteriori
30. Materiale vetri porte anteriori Plexiglas
31. Sistema d'apertura vetri porte MANUALE
32. Materiale vetri laterali posteriori

ACCESSORI E FINITURE:

38. Riscaldamento interno: sì / no
39. Condizionamento: sì / no
40. Ventilazione: sì / no
41. Sedili anteriori: tipo e rivestimento

42. Peso del sedile o sedili anteriori (con schienale, guide e supporti) 5,500 kg   lbs
43. Sedile posteriore: tipo e rivestimento

44. Paraurti anteriore: materiale   peso   kg   lbs
45. Paraurti posteriore: materiale   peso   kg   lbs

RUOTE:

50. Tipo: a raggi / disco pieno / disco fenestrato
51. Peso unitario delle ruote senza pneumatico   kg   lbs
52. Sistema di fissaggio COLONNETTE
53. Diametro del cerchione 355,6 mm   14 in
54. Larghezza del cerchione 190,5 mm   7,5 in

STERZO:

60. Tipo A CREMAGLIERA
61. Servosterzo: sì / no
62. Numero giri volante per sterzata totale nei due sensi 3,3
63. Idem con servosterzo

Timbro e firma della C.S.A.I.

Casa costruttrice: LANCIA   modello: STRATOS HF   Omologazione F.I.A. N°

SOSPENSIONI:

* 70. Sospensione anteriore (foto D), tipo RUOTE INDIPENDENTI
* 71. Tipo di molla ELICOIDALE
72. Stabilizzatore (se previsto) BARRA STABILIZZATRICE
73. Numero di ammortizzatori 2   * 74. Tipo IDRAULICI TELESCOPICI
* 78. Sospensione posteriore (foto E), tipo RUOTE INDIPENDENTI
* 79. Tipo di molla ELICOIDALE
80. Stabilizzatore (se previsto) BARRA STABILIZZATRICE
81. Numero di ammortizzatori 2   82. Tipo IDRAULICI TELESCOPICI

FRENI (foto F e G):

* 90. Sistema IDRAULICO
91. Servofreno (se previsto), tipo NO
92. Numero pompe 1 DUPLEX

	Anteriori		Posteriori	
93. Numero di cilindretti per ruota	2		2	
94. Diametro interno	48 mm	in	38 mm	in
Freni a tamburo:				
95. Diametro interno	mm	in	mm	in
96. Lunghezza guarnizioni	mm	in	mm	in
97. Larghezza guarnizioni	mm	in	mm	in
98. Numero ganasce per freno				
99. Superficie frenante per freno	cm²	sq.in	cm²	sq.in
Freni a disco:				
100. Diametro esterno	271 mm	in	271 mm	in
101. Spessore del disco	20 mm	in	20 mm	in
102. Lunghezza pattino d'attrito CIRCA	76,5 mm	in	61,5 mm	in
103. Larghezza pattino d'attrito CIRCA	56 mm	in	42 mm	in
104. Numero di pattini per freno	2		2	
105. Superficie frenante per freno	76 cm²	sq.in	48 cm²	sq.in

Timbro e firma della C.S.A.I.

Casa costruttrice __Lancia__ modello __Stratos__ Omologazione F.I.A. N° _____

MOTORE:

* 130. Ciclo __OTTO__
* 131. Numero di cilindri __6__   * 132. Disposizione cilindri __V di 65°__
* 133. Alesaggio __92,5__ mm __3,64__ in.   * 134. Corsa __60__ mm __2,36__ in
* 135. Cilindrata per cilindro __403__ cm³ __24,5__ cu.in
* 136. Cilindrata totale __2418__ cm³ __147,5__ cu.in
* 137. Materiale gruppo cilindri __GHISA__
  138. Materiale canne (se previste) _____
* 139. Materiale testa cilindri __LEGA ALLUMINIO__
  140. Luci di aspirazione testa cilindri: numero __6__
  141. Luci di scarico testa cilindri: numero __6__
  142. Rapporto di compressione __9__
  143. Volume camera di scoppio __50,4__ cm³ _____ cu.in
  144. Materiale stantuffo __LEGA ALLUMINIO__   145. Numero anelli __3__
  146. Distanza dall'asse perno al punto più alto dello stantuffo __35__ mm _____ in
* 147. Albero motore: fuso /fucinato.   * 148. Tipo albero motore __MONOLITICO__
  149. Numero supporti albero motore __4__
* 150. Materiale cappello supporti albero motore __GHISA__
  151. Sistema lubrificazione: coppa a secco / olio nella coppa.
  152. Capacità: serbatoio / coppa __7__ litri _____ pts GB _____ qts US
  153. Radiatore olio: si / no   __SCAMBIATORE DI CALORE__
* 154. Sistema raffreddamento motore __A LIQUIDO__
  155. Capacità circuito di raffreddamento __15__ litri _____ pts GB _____ qts US
  156. Diametro eventuale ventilatore __280__ mm _____ in
  157. Numero pale ventilatore __5__

Cuscinetti:

* 158. Supporti di banco, tipo __GUSCIO SOTTILE__ diametro __63__ mm _____ in
* 159. Testa di biella, tipo __CON CAPPELLO__ diametro __43,6__ mm _____ in

Pesi:

160. Volano nudo __8,100__ kg _____ lbs
161. Volano con frizione (parte rotante) __15,700__ kg _____ lbs
162. Albero motore __16,300__ kg _____ lbs
163. Biella __0,565__ kg _____ lbs
164. Stantuffo con anelli e perno __0,534__ kg _____ lbs

Timbro e firma della C.S.A.I.

Casa costruttrice __Lancia__ modello __Stratos__ Omologazione F.I.A. N° _____

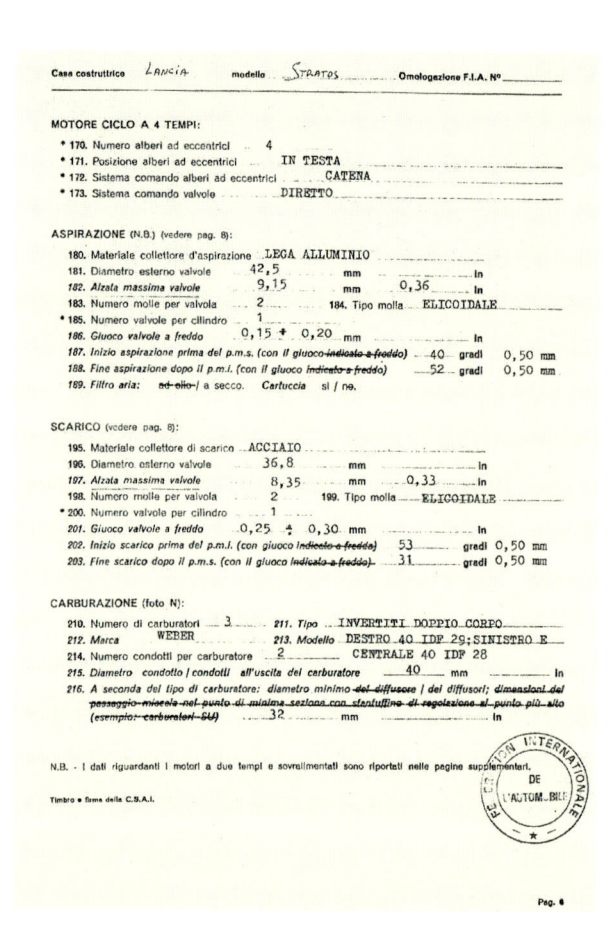

MOTORE CICLO A 4 TEMPI:

* 170. Numero alberi ad eccentrici __4__
* 171. Posizione alberi ad eccentrici __IN TESTA__
* 172. Sistema comando alberi ad eccentrici __CATENA__
* 173. Sistema comando valvole __DIRETTO__

ASPIRAZIONE (N.B.) (vedere pag. 8):

180. Materiale collettore d'aspirazione __LEGA ALLUMINIO__
181. Diametro esterno valvole __42,5__ mm _____ in
182. Alzata massima valvole __9,15__ mm __0,36__ in
183. Numero molle per valvola __2__   184. Tipo molla __ELICOIDALE__
* 185. Numero valvole per cilindro __1__
186. Giuoco valvole a freddo __0,15 ÷ 0,20__ mm _____ in
187. Inizio aspirazione prima del p.m.s. (con il giuoco indicato a freddo) __40__ gradi __0,50 mm__
188. Fine aspirazione dopo il p.m.i. (con il giuoco indicato a freddo) __52__ gradi __0,50 mm__
189. Filtro aria: ad olio / a secco.   Cartuccia si / no.

SCARICO (vedere pag. 8):

195. Materiale collettore di scarico __ACCIAIO__
196. Diametro esterno valvole __36,8__ mm _____ in
197. Alzata massima valvole __8,35__ mm __0,33__ in
198. Numero molle per valvola __2__   199. Tipo molla __ELICOIDALE__
* 200. Numero valvole per cilindro __1__
201. Giuoco valvole a freddo __0,25 ÷ 0,30__ mm _____ in
202. Inizio scarico prima del p.m.i. (con giuoco indicato a freddo) __53__ gradi __0,50 mm__
203. Fine scarico dopo il p.m.s. (con il giuoco indicato a freddo) __31__ gradi __0,50 mm__

CARBURAZIONE (foto N):

210. Numero di carburatori __3__   211. Tipo __INVERTITI DOPPIO CORPO__
212. Marca __WEBER__   213. Modello __DESTRO 40 IDF 29; SINISTRO E__
214. Numero condotti per carburatore __2__   __CENTRALE 40 IDF 28__
215. Diametro condotto / condotti all'uscita del carburatore __40__ mm _____ in
216. A seconda del tipo di carburatori: diametro minimo del diffusore / dei diffusori; dimensioni del passaggio miscela nel punto di minima sezione con stantuffino di regolazione al punto più alto (esempio: carburatori SU) __32__ mm _____ in

N.B. - I dati riguardanti i motori a due tempi e sovralimentati sono riportati nelle pagine supplementari.

Timbro e firma della C.S.A.I.

Casa costruttrice __Lancia__ modello __Stratos__ Omologazione F.I.A. N° _____

INIEZIONE (se prevista):

220. Marca pompa _____
221. Numero stantuffi _____
222. Modello e tipo pompa _____
223. Numero totale iniettori _____
224. Sistemazione iniettori _____
225. Diametro condotto d'alimentazione nel punto di sezione minima _____ mm _____ in

ACCESSORI DEL MOTORE:

230. Pompa carburante: meccanica ed / o elettrica
231. Numero pompe __1__
232. Sistema accensione, tipo __ELETTRONICA__
233. Numero distributori __1__
234. Numero bobine __1__
235. Numero candele per cilindro __1__
236. Generatore, tipo: dinamo / alternatore   Numero __1__
237. Sistema di comando __CINGHIA__
238. Tensione __12__ volt
239. Numero batterie __1__
240. Sistemazione __COFANO MOTORE LATO SINISTRO__
241. Tensione __12__ volt

PRESTAZIONI DEL MOTORE E DELLA VETTURA (secondo i dati dichiarati dalla Casa costruttrice):

250. Potenza del motore __190__ Cv (¹) __DIN__ a __7000__ girl/min
251. Regime massimo __7800__ girl/min   Potenza corrispondente _____ Cv (¹)
252. Coppia massima __23__ kgm   a __4000__ girl/min
253. Velocità massima della vettura __OLTRE 230__ km/h _____ miglia/h

255.

Eccentrico d'aspirazione:
S = __23,0__ mm _____ in
T = __13,7__ mm _____ in
U = __27,4__ mm _____ in

Eccentrico di scarico:
S = __22,3__ mm _____ in
T = __13,7__ mm _____ in
U = __27,4__ mm _____ in

R = Centro albero ad eccentrici

(¹) Precisare se CV DIN, SAE, ecc.

Timbro e firma della C.S.A.I.

Casa costruttrice __Lancia__ modello __Stratos HF__ Omologazione F.I.A. N° _____

Disegno o foto luci condotti d'aspirazione, lato testa cilindri.
Indicare la scala o le dimensioni, e le tolleranze di lavorazione.

Disegno o foto luci d'aspirazione testa cilindri.
Indicare la scala o le dimensioni, e le tolleranze di lavorazione.

Disegno o foto luci collettore di scarico, lato testa cilindri.
Indicare la scala o le dimensioni, le tolleranze di lavorazione ed il diametro dell'uscita.

Disegno o foto luci scarico testa cilindri.
Indicare la scala o le dimensioni, e le tolleranze di lavorazione.

Timbro e firma della C.S.A.I.

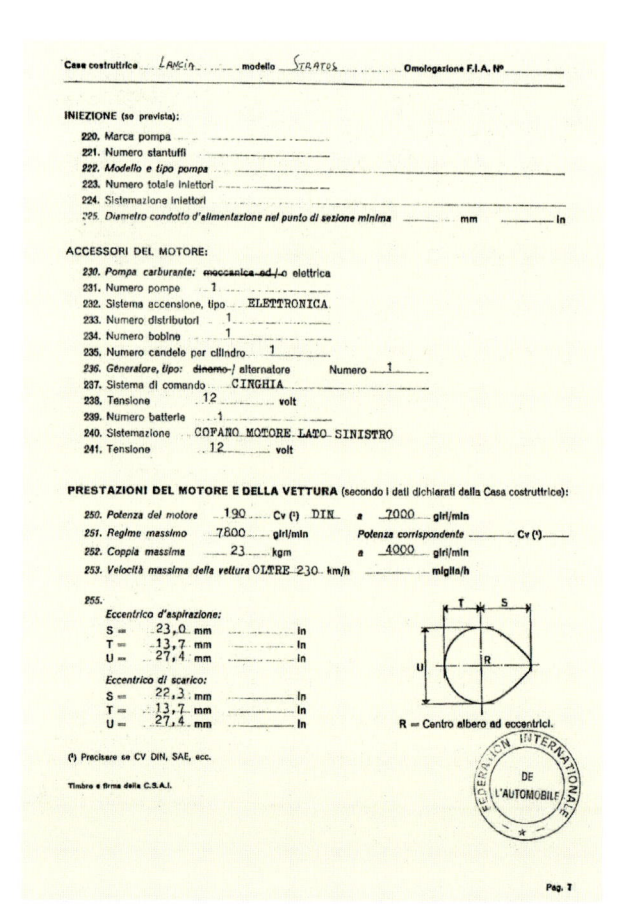

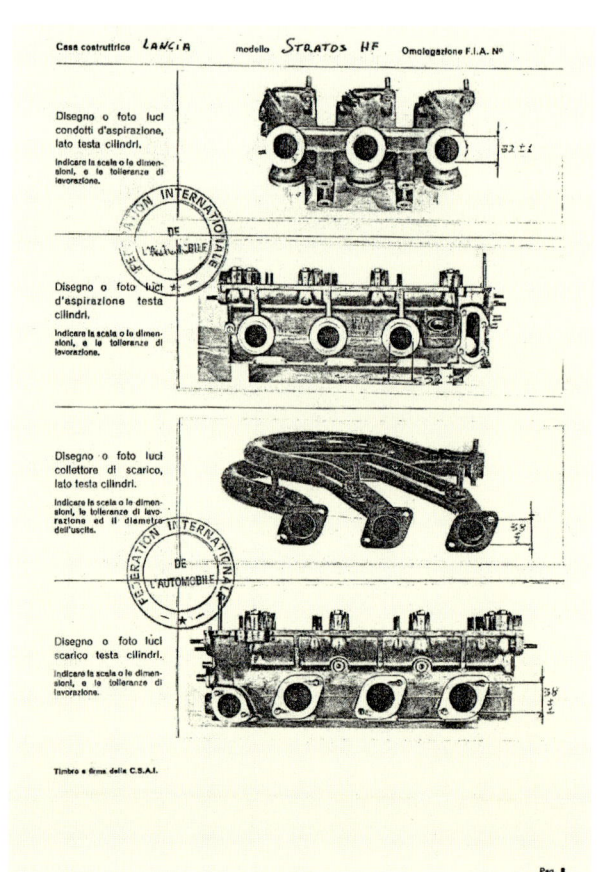

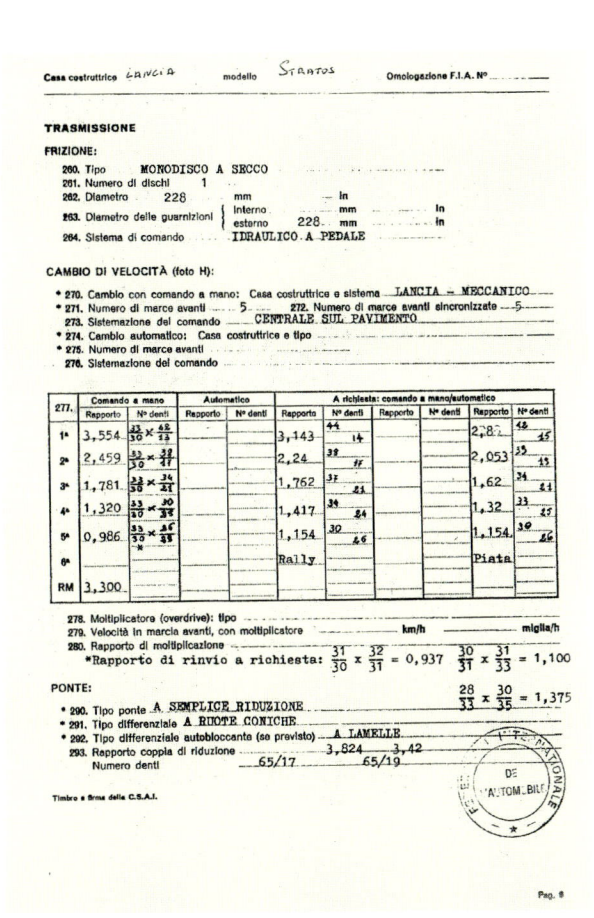

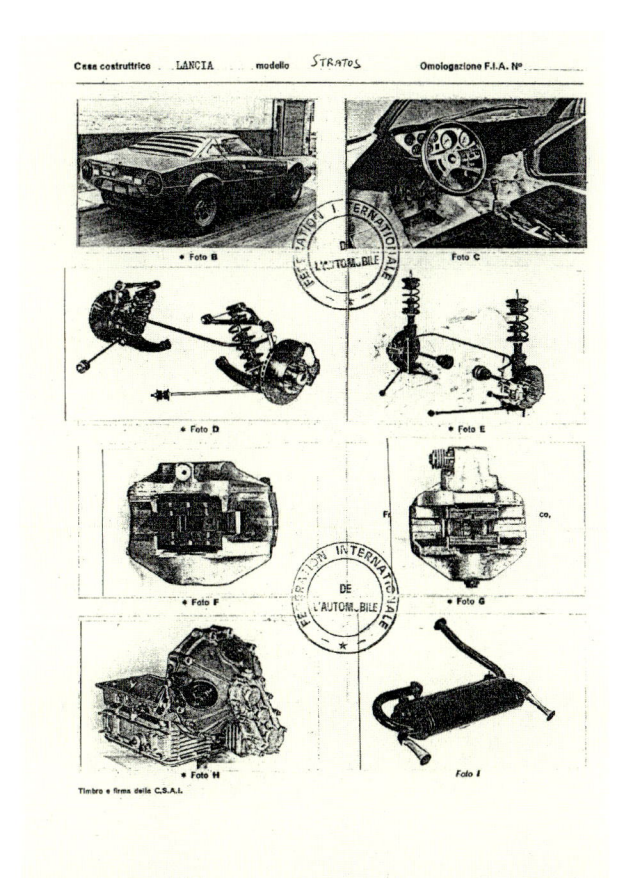

Casa costruttrice LANCIA   **modello** Stratos   **Omologazione F.I.A. N°**

TRASMISSIONE

FRIZIONE:
- 260. Tipo MONODISCO A SECCO
- 261. Numero di dischi 1
- 262. Diametro 228 mm — in
- 263. Diametro delle guarnizioni { Interno — mm — in ; esterno 228 mm — in }
- 264. Sistema di comando IDRAULICO A PEDALE

CAMBIO DI VELOCITÀ (foto H):
- *270. Cambio con comando a mano: Casa costruttrice e sistema LANCIA - MECCANICO
- *271. Numero di marce avanti 5   272. Numero di marce avanti sincronizzate 5
- 273. Sistemazione del comando CENTRALE SUL PAVIMENTO
- *274. Cambio automatico: Casa costruttrice e tipo
- *275. Numero di marce avanti
- 276. Sistemazione del comando

277.	Comando a mano		Automatico		A richiesta: comando a mano/automatico					
	Rapporto	N° denti	Rapporto	N° denti	Rapporto	N° denti	Rapporto	N° denti	Rapporto	N° denti
1ª	3,554	33/30 × 42/13			3,143	44/14			2,782	42/15
2ª	2,459	33/30 × 32/11			2,24	38/17			2,053	35/17
3ª	1,781	33/30 × 34/21			1,762	37/21			1,62	34/21
4ª	1,320	33/30 × 30/25			1,417	34/24			1,32	33/25
5ª	0,986	33/30 × 26/29			1,154	30/26			1,154	30/26
6ª					Rally				Pista	
RM	3,300									

- 278. Moltiplicatore (overdrive): tipo
- 279. Velocità in marcia avanti, con moltiplicatore — km/h — miglia/h
- 280. Rapporto di moltiplicazione
  *Rapporto di rinvio a richiesta: $\frac{31}{30} \times \frac{32}{31} = 0,937$ $\frac{30}{31} \times \frac{31}{33} = 1,100$

PONTE:
- *290. Tipo ponte A SEMPLICE RIDUZIONE $\frac{28}{33} \times \frac{30}{35} = 1,375$
- *291. Tipo differenziale A RUOTE CONICHE
- *292. Tipo differenziale autobloccante (se previsto) A LAMELLE
- 293. Rapporto coppia di riduzione 3,824   3,42
  Numero denti 65/17   65/19

Timbro e firma della C.S.A.I.

Casa costruttrice LANCIA   **modello** Stratos   **Omologazione F.I.A. N°**

IMPORTANTE - Quando una vettura è stata inclusa nel gruppo 2 (Turismo) o gruppo 3 (Gran Turismo) non deve essere controllata la conformità della stessa alle voci e foto della presente Scheda di Omologazione con titoli stampati in carattere corsivo ed a tutti i disegni o foto di pag. 8.

Quando si tratti d'una vettura inclusa nel gruppo 4 (Sport) solamente le voci e le foto contraddistinti da un asterisco * devono essere controllate durante la verifica tecnica del veicolo.

ACCESSORI E FORNITURE SUPPLEMENTARI montati in serie e ~~fornibili a richiesta~~ (devono essere indicati i numeri dei punti ai quali si riferiscono gli stessi):

CENTINA DI SICUREZZA

ARCEAU DE SICURITE

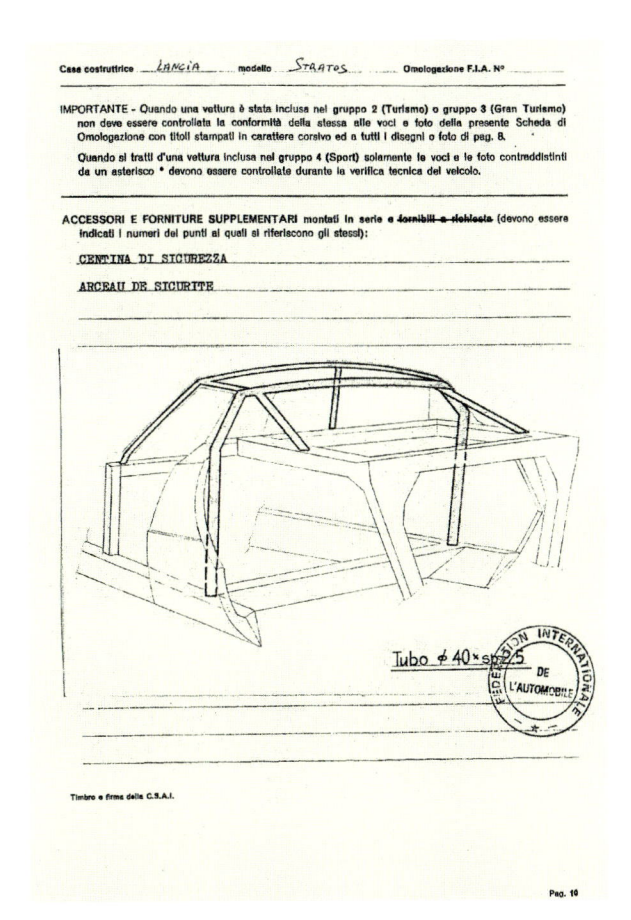

Tubo ⌀ 40 × sp 2,5

Timbro e firma della C.S.A.I.

Casa costruttrice LANCIA   **modello** Stratos   **Omologazione F.I.A. N°**

*Foto B   Foto C
*Foto D   *Foto E
*Foto F   *Foto G
*Foto H   Foto I

Timbro e firma della C.S.A.I.

Casa costruttrice LANCIA   **modello** Stratos   **Omologazione F.I.A. N°**

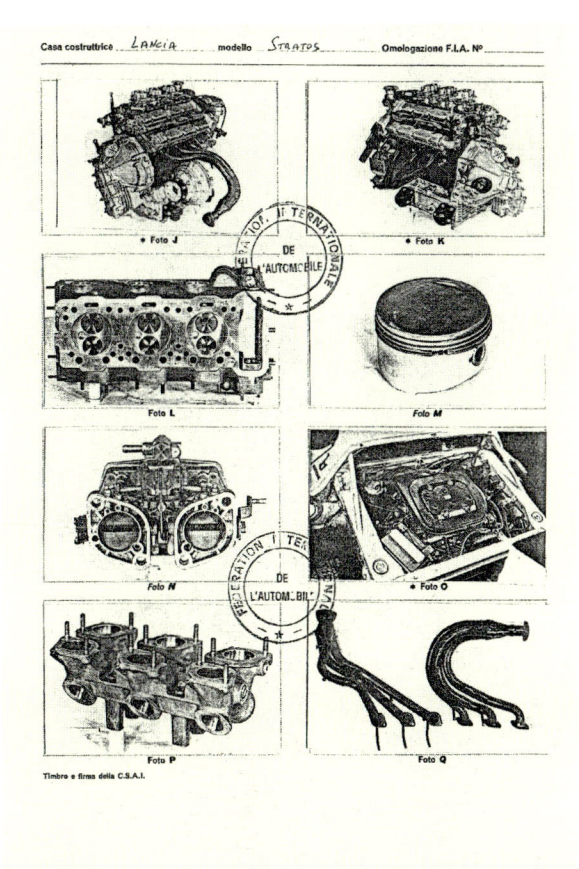

*Foto J   *Foto K
Foto L   Foto M
Foto N   Foto O
Foto P   Foto Q

Timbro e firma della C.S.A.I.

Omologazione F.I.A. N°. 640 1/IV
Omologazione C.S.A.I. N°.
Gruppo 4
Vettura G. TURISMO

AUTOMOBILE CLUB D'ITALIA
COMMISSIONE SPORTIVA AUTOMOBILISTICA ITALIANA
FEDERATION INTERNATIONALE DE L'AUTOMOBILE

Scheda di estensione d'Omologazione
secondo l'allegato J al Codice Sportivo Internazionale

Casa costruttrice LANCIA Modello
N° di serie d'inizio delle modifiche (¹) descritte — autotelaio — motore
Data di applicazione delle modifiche 19
Denominazione commerciale dopo l'applicazione delle modifiche:

La presente estensione d'omologazione deve essere considerata come:
variante /
Omologazione valida dal 1 10 1974 Lista

COMPLESSIVO FRIZIONE 82310314
EMBRAYAGE 82310314

VOLANO MOTORE 82301992
VOLANT DE MOTEUR 82301992

Timbro e firma della C.S.A.I. Timbro e firma della F.I.A.

Pag. 1 /

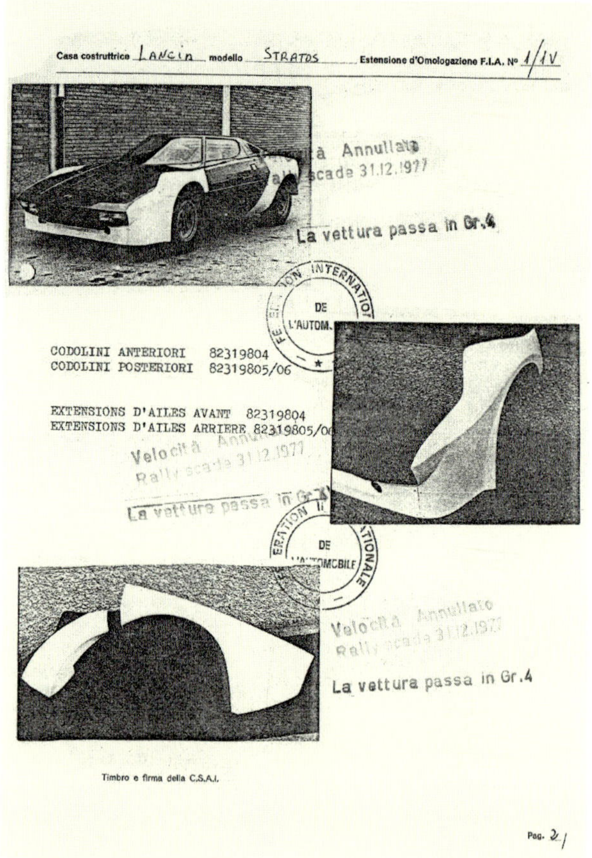

Casa costruttrice LANCIA modello STRATOS Estensione d'Omologazione F.I.A. N° 1/IV

Velocità Annullato
Rally scade 31.12.1977
La vettura passa in Gr.4

CODOLINI ANTERIORI 82319804
CODOLINI POSTERIORI 82319805/06

EXTENSIONS D'AILES AVANT 82319804
EXTENSIONS D'AILES ARRIERE 82319805/06

Timbro e firma della C.S.A.I.

Pag. 2 /

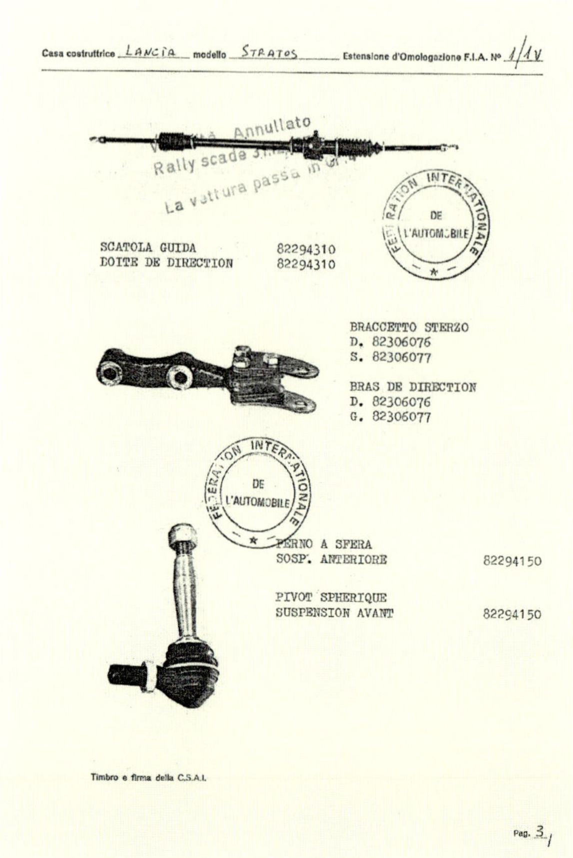

Casa costruttrice LANCIA modello STRATOS Estensione d'Omologazione F.I.A. N° 1/IV

SCATOLA GUIDA 82294310
BOITE DE DIRECTION 82294310

BRACCETTO STERZO
D. 82306076
S. 82306077

BRAS DE DIRECTION
D. 82306076
G. 82306077

PERNO A SFERA
SOSP. ANTERIORE 82294150

PIVOT SPHERIQUE
SUSPENSION AVANT 82294150

Timbro e firma della C.S.A.I.

Pag. 3 /

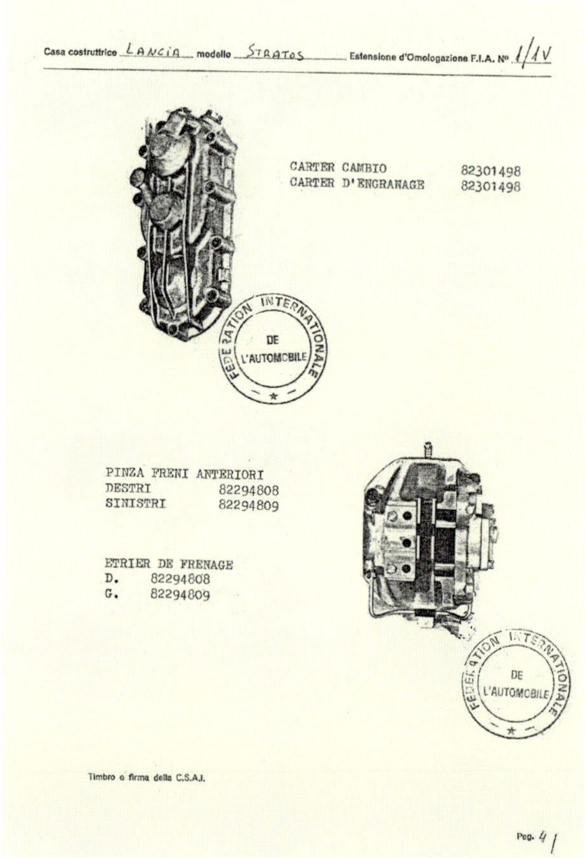

Casa costruttrice LANCIA modello STRATOS Estensione d'Omologazione F.I.A. N° 1/IV

CARTER CAMBIO 82301498
CARTER D'ENGRANAGE 82301498

PINZA FRENI ANTERIORI
DESTRI 82294808
SINISTRI 82294809

ETRIER DE FRENAGE
D. 82294808
G. 82294809

Timbro e firma della C.S.A.I.

Pag. 4 /

Casa costruttrice LANCIA modello STRATOS HF Estensione d'Omologazione F.I.A. N° 1/IV

TESTATA A 4 VALVOLE	DESTRA	82315004
TESTATA A 4 VALVOLE	SINISTRA	82315005
COULASSE 4 SOUPAPES	D.	82315004
COULASSE 4 SOUPAPES	G.	82315005

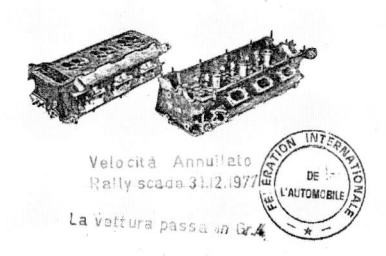

Velocità Annullato
Rally scade 31.12.1977

La vettura passa in Gr.4

SOSTITUZIONE DEL COMANDO ELETTRICO ALZAFARI CON SISTEMA MANUALE.
REMPLACEMENT DU SYSTEME SOULEVEMENT ELECTRIQUE DES PHARES AVEC SISTEME MANUEL.

Timbro e firma della C.S.A.I.

Pag. 5./

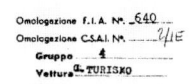

Omologazione F.I.A. N° 640
Omologazione C.S.A.I. N° 2/IE
Gruppo 4
Vettura TURISMO

AUTOMOBILE CLUB D'ITALIA
COMMISSIONE SPORTIVA AUTOMOBILISTICA ITALIANA
FEDERATION INTERNATIONALE DE L'AUTOMOBILE

Scheda di estensione d'Omologazione
secondo l'allegato J al Codice Sportivo Internazionale

Casa costruttrice LANCIA BERTONE   Modello STRATOS HF
N° di serie d'inizio delle autotelaio 829 AR. 0
modifiche (¹) descritte   motore   829 AR. 000
Data di applicazione delle modifiche ... 19 ..
Denominazione commerciale dopo l'applicazione delle modifiche:

La presente estensione d'omologazione deve essere considerata come:
variante / EVOLUZIONE NORMALE DEL TIPO
Omologazione valida dal 1.1. 1975   Lista

Descrizione delle modifiche: Dal 1.11.74 vetture fornite con deviatore flusso aria e spoiler posteriore.
Depuis 1.11.74 voitures fournis avec aileron deviateur d'air et spoiler arrier.

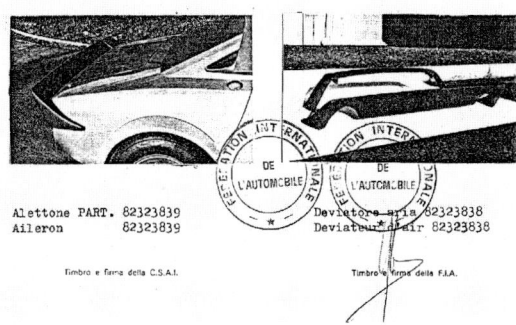

Alettone PART. 82323839
Aileron   82323839

Deviatore aria 82323838
Deviateur d'air 82323838

Timbro e firma della C.S.A.I.   Timbro e firma della F.I.A.

Pag. 1/

Casa costruttrice LANCIA modello STRATOS HF Estensione d'Omologazione F.I.A. N° 640 2/IE

PORTA MOZZO RUOTA POST.	D. e S.	82321178
DISCO FRENO POST.	D. e S.	82319461/62
PINZE FRENO POST.	D. e S.	82321179/80
MOYEU DE ROUE AVANT	D. e G.	82321178
DISQUE DE FREIN AVANT	D. e G.	82319461/62
ETRIER DE FRE-IN AVANT	D. e G.	82321179/80

DISCO FRENO ANT.	D. e S.	82319461/62
PINZE FRENO ANT.	D. e S.	82319235/36
DISQUE DE FREIN AVANT	D. e G.	82319461/62
ETRIER DE FREIN AVANT	D. e G.	82319235/36

Freno a mano agente sulle 4 ruote
Frein de secour sur les 4 roues/

Timbro e firma della C.S.A.I.

Pag. ./

Omologazione F.I.A. N° 640
Omologazione C.S.A.I. N° 3/DV
Gruppo 4
Vettura G. TURISMO

AUTOMOBILE CLUB D'ITALIA
COMMISSIONE SPORTIVA AUTOMOBILISTICA ITALIANA
FEDERATION INTERNATIONALE DE L'AUTOMOBILE

Scheda di estensione d'Omologazione
secondo l'allegato J al Codice Sportivo Internazionale

Casa costruttrice LANCIA – Bertone   Modello STRATOS HF
N° di serie d'inizio delle { autotelaio 829 AR.0
modifiche (¹) descritte { motore   829 A. 000
Data di applicazione delle modifiche 19
Denominazione commerciale dopo l'applicazione delle modifiche:

La presente estensione d'omologazione deve essere considerata come:
variante / ~~evoluzione del tipo / inclusione~~
Omologazione valida dal 1 4 19 75   Lista

Cruscotto	part.	n. 82324045
Tableau de bord	"	n. 82324045
Cruscotto	"	n. 82324046
Tableau de bord	"	n. 82324046

82324045

Timbro e firma della C.S.A.I.

Omologazione F.I.A. N° 640
Omologazione C.S.A.I. N° 4/3V
Gruppo 4
Vettura G. TURISMO

AUTOMOBILE CLUB D'ITALIA
COMMISSIONE SPORTIVA AUTOMOBILISTICA ITALIANA
FEDERATION INTERNATIONALE DE L'AUTOMOBILE

Scheda di estensione d'Omologazione
secondo l'allegato J al Codice Sportivo Internazionale

Casa costruttrice LANCIA   Modello STRATOS HF
N° di serie d'inizio delle { autotelaio 829.AR.0
modifiche (¹) descritte { motore   829.A. 000
Data di applicazione delle modifiche 19
Denominazione commerciale dopo l'applicazione delle modifiche:
INVARIATA – INCHANGEE

La presente estensione d'omologazione deve essere considerata come:
variante / ~~evoluzione del tipo / inclusione~~
Omologazione valida dal 1.10 19 75   Lista

Descrizione delle modifiche:
COMPLESSIVO FRIZIONE – part. 82325563
EMBRAYAGE   – n°

La vettura passa in Gr.4

Timbro e firma della C.S.A.I.

Casa costruttrice LANCIA   modello STRATOS HF   Estensione d'Omologazione F.I.A. N° 4/3V

BRACCI INFERIORI SOSPENSIONI ANTERIORI
RINFORZATI
BRAS INFERIEURS SUSPENSIONS AVANT
RENFORCES

part. n° 82324064

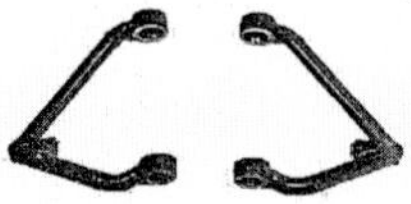

BRACCI SUPERIORI SOSPENSIONI ANTERIORI
RINFORZATI
BRAS SUPERIEURS SUSPENSIONS AVANT
RENFORCES

part. n°   a.D. 82324059
            s.G. 82324060

FISSAGGIO PORTAMOLLE PER IL MONTAGGIO
DELL'UNIBALL
FIXAGE PLAT RESSORTS POUR MONTAGE
UNIBALL

Timbro e firma della C.S.A.I.

Casa costruttrice LANCIA modello STRATOS HF Estensione d'Omologazione F.I.A. N° 4/34

ADATTAMENTO PARATIA PER MONTAGGIO
DOPPIA POMPA FRENI
MODIFICATION POUR MONTAGE DOUBLE
POMPE FREINS

PRESE ARIA PER ABITACOLO E/O PER
FRENI
PRISE D'AIR POUR HABITACLE ET/OU
POUR FREINS

RAPPORTI DI RINVIO

$$\frac{31}{30} \times \frac{25}{31} = 0,86 \qquad \frac{29}{27} \times \frac{31}{35} = 0,951 \qquad \frac{30}{31} \times \frac{32}{31} = 1,001$$

$$\frac{30}{31} \times \frac{31}{29} = 1,034 \qquad \frac{28}{33} \times \frac{31}{32} = 1,217$$

Timbro e firma della C.S.A.I.

Casa costruttrice LANCIA modello STRATOS HF Estensione d'Omologazione F.I.A. N° 4/34

INCERNIERAMENTO PER APERTURA ALETTATURA
POSTERIORE

ARTICULATION POUR OUVERTURE LUNETTE
ARRIERE A LAMELLES

ATTACCHI AMMORTIZZATORI ANTERIORI TIPO
SAFARI - I PUNTI DI ATTACCO DELLA SO-
SPENSIONE RIMANGONO INVARIATI

FIXAGE AMORTISSEURS AVANT TYPE SAFARI
LES POINTS DE FIXAGE DE LA SUSPENSION
SONT INVARIES

PER RAGIONI DI SICUREZZA AD EVITARE
INTERFERENZE DELLA ESCURSIONE DEL-
L'AMMORTIZZATORE VENGONO MODIFICATE
LE LONGHERINE ANTERIORI PER PASSAGGIO
LEVE STERZO.

POUR RAISONS DE SECURITE POUR EVITER
DES INTERFERENCES PROVOQUEES PAR LE
MOUVEMENT DE L'AMORTISSEUR SONT MODI-
FIES LES BRANCARDS AVANT POUR LE
PASSAGE DU LEVIER DE DIRECTION.

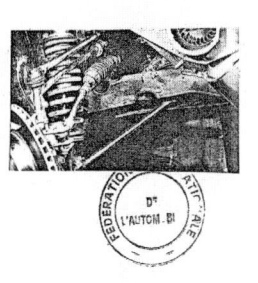

Timbro e firma della C.S.A.I.

Casa costruttrice LANCIA modello STRATOS HF Estensione d'Omologazione F.I.A. N° 4/34

INCERNIERAMENTO COFANI CON SPINE
ARTICULATION CAPOTS AVEC GOUPILLES

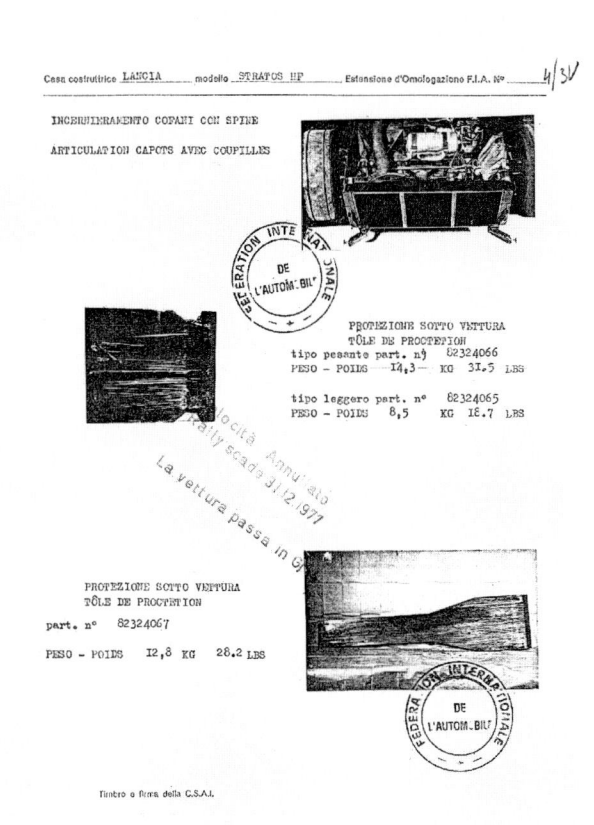

PROTEZIONE SOTTO VETTURA
TÔLE DE PROTECTION
tipo pesante part. n° 82324066
PESO - POIDS 14,3 KG 31.5 LBS

tipo leggero part. n° 82324065
PESO - POIDS 8,5 KG 18.7 LBS

PROTEZIONE SOTTO VETTURA
TÔLE DE PROTECTION
part. n° 82324067
PESO - POIDS 12,8 KG 28.2 LBS

Timbro e firma della C.S.A.I.

Casa costruttrice LANCIA modello STRATOS HF Estensione d'Omologazione F.I.A. N° 4/34

PRESA ARIA PER AERAZIONE ABITACOLO
PRISE D'AIR POUR HABITACLE

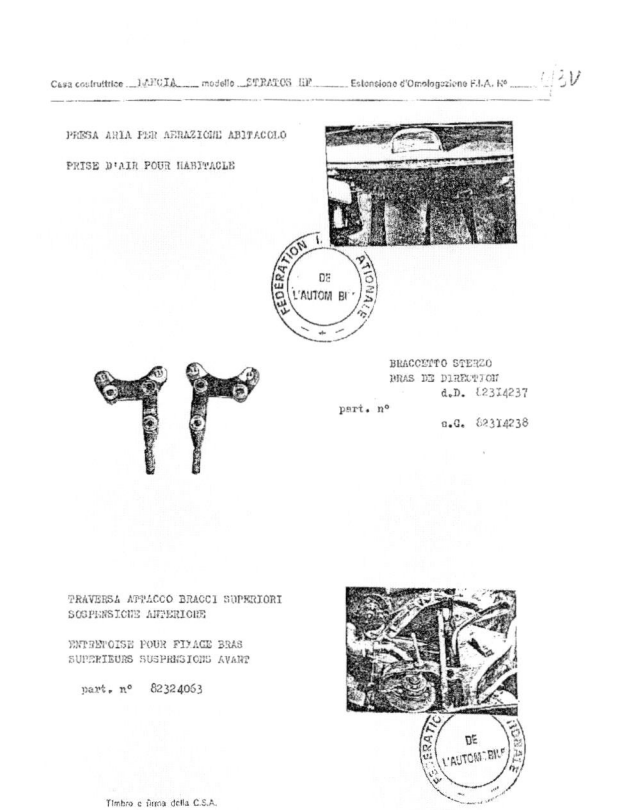

BRACCETTO STERZO
BRAS DE DIRECTION
              d.D. 82314237
part. n°
              s.G. 82314238

TRAVERSA ATTACCO BRACCI SUPERIORI
SOSPENSIONE ANTERIORE

ENTRETOISE POUR FIXAGE BRAS
SUPERIEURS SUSPENSIONS AVANT

part. n° 82324063

Timbro e firma della C.S.A.I.

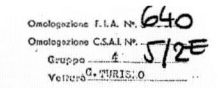

Omologazione F.I.A. N° 640
Omologazione C.S.A.I. N° 5/2E
Gruppo 4
Vettura G. TURISMO

AUTOMOBILE CLUB D'ITALIA
COMMISSIONE SPORTIVA AUTOMOBILISTICA ITALIANA
FEDERATION INTERNATIONALE DE L'AUTOMOBILE

Scheda di estensione d'Omologazione
secondo l'allegato J al Codice Sportivo Internazionale

Casa costruttrice LANCIA Modello STRATOS HP
N° di serie d'inizio delle modifiche (?) descritte { autotelaio 829 AR.0
motore 829 A. 000
Data di applicazione delle modifiche _____ 19 __
Denominazione commerciale dopo l'applicazione delle modifiche:
INVARIATA - INCHANGEE

La presente estensione d'omologazione deve essere considerata come:
~~variante~~ / evoluzione normale del tipo
Omologazione valida dal 1.10 1975 Lista ____

Descrizione delle modifiche:
A partire dal 1.1.1975

BRACCI INFERIORI SOSPENSIONI ANTERIORI RINFORZATI

part. n° { d. D. 42304261
S. C. 42304262

Timbro e firma della C.S.A.I.

Pag. 1/2

Casa costruttrice LANCIA modello STRATOS HP Estensione d'Omologazione F.I.A. N° 5/2E

A partire dal 1.4.1975

COFANO POSTERIORE SENZA RIPARO MOTORE SOTTO L'ALETTATURA

Timbro e firma della C.S.A.I.

Pag. 2/2

Omologazione F.I.A. N° 640
Omologazione C.S.A.I. N° 6/4V
Gruppo 4
Vettura G. TURISMO

AUTOMOBILE CLUB D'ITALIA
COMMISSIONE SPORTIVA AUTOMOBILISTICA ITALIANA
FEDERATION INTERNATIONALE DE L'AUTOMOBILE

Scheda di estensione d'Omologazione
secondo l'allegato J al Codice Sportivo Internazionale

Casa costruttrice LANCIA Modello STRATOS HP
N° di serie d'inizio delle modifiche (?) descritte { autotelaio
motore
Data di applicazione delle modifiche Per tutte le vetture prodotte - pour toutes les voitures fabriquées
Denominazione commerciale dopo l'applicazione delle modifiche:
invariata - inchangée

La presente estensione d'omologazione deve essere considerata come:
variante / ~~evoluzione normale del tipo~~ di fornitura
Omologazione valida dal 1.4 1976 Lista ____

Descrizione delle modifiche: COPERCHIO CAMPANA FRIZIONE
COUVERCLE CLOCHE EMBRAYAGE

N. 82301498   N. 82307691

Timbro e firma della C.S.A.I.   Timbro e firma della F.I.A.

Pag. 1/

Omologazione F.I.A. N° 640
Omologazione C.S.A.I. N° _____
Gruppo 4
Vettura G. TURISMO

7/3 E

AUTOMOBILE CLUB D'ITALIA
COMMISSIONE SPORTIVA AUTOMOBILISTICA ITALIANA
FEDERATION INTERNATIONALE DE L'AUTOMOBILE

Scheda di estensione d'Omologazione
secondo l'allegato J al Codice Sportivo Internazionale

Casa costruttrice LANCIA   Modello STRATOS HF
N° di serie d'inizio delle modifiche (¹) descritte:
 autotelaio 829 AR 0
 motore 829 A 000
Data di applicazione delle modifiche _____ 19 __
Denominazione commerciale dopo l'applicazione delle modifiche:
invariata – inchangée
La presente estensione d'omologazione deve essere considerata come:
~~variante / modello / tipo / serie~~
Omologazione valida dal -1 JAN 1977 19 7   Lista _____

Descrizione delle modifiche: ERRATA CORRIGE

PAG. 4   FRENI – FREINS

101. Spessore del disco – ant.: leggere   mm 22   anziché mm 20
     Epaisseur du disque – avant: lire   au lieu de

Estensione di omologazione   5/2 E
Extension d'homologation

PAG. 1 Bracci inferiori sospensione anteriori rinforzati
        Bras inférieures suspension avant renforcées

n. part. leggere   82304261 e 82304262   anziché 42304261 e 42304262
          lire   au lieu de

Timbro e firma della C.S.A.I.

Casa costruttrice LANCIA modello STRATOS HF Estensione d'Omologazione F.I.A. N° 640

7/3 E

ESTENSIONE DI OMOLOGAZIONE 2/1 E
EXTENTION D'HOMOLOGATION

FRENI – FREINS

	ant. – avant	post. – arrière
93. N. cilindri per ruota – N. cylindres par roue	4	4
94. Diametro interno – Alésage	44.45 mm – 1¾ inc	38.1 mm – 1½ inc

FRENI A DISCO – FREINS A' DISQUE

100. Diametro esterno – Diamètre éxterieur	267 mm	267 mm
101. Spessore del disco – Epaisseur du disque	28 mm	28 mm
102. Lunghezza pattino – Longeur des sabots	132 mm	122 mm
103. Larghezza pattino – Largeur des sabots	50 mm	50 mm
104. N. pattini per freno – N. sabots par frein	2	2
105. Superficie frenante per freno – Surface de freinage par frein	116 cm²	108 cm²

Timbro e firma della C.S.A.I.

Omologazione F.I.A. N° 640
Omologazione C.S.A.I. N° _____
Gruppo 4
Vettura G. TURISMO

8/5 V

AUTOMOBILE CLUB D'ITALIA
COMMISSIONE SPORTIVA AUTOMOBILISTICA ITALIANA
FEDERATION INTERNATIONALE DE L'AUTOMOBILE

Scheda di estensione d'Omologazione
secondo l'allegato J al Codice Sportivo Internazionale

Casa costruttrice LANCIA   Modello STRATOS HF
N° di serie d'inizio delle modifiche (¹) descritte:
 autotelaio 829 AR 0
 motore 829 A 000
Data di applicazione delle modifiche _____ 19 __
Denominazione commerciale dopo l'applicazione delle modifiche:
invariata – inchangée
La presente estensione d'omologazione deve essere considerata come:
variante / ~~modello / tipo / serie~~
Omologazione valida dal 1.4 1977   Lista _____

Descrizione delle modifiche:

Bracci inferiori sospensioni anteriori rinforzati
Bras inférieures suspensions avant renforcées

Part. N.   d. D. 82324070   "valable en Groupe 4 uniquement"
           s. G. 82324071   "valid for Group 4 only"

Timbro e firma della C.S.A.I.

Casa costruttrice LANCIA modello STRATOS HF Estensione d'Omologazione F.I.A. N° 640 8/5 V

Braccio inferiore sospensione posteriore rinforzato
Bras inférieur suspension arrière renforcée

part. N. 82324072   "valable en Groupe 4 uniquement"
                     "valid for Group 4 only"

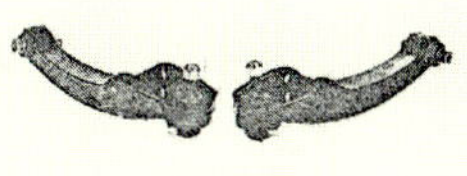

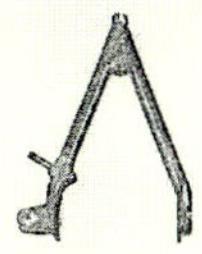

Timbro e firma della C.S.A.I.

A few road tests

In the early Sixties the two principal British car magazines, «The Autocar» and «The Motor», launched the idea of performing test drives on competition cars. While «The Motor» conducted only two broad tests of Touring cars that had won their class at the 6 Hours of Brands Hatch in 1962 and 1963, organized by that same magazine, Graham Robsam of its sister publication initiated a popular column *"Given The Works"*, which published the results of cars used by the official teams, especially rally cars. Of course, most of the issues were devoted to British cars, but as a result of the insistent victories of Lancia, reports also appeared on its cars subjected to testing on Britain's famed MIRA proving ground. This custom also spread to the special «Quattroruote Sport» issue published once a year by «Quattroruote» magazine, which presented the results of some tests conducted at ISAM, the equivalent Italian institute.

Although the results published at the time by the two periodicals have the merit of being certain, because of the integrity of the institutes that produced them, they cannot be taken as an indication of the top performance of the cars that generated them, only an indicative curiosity.

First of all, nothing is known about the condition of the cars tested, in the British case often at the end of a grueling competition and in all cases under the vigilant eye of the teams, which required total compliance with ultra-conservative engine speeds. They are therefore not as dependable as the data obtained on series cars, measured after a proper breaking-in and with the cars in the best state of repair.

Normally, the cars to be tested were furnished with the final drive ratios used in racing, and thus extremely "short". This casts some doubts on the acceleration tests, since the drive wheels could easily spin and thus penalize the performance figures. The measurement of top speed was also of no practical value, since the rpm-limiter prevented the cars from achieving the best results possible at full engine speeds.

Nor can the results of «Quattroruote Sport» be compared with those of «The Autocar», since the former were reported in metric distances, while the latter were in British units (with an asterisk *), so that for the latter 160 mph was equal to 160,93 kph while the quarter-mile was equal to 402.34 m. Consequently the exit speed from the base, also affected by the difficulties mentioned earlier, was measured more than two meters later.

The fact remains, however, that the Fulvia 1.6 HF used in the 1969 RAC Rally required more than twice the time of the Stratos HF to accelerate from zero to 160 kph, while there was virtual parity between the preparation of Claudio Maglioli on the car tested by «Quattroruote Sport» in 1979 and that of University Motors of Genoa for Britain's *The Chequered Flag* team, subjected again to the fifth-wheel test in 1982 after the tests in 1975 and 1978.

It would be interesting to be able to compare the final versions of the Stratos HF with its heir the Rally 037, but unfortunately the only usable figure is the 1.4 seconds less the latter required to reach 160 kph (but with what final drive ratio?). Since the base used by «Quattroruote Sport» was only 300 m, however, this explains both the shorter time it required (with two asterisks**) but also the exit speed almost 10 kph slower (with two asterisks) than the Stratos. Lacking the results of tests timed with a clothoid or steering pad for both cars, any judgment, for what it might be worth, must be suspended, and the Stratos-slayers will continue forever to speak of a valid car that had come to its natural terminus.

	Fulvia 1.6 HF 1969	Stratos HF 1975	Stratos HF 1978	Stratos HF 1979	Stratos HF 1982	Rally 037 1982
Top speed (kph)	163	nd	nd	nd	nd	163.75
0-160 kph (s)	29,7*	14,5*	13,9*	12,4	12,4*	11,0
400 m (s)	16,7*	14,2*	nd	13,2	13,2*	10,9**
Exit speed (kph)	132	159,3	nd	166,5	167,4	158,9**

nd=not determined

Results

in collaboration with Luca Ronchi

Listed on the following pages, divided by year, are the results obtained by the Lancia Stratos HF in the championships, trophies and cups sanctioned by the FIA during the ten-year period 1 Jan 1973-31 Dec 1982 (the date its homologation expired). The list does not include the car's victories or placements in events not valid for FIA titles, nor placements that brought no points to the crew and/or car in valid events.

Each event the Stratos participated in is shown in the table as follows, complying with the standard used for decades by the Fédération Internationale de l'Automobile. From left to right: date, type of event, original name of the event, the racing symbol of the organizing country, crew and placement. Example: 6-8/April, ERC, Firestone Rally (P), Munari-Mannucci, 1st.

1973
WCM WORLD CHAMPIONSHIP FOR MAKES
Technical regulations
Open to Group 5 Sports cars up to 3000 cc and Grand Touring cars without displacement limitation that also compete in an international cup
Point system
20-15-12-10-8-6-4-3-2-1 points to the first 10 cars classified (one per make). The 7 best results are considered

Number events
10

ERC EUROPEAN RALLY CHAMPIONSHIP FOR DRIVERS
Technical regulations
Open to cars of Groups 1 (series Touring) to 5 (Sport)

Point system
20-15-12-10-8-6-4-3-2-1 points to the first 10 classified. The 6 best results are considered. Each driver can only consider two events held in the same country
Number events
20
Event characteristics
total distance longer than 1000 kms and at least 5 special stages totaling 100 km

DATE	TYPE OF EVENT	NAME OF EVENT	COUNTRY SYMBOL	CREW	PLACEMENT
6-8/April	ERC	Firestone Rally	(P)	Munari-Mannucci	1st
13-May	WCM	Targa Florio	(I)	Munari-Andruet	2nd
14-22/September	ERC	Tour de France	(F)	Munari-Mannucci	1st

Official final classification of the WCM
1st Matra-Simca 124 points
7th Lancia 15 points
Official final classification of the ERC
1st Munari-Mannucci (Lancia Fulvia 1.6 HF + Lancia Stratos HF) 71+40=111 points

1974
WRC WORLD RALLY CHAMPIONSHIP FOR MAKES
Technical regulations
Open to car of Groups 1 (series Touring) to 4 (special Grand Touring)

Point system
20-15-12-10-8-6-4-3-2-1 points to the first 10 cars (one per make). The 6 best results are considered
Number events
8

Event characteristics
total distance longer than 3,000 kms, including at least 1,000 of road sections and 200 of special stages. To compute the total conventional distance of a rally, 1 km of special stage is considered equivalent to 5 kms of road section

DATE	TYPE OF EVENT	NAME OF EVENT	COUNTRY SYMBOL	CREW	PLACEMENT
2-5/October	WRC	Rally Sanremo	(I)	Munari-Mannucci	1st
16-20/October	WRC	Rally Rideau Lakes	(CDN)	Munari-Mannucci	1st
15-20 November	WRC	RAC Rally of Great Britain	(GB)	Munari-Sodano	3rd
30 November-1/December	WRC	Tour de Corse	(F)	Andruet-"Biche"	1st

Official final classification of the WRC
1st Lancia (Lancia Beta Coupe+ Lancia Stratos HF) 22+72=94 points

1975

WRC WORLD RALLY CHAMPIONSHIP FOR MAKES

Technical regulations
Open to cars of Groups 1 (series Touring) to 4 (special Grand Touring)

Point system
20-15-12-10-8-6-4-3-2-1 points to the first 10 cars (one per make). The 8 best results are considered

Number events
10

Event characteristics
total distance longer than 3,000 kms, including at least 1,000 of road sections and 200 of special stages. To compute the total conventional distance of a rally, 1 km of special stage is considered equivalent to 5 kms of road section

ECGT EUROPEAN CHAMPIONSHIP FOR GRAND TOURING CARS

Technical regulations
Open to cars of Groups (series Grand Touring) and 4 (special Grand Touring)

Point system
20-15-12-10-8-6-4-3-2-1 points to the first 10 classified.

Number of events
7

ERC EUROPEAN RALLY CHAMPIONSHIP FOR DRIVERS

Technical regulations
Open to cars of Groups 1 (series Touring) to 4 (special Grand Touring)

Point system
20-15-12-10-8-6-4-3-2-1 points to the first 10 classified. The 8 best results are considered

Number of events
38 events of which 5 with coefficient 4, 10 with coefficient 3, 10 with coefficient 2, and 13 with coefficient 1

Event characteristics
minimum road sections 700 kms, minimum total distance of special stages 150 kms

Minimum number of special stages
5

DATE	TYPE OF EVENT	NAME OF EVENT	COUNTRY SYMBOL	CREW	PLACEMENT
15-24/January	WCR	Rally of Montecarlo	(MC)	Munari-Mannucci	1st
13-15/February	WCR	Rally of Sweden	(S)	Waldegaard-Thorszelius	1st
27-31/March	WCR	East African Safari	(EAK)	Munari-Drews	2nd
				Waldegaard-Thorszelius	3rd
30-31/May	ERC (1)	Rally 4 Regioni	(I)	Munari-Mannucci	1st
				De Eccher-Garzoglio	7th
28-29/June	ERC (1)	Rally delle Alpi orientali	(I)	Pinto-Bernacchini	4th
29-June	ECGT	Norisring	(D)	Facetti	9th
28-30/August	ERC (4)	Rally San Martino di Castrozza	(I)	Pinto-Bernacchini	1st
				"Tony"-De Marco	5th
28-September	ECGT	6 Ore di Monza	(I)	Facetti-Brambilla	4th
1-4/October	WRC	Rally Sanremo	(I)	Waldegaard-Thorszelius	1st
8-9/November	WRC	Tour de Corse	(F)	Darniche-Mahé	1st
21-26/November	WRC	RAC Rally of Great Britain	(GB)	Munari-Mannucci	4th

Official final classification of the WRC
1st Lancia (Lancia Stratos HF) 96 points

Official final classification of the ECGT
1st Hartwig Bertrams (Porsche Carrera RSR) 67 points
14th Carlo Facetti (Lancia Stratos HF) 11 points

Semi-official final classification of the ERC
1st Maurizio Verini (FIAT 124 Abarth) 390 points
13th Raffaele Pinto (Lancia Stratos HF) 90 points

1976

WCM WORLD CHAMPIONSHIP FOR MAKES
Technical regulations
A World Championship for Makes is contended in parallel with a World Sport Championship. World Championship for Makes: reserved to cars of Groups 1 to 5 (1 series Touring, 2 Touring, 3 series Gran Touring, 4 Gran Touring, and 5 special Production which, though no minimum production is required, must be based on a model belonging to the other four Groups, hence the designation "silhouette")

Point system
20-15-12-10-8-6-4-3-2-1 points to the first 10 cars classified (one per make). The 5 best results are considered
Number of events
7

WRC WORLD RALLY CHAMPIONSHIP FOR MAKES
Regulations identical to previous year

ECGT EUROPEAN CHAMPIONSHIP FOR GRAND TOURING CARS
Regulations identical to previous year

ERC EUROPEAN RALLY CHAMPIONSHIP FOR DRIVERS
Regulations identical to previous year
Number of events
39 scheduled, 35 contended, including 5 with coefficient 4, 10 with coefficient 3.

DATE	TYPE OF EVENT	NAME OF EVENT	COUNTRY SYMBOL	CREW	PLACEMENT
16-24/January	WRC	Rally of Montecarlo	(MC)	Munari-Maiga	1st
				Waldegaard-Thorszelius	2nd
				Darniche-Mahé	3rd
19-22/February	WRC	Rally of Sweden	(S)	Lampinen-Hertz	4th
4-6/March	ERC (4)	Rally Stuttgart-Lyon-Charbonnières	(D)	Darniche-Mahé	1st
10-14/March	WRC	Rally of Portugal	(P)	Munari-Maiga	1st
				Pinto-Bernacchini	4th
27-28/March	ERC (1)	Rally di Sicilia	(I)	Pregliasco-Sodano	1st
4-April	WCM	6 Ore di Vallelunga	(I)	Ricci-Zorzi	8th
21-23/May	ERC (3)	Criterium Alpin	(F)	Jaroszewicz-Zyskowsky	3rd
4-6/June	ERC (3)	Rally 4 Regioni	(I)	Darniche-Mahé	1st
				"Tony"-Mannini	3rd
7-June	ECGT	Oesterreichring	(A)	Gianfranco Ricci	5th
19-21/June	ERC (3)	Rally Zlatni Piassatzi	(BG)	Jaroszewicz-Zyskowsky	1st
22-29/June	WRC	Rally Marocco		Munari-Maiga	3rd
25-27/June	ERC (3)	Criterium d'Antibes	(F)	Darniche-Mahé	1st
11-13/July	ERC (4)	Rallye de Pologne	(PL)	Jaroszewicz-Zyskowsky	1st
1-August	ECGT	Euro GT Misano	(I)	Gianfranco Ricci	3rd
2-4/September	ERC (4)	Rally San Martino di Castrozza	(I)	Darniche-Mahé	1st
				"Tony"-Mannini	3rd
5-September	ECGT	6 Ore di Monza	(I)	Ricci-Facetti	6th
19-September	ECGT	Coppa Bevilacqua	(I)	Gianfranco Ricci	8th
8-11/September	ERC (2)	Sachs Rallye Baltic	(D)	Darniche-Mahé	1st
				Jaroszewicz-Zyskowsky	3rd
6-9/October	WRC	Rally Sanremo	(I)	Waldegaard-Thorszelius	1st
				Munari-Maiga	2nd
				Pinto-Bernacchini	3rd
				"Tony"-Mannini	4th
6-7/November	WRC	Tour de Corse	(F)	Munari-Maiga	1st
				Darniche-Mahé	2nd
22-24/November	ERC (4)	Rallye de Espana	(E)	De Bragation-Barbeito	1st
				Darniche-Mahé	2nd
26 November/1 December	WCR	RAC Rally of Great Britain	(GB)	Munari-Maiga	4th

Official final classification of the WRC
1st Porsche 95 points
5th Lancia (Lancia Stratos HF) 3 points

Official final classification of the World Rally Championship for Makes
1th Lancia (Lancia Stratos HF) 96 points

Official final classification of the ECGT
1st Toine Hezemans (Porsche 934) 100 points
9th Gianfranco Ricci (Lancia Stratos HF) 29 points

Official final classification of the ERC
1st Bernard Darniche-Alain Mahé (Lancia Stratos HF) 380 points
3rd Andrej Jaroszewicz (FIAT 124 Abarth-Lancia Stratos HF) 254 points
11th "Tony" Fassina 84 points

1977

WRC WORLD RALLY CHAMPIONSHIP FOR MAKES
Technical regulations
Open to cars of Groups 1 (series Touring) to 4 (special Grand Touring). No four-wheel-drive cars admitted
Point system
10-9-8-7-6-5-4-3-2-1 points to the first 10 cars classified overall (one per make);. 8-7-6-5-4-3-2-1 points to the first 8 cars classified in their respective groups (also within the overall classification) added to those earned for the overall classification. The 8 best results are considered
Number of events
11
Event characteristics
Total distance greater than 3,000 kms, including at least 1,000 of road sections and 200 of special stages. To calculate the conventional total distance of a rally, 1 km of special stage is considered equivalent to 5 kms of road section

FIACRD FIA CUP FOR RALLY DRIVERS
Point system
9-6-4-3-2-1 points to the first 6 drivers in the overall classification

Number of events
Divided into three categories: category A (all WRC events), category B (all ERC rallies with coefficient 4), and category C (Giro d'Italia, Total Rally of South Africa, Total Southern Cross Rally and Bandama Rally). Participation in at least one category C rally is mandatory

ERC EUROPEAN RALLY CHAMPIONSHIP FOR DRIVERS
Regulations identical to previous year
Number of events
43 scheduled. 41 contended, including 5 with coefficient 4, 10 with coefficient 3

DATE	TYPE OF EVENT	NAME OF EVENT	COUNTRY SYMBOL	CREW	PLACEMENT
22-29/January	WRC	Rally of Montecarlo	(MC)	Munari-Maiga	1st
4-6/February	ERC (1)	Galway Rally	(GB)	Coleman-O'Donoghue	4th
18-20/February	ERC (3)	Costa Brava	(E)	Darniche-Mahé	1st
25-27/March	ERC (2)	Rally of Sicilia	(I)	Darniche-Mahé	1st
				Vudafieri-De Antoni	4th
7-11/April	WRC	East African Safari	(EAK)	Munari-Sodano	3rd
8-12/April	ERC (3)	Circuit of Ireland	(EIR)	Coleman-Scott	2nd
21-23/April	ERC (3)	Rally Isola d'Elba	(I)	Darniche-Mahé	1st
29-1/May	ERC (3)	Firestone Rally	(P)	Darniche-Mahé	1st
7-8/May	ERC (3)	Criterium Alpin	(F)	Darniche-Mahé	1st
13-15/May	ERC (2)	Criterium Lucien Bianchi	(B)	Darniche-Mahé	1st
3-5/June	ERC (3)	Rally 4 Regioni	(I)	Darniche-Mahé	1st
				Pregliasco-Reisoli	2nd
12-17/June	FIACRD	Giro d'Italia	(I)	De Angelis-Del Fante	10th
24-25/June	ERC (3)	24 Uren van Ieper	(B)	Darniche-Mahé	1st
				Coleman-Richards	4th

DATE	TYPE OF EVENT	NAME OF EVENT	COUNTRY SYMBOL	CREW	PLACEMENT
1-3/July	ERC (2)	Rally Campagnolo	(I)	Carello-Perissinot	1st
				Vudafieri-Bonaga	2nd
5-9/July	FIACRD	Total Rally	(ZA)	Munari-Sodano	1st
8-10/July	ERC (4)-FIACRD	Rallye de Pologne	(PL)	Darniche-Mahé	1st
2-4/September	ERC (4)-FIACRD	Rally San Martino di Castrozza	(I)	Munari-Sodano	1st
				Pregliasco-Reisoli	2nd
15-24/September	ERC (4)	Tour de France	(F)	Darniche-Mahé	1st
5-8/October	WRC	Rally Sanremo	(I)	Pregliasco-Reisoli	4th
15-16/October	ERC (1)-FIACRD	Rallye of La Chataigne	(F)	Darniche-Mahé	1st
5-6/November	WRC	Tour de Corse	(F)	Pinto-Bernacchini	2nd
				Carello-Perissinot	4th

Official final classification of the WRC
1st FIAT (FIAT 131 Abarth) 136 points
5th Lancia (Lancia Stratos HF) 60 points

Official final classification of the FIACRD
1st Sandro Munari (Lancia Stratos HF) 31 points
3rd Bernard Darniche (Lancia Stratos HF) 28 points

Official final classification of the ERC
1st Bernard Darniche (Lancia Stratos HF) 500 points
7th Billy Coleman (Lancia Stratos HF) 125 points
11th Mauro Pregliasco (Lancia Stratos HF) 105 points
15th Sandro Munari (Lancia Stratos HF) points 80

1978

WRC WORLD RALLY CHAMPIONSHIP FOR MAKES
Regulations identical to previous year

FIACRD FIA CUP FOR RALLY DRIVERS
Regulations identical to previous year

ERC EUROPEAN RALLY CHAMPIONSHIP FOR DRIVERS
Regulations identical to previous year

Number of events
48 scheduled. 44 contended, including 5 with coefficient 4, 11 with coefficient 3

DATE	TYPE OF EVENT	NAME OF EVENT	COUNTRY SYMBOL	CREW	PLACEMENT
21-28/January	WRC	Rally of Montecarlo	(MC)	Mouton-Conconi	7th
				Bacchelli-Bernacchini	10th
10-12/February	WRC	Rally of Sweden	(S)	Blomqvist-Sylvan	4th
10-12/February	ERC (2)	Galway Rally	(GB)	Coleman-O'Donoghue	5th
17-19/February	ERC (3)	Rally Costa Brava	(And)	Carello-Perissinot	1st
14-16/April	ERC (1)	Saarland Rally	(D)	Rohrl-Geistdorfer	1st
23-25/March	ERC (2)	Rally Targa Florio	(I)	Carello-Perissinot	1st
				Vudafieri-De Antoni	2nd
				Cambiaghi-Meli	6th
4-6/May	ERC (3)	Rally Isola d'Elba	(I)	Vudafieri-Mannini	1st
6-7/May	ERC (3)	Criterium Alpin	(F)	Darniche-Mahé	1st
19-21/May	ERC (3)	Rally 4 Regioni	(I)	Carello-Perissinot	1st
				Vudafieri-Mannini	2nd
				Codognelli-Rancati	9th

DATE	TYPE OF EVENT	NAME OF EVENT	COUNTRY SYMBOL	CREW	PLACEMENT
19-21/May	ERC (1)	Rally of Lorena	(F)	Darniche-Mahé	1st
16-18/June	ERC (3)	Rally d'Antibes	(F)	Darniche-Mahé	1st
				Bettega-Vacchetto	2nd
23-25/June	ERC (3)	24 Uren van Ieper	(B)	Carello-Perissinot	3rd
				Coleman-Scott	6th
1-2/July	ERC (2)	Rally del Friuli e delle Alpi orientali	(I)	Carello-Perissinot	1st
21-23/July	ERC (1)	Rally Hunsruck	(D)	Rohrl-Geistdorfer	1st
				Bettega-Vacchetto	2nd
9-11/September	ERC (3)	Rally Halkidikis	(GR)	Carello-Perissinot	1st
				"Siroco"-Makrinos	2nd
4-7/October	WRC	Rally of Sanremo	(I)	Alen-Kivimaki	1st
13-15/October	ERC (2)	OeASC	(A)	Carello-Perissinot	1st
14-15/October	ERC (1)	Rally of La Chataigne	(F)	Darniche-Giroux	1st
14-17/October	FIACRD	Giro d'Italia	(I)	Alen-Pianta-Kivimaki	1st
				Magnani-Pittoni-Cresto	3rd
20-22/October	ERC (3)	Rally de Espana	(E)	Carello-Perissinot	1st
				De Bragation-Llopis	3rd

Official final classification of the WRC
1st FIAT (FIAT 131 Abarth) 134 points
7th Lancia (Lancia Stratos HF) 49 points

Official final classification of the FIACRD
1st Markku Alen (FIAT 131 Abarth + Lancia Stratos HF) 52 points
5th Bernard Darniche (Lancia Stratos HF) 13 points

Semi-official final classification of the ERC
1st "Tony" Carello (Lancia Stratos HF) 416 points
6th Bernard Darniche (Lancia Stratos HF) 160 points
8th Adartico Vudafieri (Lancia Stratos HF) 135 points

1979

WRC WORLD RALLY CHAMPIONSHIP FOR MAKES
Regulations identical to 1977
Number of events
12

THE FIA CUP FOR RALLY DRIVERS BECOMES WORLD CHAMPIONSHIP FOR RALLY DRIVERS
Point system
20-15-12-10-8-6-4-3-2-1 points to the first 10 drivers in the overall classification
Number of events
12. The same as the WRC. The 7 best results considered valid for both titles.

ERC EUROPEAN RALLY CHAMPIONSHIP FOR DRIVERS
Regulations identical to previous year
Number of events
47 scheduled. 46 contended, including 6 with coefficient 4 and 10 with coefficient 3

DATE	TYPE OF EVENT	NAME OF EVENT	COUNTRY SYMBOL	CREW	PLACEMENT
20-26/January	WRC	Rally of Montecarlo	(MC)	Darniche-Mahé	1st
18/19/March	ERC (2)	Rally di Sicilia/Targa Florio	(I)	Cambiaghi/Vittadello	6th
4-7/April	ERC (1)	Rally Costa Smeralda	(I)	Cambiaghi/Vittadello	7th
7-9/April	ERC (4)	Zlatni Piassatzi	(BG)	"Siroco"-Fertakis	2nd
26-28/April	ERC (4)	Rally Isola d'Elba	(I)	"Tony"-Mannini	1st
				Betti-Betti	6th

DATE	TYPE OF EVENT	NAME OF EVENT	COUNTRY SYMBOL	CREW	PLACEMENT
27-29/April	ERC (2)	Criterium Lucien Bianchi	(B)	Neri-Materne	9th
22-23/June	ERC (1)	Rally Il Ciocco	(I)	"Nico"-Barban	8th
23-24/June	ERC (1)	Rally Orense	(E)	De Bragation-Llopis	1st
18-19/August	ERC (1)	Volta de Madeira	(E)	"Tony"-Mannini	1st
15-20/September	ERC (4)	Tour de France	(F)	Darniche-Mahé	1st
2-6/October	WRC	Rally di Sanremo	(I)	"Tony"-Mannini	1st
				"Nico"-Barban	9th
19-21/October	ERC (3)	Rally de Espana	(E)	De Bragation-Llopis	1st
2-4/November	WRC	Tour de Corse	(F)	Darniche-Mahé	1st

Official final classification of the WRC
1st Ford (Ford Escort RS) 122 points
4th Lancia (Lancia Stratos HF) 65 points

Official final classification of the World Championship for Rally Drivers
1st Bjorn Waldegaard (Ford Escort RS) 112 points
3rd Markku Alen (FIAT 131 Abarth + Lancia Stratos HF) 68 points
6th Bernard Darniche (Lancia Stratos HF) 40 points
10th "Tony" Fassina (Lancia Stratos HF) 20 points

Official final classification of the ERC
1st Jochi Kleint (Opel Ascona) 375 points
14th "Tony" Fassina (Lancia Stratos HF) 96 points
23rd Jorge De Bragation (Lancia Stratos HF) 80 points
Bernard Darniche (Lancia Stratos HF) 80 points
37th "Siroco" (Lancia Stratos HF) 60 points

1980

WRC WORLD RALLY CHAMPIONSHIP FOR MAKES
Regulations identical to 1977, except for admission to 4WD cars if homologated
Number of events
10

WORLD CHAMPIONSHIP FOR RALLY DRIVERS
Regulations identical to 1979
Number of events
12. The same as the WRC, plus the Rallies of Sweden and the 1,000 Lakes. The 7 best results considered valid for both titles.

ERC EUROPEAN RALLY CHAMPIONSHIP FOR DRIVERS
Regulations identical to previous year
Number of events
48 scheduled. 46 contended, including 8 with coefficient 4 and 8 with coefficient 3

DATE	TYPE OF EVENT	NAME OF EVENT	COUNTRY SYMBOL	CREW	PLACEMENT
19-25/January	WRC	Rally of Montecarlo	(MC)	Darniche-Mahé	2nd
6-10/February	ERC (3)	Rally Costa Brava	(E)	De Bragation-Llopis	2nd
7-9/March	ERC (2)	Rally Targa Florio	(I)	Montalto-"Flay"	9th
26-29/March	ERC (2)	Rally Costa Smeralda	(I)	Darniche-Mahé	1st
				Cunico-Ravizza	3rd
17-19/April	ERC (2)	Rally Isola d'Elba	(I)	Volpi-Piacani	9th
14-18/May	ERC (4)	Rally 4 Regioni	(I)	Tabaton-Radaelli	2nd
26-29/May	WRC	Rally of Acropolis	(GR)	"Siroco"-Makrinos	9th
21-22/June	ERC (1)	Rally Orense	(E)	Balcazar-Martin	1st
26-28/June	ERC (2)	Rally Il Ciocco	(I)	Cunico-Meggiolan	3rd
18-20/July	ERC (2)	Firestone Rally	(P)	De Bragation-Llopis	1st
				Balcazar-Martin	3rd

DATE	TYPE OF EVENT	NAME OF EVENT	COUNTRY SYMBOL	CREW	PLACEMENT
8-10/August	ERC (2)	Rally Hunsruck	(D)	Fritzinger-Schwagerl	7th
11-13/September	ERC (1)	Manx Trophy	(GB)	Dawson-Gormley	5th
14-21/September	ERC (4)	Tour de France	(F)	Darniche-Mahé	1st
17-19/October	ERC (3)	Rally de Espana	(E)	De Bragation-Llopis	3rd

Official final classification of the WRC
1st FIAT (FIAT 131 Abarth) 120 points
10th Lancia (Lancia Stratos HF) 20 points

Official final classification of the World Championship for Rally Drivers
1st Walter Röhrl (FIAT 131 Abarth) 118 points
16th Bernard Darniche (Lancia Stratos HF) points 15

Official final classification of the ERC
1st Antonio Zanini (Porsche 911 SC) 456 points
11th Jorge De Bragation (Lancia Stratos HF) 136 points
14th Bernard Darniche (Lancia Stratos HF) 120 points

1981

WRC WORLD RALLY CHAMPIONSHIP FOR MAKES
Regulations identical to previous year
Number of events
9

WORLD CHAMPIONSHIP FOR RALLY DRIVERS
Regulations identical to previous year
Number of events
11. The same as the WRC, plus the Rallies of Sweden and Brazil. The 7 best results considered valid for both titles.

ERC EUROPEAN RALLY CHAMPIONSHIP FOR DRIVERS
Regulations identical to previous year
Number of events
46 scheduled. 44 contended, including 7 with coefficient 4 and 8 with coefficient 3

DATE	TYPE OF EVENT	NAME OF EVENT	COUNTRY SYMBOL	CREW	PLACEMENT
24-31/January	WRC	Rally of Montecarlo	(MC)	Darniche-Mahé	6th
13-15/March	ERC (2)	Rally of Sicilia	(I)	"Dielis"-Spataro	8th
20-22/March	ERC (3)	Rally of RACE	(E)	De Bragation-Sabater	2nd
				Balcazar-Martin	4th
10-12/April	ERC (1)	Maspalomas		De Bragation-Sabater	1st
1-3/May	WRC	Tour de Corse	(F)	Darniche-Mahé	1st
1-3/May	ERC (2)	Rally CS	(E)	De Bragation-Sabater	1st
				Balcazar-Martin	3rd
15-20/September	ERC (4)	Tour de France	(F)	Darniche-Mahé	2nd
21-22/November	ERC (2)	Cataluna	(E)	De Bragation-Sabater	2nd

Official final classification of the WRC
1st Talbot (Talbot Sunbeam Lotus) 117 points
10th Lancia (Lancia Stratos HF) 28 points

Official final classification of the World Championship for Rally Drivers
1st Ari Vatanen (Ford Escort RS) 118 points
12th Bernard Darniche (Lancia Stratos HF) 26 points

Official final classification of the ERC
1st Adartico Vudafieri (FIAT 131 Abarth) 420 points
11th Jorge De Bragation (Lancia Stratos HF) 115 points
14th Bernard Darniche (Lancia Stratos HF) 120 points

1982
ERC EUROPEAN RALLY CHAMPIONSHIP FOR DRIVERS

Regulations identical to previous year

Number of events

49 scheduled. 45 contended, including 8 with coefficient 4 and 7 with coefficient 3

DATE	TYPE OF EVENT	NAME OF EVENT	COUNTRY SYMBOL	CREW	PLACEMENT
1-3/April	ERC (3)	Rally Costa Smeralda	(I)	Tabaton-Todeschini	2nd
22-25/April	ERC (3)	Rally Isola d'Elba	(I)	Tabaton-Todeschini	1st
1-3/July	ERC (2)	Rally of the Ciocco	(I)	Tabaton-Todeschini	5th
24-27/August	ERC (4)	Rally Halkidikis	(GR)	"Benny"-Stefanis	6th
10-12/December	ECR (3)	Rally of Valle d'Aosta	(I)	Tabaton-Todeschini	1st

Semi-official final classification of the ERC

1st "Tony" Fassina (Opel Ascona 400) 446 points
16th Fabrizio Tabaton (Lancia Stratos HF) 121 points

Acknowledgements

Just pronouncing the name "Stratos" brought forth spontaneous offers from many persons, even some I did not know, to help me in various ways. Such is the passion this magical car still automatically evokes.

I would like to thank, first of all, Pier Ugo Gobbato, Cesare Fiorio and Sandro Munari for helping me accurately reconstruct many events. No less merit must go to Nicola "Nick" Bianchi and Gianni Tonti.

Competing in courtesy among the tuners were Mauro Ambrogi, with his daughter Marianna, of University Motors of Genoa, and brother Carlo and Giuliano Facetti, not to mention Claudio Maglioli: grand "wizards" prior to the Stratos, during its reign and afterward.

Giovannino Fabbri, traditional and lovable luncheon companion of "our" Monday table at Emilio Cecchi's "Borghetto", assisted me with personal photos and memories to comment that exciting exploit against the hordes of Porsches conducted by the small, solitary Stratos of the Team Rino Fabbri Editore, managed by him at the time.

Speedsters Francesco Capuzzo, Luciano Dal Ben and Claudio Magnani, at a distance of over 20 years, clashed once again in competition, no longer on the circuits but in generosity in providing me information and stupendous photos, equaled in this ideal sprint of passion and friendship by Luigi "Chicco" Cabella with his many aliases, historical pillar and driver first of the original Hi.Fi. Sport, then of the HF Squadra Corse from its formation, and by Giorgio Pianta. My sincere gratitude to all of them.

I am also indebted to Leo Pittoni and Giancarlo Biasuzzi, those unforgotten Stratos rally drivers, for their impartial assistance that, along with the aid of Thomas Popper, enabled me to complete the wealth of images made available to me by Carrozzeria Bertone's efficient Direzione della Comunicazione, through their kind and enthusiastic Elisabetta Farmeschi, and by the FIAT Archives, through the expert assistance of Massimo Castagnola.

My inimitable ambassador and the diligent manager of most of my contacts was Enrico Masala, former director of policy and strategy for Lancia and fervent Lancia-lover in life, but I also wish to thank Luca De Meo, current marketing manager of the Lancia Division, for having considered this volume and facilitated the iconographic research.

Particular merit goes to Franco Varisco who, while at his home in those days, upon hearing the roar of cars testing on the national autodrome of Monza, would rush to the track with his cameras and photograph everything. Today he possesses an unpublished archive unlike any other and made it available for this volume with a gentility of yore.

To my friends at AISA, Associazione Italiana della Storia dell'Automobile, to the president and his steering committee, goes all my admiration for having organized, as part of the association's institutional activity, that memorable, oft-cited conference that was the primary source and stimulus for this volume.

Friendship and a shared passion for autoracing also moved two others to help me: Roberto Rettani and especially Luca Ronchi, who was a fundamental support in my biographical research and in compiling the "Results" of the Stratos. In all respects, Luca must be considered the coauthor of this book. Thanks again! Last but not least, without Fulvio Miglia and empassioned philatelist Giordano Falciatori I would never have come to possess the original stamp of the Stratos issued by Monaco.

Many thanks also to Luciano Greggio, the "historian" of Bertone and passionate author of book's chapter four. And, lastly, to Leonardo Acerbi, who put up with my bad moods and never batted an eye. Once again, I thank you all. Without you, I could never have completed the manuscript.

The Author

Bibliography

Alder Trevor (ed.), *Lancia Stratos Road tests & Articles*, Ipswich, Transport Source Books, n.d.

Amatori Franco et al., *Storia della Lancia Impresa Tecnologia Mercati 1906-1969*, Milan, Fabbri, 1992

Boscarelli Lorenzo (ed.), *La Lancia Stratos*, conferenza dell'ing. Pierugo Gobbato, Milano, Museo Nazionale della Scienza e della Tecnica, 11 marzo 2000, monography containing the stenographic text of the meeting, reserved to the members of the Associazione Italiana per la Storia dell'Automobile (AISA)

Buhlmann Klaus-Klein Reinhard, *40 Jahre Rallyesport. Die Geschichte der Lenkradartisten von Mini-trip zum Allrad-Ritt*, Stuttgart, Motorbuch, 2002

Casucci Piero, *Lancia Stratos*, Milan, Domus-Libreria dell'Automobile, 1983

Clarke R M (ed.), *Lancia Stratos Gold Portfolio 1972-1985*, Brooklands Books, 1995

Curtis Anthony, *Ferrari Dino The Complete Story*, Marlborough, Crowood Autoclassics, 2002

Faure Eric- Léonard Christian, *Les reines des rallyes. 25 ans de Championnat du Monde des rallyes*, sl, Lamaco, 1998

Gabriel Jean-Pierre, *Dino Le altre Ferrari*, Milan, Giorgio Nada, 1989 (Italian ed. of Dino: *Ferrari, Fiat et Lancia*, Paris, EPA, 1984)

Gary Pierre-Bedei Christian-Moity Christian, *Lancia au volant*, Sèvres, La Sirène, 1993

Giacosa Dante, *I miei 40 anni di progettazione alla Fiat*, Milan, Automobilia, 1979

Klein Reinhard et al., *Rally*, Köln, Könemann, sd

Klein Reinhard, *Rally Cars*, Köln, Könemann, 2000

Manganaro Alfio-Vinai Paolo, *Lancia corse*, Milan, Automobilia, 1988

Pitt Colin (ed.), *Lancia Stratos*, Hockley, Unique Motor Books, s.d.

Robson Graham, *Lancia Stratos Super Profile*, Yeovil, Haynes, 1983

Trow Nigel, Lancia Stratos: *World Champion Rally Car*, London, Osprey, 1990

Trow Nigel, *Lancia Racing*, London, Osprey, 1987

Weernink Wim Oude, *La Lancia*, Milan, Giorgio Nada, 1994 (Italian ed. expanded and updated of *La Lancia*, Croydon, MRP, 1979 I ed, 1991 II ed. updated and expanded)

Yearbooks

Fédération Internationale de L'Automobile (ed.), *FIA annuaire du sport automobile*, Cambridge, Patrick Stephens, 1970-1982

Fenu Michele-Rizzo Pietro (ed.), *Velocità & rally*, Milan, Studio Erre, 1977-1982

Greasley Mike (ed.), *Rallycourse 1982-83*, Richmond, Hazleton, sd

Holmes Martin-Bishop Hugh, *Rothmans World Rallying*, London, Osprey, 1978-1982

Periodicals

Autosprint, Autosprint Anno, Autosprint Mese, Auto Italiana, Il pilota, Quattroruote, Quattroruote Sport, Rallysprint, Rombo, Ruoteclassiche

Printed by Bolis Poligrafiche SpA
Bergamo, Italy, July 2003